BAPTISM AT
BULL RUN

BAPTISM AT BULL RUN

BY JAMES P. REGER

HARBOR
HOUSE

BAPTISM AT BULL RUN
By James P. Reger
A Harbor House Book/2004

For information address:
         HARBOR HOUSE
         3010 STRATFORD DRIVE
         AUGUSTA, GEORGIA 30909

Jacket Design by Jane H. Carter
Author photo by Michael Armbrust

Cataloging-in-Publication Data
Reger, James P.
Baptism at Bull Run / by James P. Reger.
p. cm.
ISBN 1-891799-14-2
1. Virginia--History--Civil War, 1861-1865--Fiction.
2. Bull Run, 1st Battle of, Va., 1861--Fiction. I. Title.

PS3618.E448B37 2004
813'.6--dc22

                                        2003027507

Printed in the United States of America
10 9 8 7 6 5 4 3 2 1

This book is dedicated to:

My son, Grayson, whose ten frolicking years of life
have added an eternity of joy to my own.

My big brother, Bill, whom I idolized like a god
until he became all too mortal in the killing fields of Vietnam.

Acknowledgements:

I would like to thank the following people whose welcomed encouragement, input, and feedback made this book possible: Bob Reger, Jack Reger, Pam Reger, Don Pratt, Rosalind Jimenez, Rosemarie Mosler, A.J. Curmaci, Jayne Anne Phillips, Stephen Coonts, Michael Oldaker, Jani Poundstone, Harvey Simon, Bonnie Szumski, Philip Comer, Ron Raposa, Jerry LaRussa, George Ohnesorgen, Lee Butler, and, of course, Bonnie ZoBell.

CHAPTER ONE

CONFEDERATE GENERAL PIERRE GUSTAVE TOUTANT BEAUREGARD STOOD on the balcony of his headquarters and looked out at Fort Sumter. He could see flames and billowy black smoke pouring out of the brick fortress and hear the delight of his staff and couriers on the balcony below, but the General himself, alone and not wanting to be disturbed, was not at all pleased.

For a day and a night now, his forty-three guns had been pummeling the fort, blowing great craters in its walls and zipping shards throughout its interior. The tiny Union garrison was managing to fight back weakly, but Beauregard knew that they had to be on the brink of surrender. He just wished they would give up before any more lives had to be needlessly lost. The life of Major Robert Anderson, the commander of Fort Sumter and Beauregard's long-time friend, concerned him most.

"Why are you doing this, mon frere," he murmured in his French Creole accent. "Why are you bringing this agony upon yourself?" A dozen-odd Southern guns went off at once, jarring the mansion and his nerves.

"Please, Robert. You have done all that honor requires. Give up." But he knew his friend too well to believe that he would. Their bond went back to

West Point where Robert Anderson had taught him artillery tactics and the military code of ethics. Twenty-year-old Beauregard stayed on at the Academy after graduation in 1838 to assist Anderson in the drill of younger cadets.

"I know how you feel about surrender, Robert, but I have offered you honorable terms." Siege guns pounded below. Their smoke swirled upward and he tasted the pungent sulfur.

"How can anyone be alive...it is an inferno." He closed his eyes and flashed on charred bodies, the stench of burning flesh, men choking out their last breaths, flapping at their flaming arms and legs. He saw Mexico.

He eased back into a chair and rubbed his dusky face. Avoiding the pasted curls that adorned each temple, he ran his hand through black, wavy hair, then stroked his mustache and the spear of beard below his lower lip. He caught a glimmer of his high cheekbones and doe-like eyes in a windowpane and admired himself for a moment.

He really was a peacock, this New Orleans Creole. Since his youth, he had reveled in his plumage and offered apologies to no one for doing so. After all, his descendants had come from the finest French and Italian aristocracy. Just because his father had squandered the family wealth did not mean that Gustave was not heir to the legacy of noble blood.

After graduating from West Point with high standing, he earned promotions for bravery under fire during the Mexican War and advanced through the ranks of the Officer Corps after the war.

In 1860, his career in the Old Army peaked when the War Department gave him one of its most prized assignments: commandant of the United States Military Academy. This proved to be his final service to the Federal government. Shortly after taking over at West Point, the deep Southern states seceded and he resigned to go South in search of a Confederate commission. When a bureaucratic oversight delayed his receiving one, he enlisted as a private in a New Orleans company of volunteers. He did not remain long. The Confederacy soon realized its error and made him a general, the general in charge of removing the Unionist garrison from Fort Sumter, the general now sitting on this third floor mansion balcony awash in the fatigue of thirty-six sleepless hours.

Escaping for a moment, he closed his eyes and drifted to thoughts of a young woman he had known in New Orleans. It was her back and the dips in her waist he remembered, the sheen of her skin in the candle light. He had always considered himself one of the most handsome officers in the Old Army and, of late, the Provisional Confederate Army; he had prided himself in being a coup for any belle on the dance floor or in the steamy salons above.

But he felt so tired and worn now, a man not only incapable of succoring women but one in shameful need of their succor.

He had long since exhausted the anger that had boiled over in his gut for the thousands of celebrants packing Battery Park below and the rooftops above. He now dismissed them as fools, the fancy fluff of this pastel city whose knowledge of war came from fire-eating screeds and romantic novels by Sir Walter Scott.

He was, on the other hand, glad to hear his artillerists celebrating. He knew that the skin-sizzling, brain-addling job they had been performing without stop was the one he had assigned them, the one President Jefferson Davis had assigned him, and that it was a job that had to be done no matter how distasteful it was to him personally. Charleston Harbor was the sovereign territory of the Confederate States of America now, and a foreign military installation like Fort Sumter could not be allowed to remain within her borders. But still, he thought, why did he have to be the one to fight his dearest friend to settle the matter.

"Why," he muttered, "why?"

Suddenly, a primordial eruption, leg-shaking earthquake nearly shook him out of his chair. The detonation blotted out the sounds of mere cannon fire. It was volcanic, creationistic, a scorching, devastating, apocalyptic roar. It rolled over the harbor, booming, smothering, feeding on its own ruthless force. The thunder tumbled and rushed, howled and bellowed. It split his ears and shocked his senses. He saw men and women driven to the ground as if flicked by giant fingers. Perhaps Christ had returned, his panicked mind raced, or Satan.

He rushed to the banister. "Sweet Mother of Jesus! What was that?" The explosion was tapering off by the time he found his field glass and only mist and white smoke remained when he had it focused.

A triple-buttoned cadet in gray bolted out onto the balcony, knocking over a chair in his clamor. "We must have hit the powder magazine," the whiskerless boy shouted. "We must have blown every last one of those damn Yankees to glorious bits with that one!"

"The powder magazine," Beauregard muttered to himself. "Good God not that. Not Robert."

Grinning irrepressibly, the cadet said, "But look at that smoke, sir. How could anyone even breathe in such a place? Surely they are all dead from that alone!"

"Silence!" Beauregard snapped. He scanned the cadet repugnantly. "What is your name again, boy?"

"Why, it's Bagwell, sir. Lieutenant Archie Bagwell. At your service, sir." He offered an enthusiastic salute that the General ignored.

"Well, Lieutenant *Bagwell*," Beauregard growled. "I will not have you yelping at those Unionists out there like some hound dog at a treed animal. They are men, brave men, and I expect you regard them with all the honors they are due."

"But sir, this is war," Archie said. "And war means killing."

"And what do you know of war, boy?" Beauregard fired. "Or killing. How many dead men have you seen in your tenure as a soldier? How many bodies have you seen ripped apart and seared like so much meat?"

"Why, none, sir. I was only in my second year at the Citadel when I received my commission."

"I am fully aware, *Lieutenant*, of your inexperience and I am also aware of how your rich daddy pulled strings to get you assigned to me to keep you from getting killed on the front lines. Do you know what that makes me, Lieutenant Bagwell?"

"Uh, no, sir, I guess I don't, sir."

"That makes me your mammy, boy, your mammy, and I am not at all happy about it. You can rest assured that none of those men out in that fort have mammies and from the looks of it, I would say that many of them do not have heads or limbs either."

"But they're Yankees, sir."

Beauregard erupted. "They are men, Lieutenant, men, quite unlike yourself!" He turned away, whipping his field glass to his eyes.

Archie looked away, hurt. It always hurt him when people did not like him, especially when he tried so hard to make them. It had been that way all his life, beginning at home on the family rice plantation along the Carolina coast. The Bagwell patriarch, Benjamin, had sired two sons, Amos and Micah, by his first wife and had groomed them to take over the plantation. They were serious boys with a natural bent toward the proper management of slaves, land, and money, and their father had always been backslapping proud of them, introducing them to whiskey and slave girls at an early age. Upon their mother's passing, Benjamin did not remarry for twenty years, preferring instead to raise his two sons in the rice growing business and personally increase his work force with several mulatto children.

His widower status changed, though, when a neighbor's offer of adjacent land and enough slaves to finally put him over the one-hundred-man mark proved too irresistible to pass up. All Benjamin had to do was marry the neighbor's daughter: a homely twenty-six year-old who had never had a suitor and probably never would. Her name was Julia and, within a year, she gave birth to Archibald Clinton Bagwell.

With Archie being two decades younger than his half-brothers and lacking the practical mind necessary to earn his father's love, Julia took her only child to herself and doted on him, perhaps to make up for her aging husband's chronic belittling of them both. She spent hours each day reading to Archie, nurturing his rich fantasy life and imbuing him with a love of books and beauty. By the time he could read them for himself, he had developed a passion for stories of glorious, bloodless war. He devoured every printed page he could find concerning the likes of Julius Caesar, the knights of old, George Washington, the Indian fighters, and Napoleon, playing out lessons learned in swordfights and gun battles with imaginary foemen.

When it came time for Benjamin Bagwell to find something that his young son could do for a living, he applied enough political pressure to get him admitted to the South Carolina Military Institute, first at the Arsenal in Columbia and then at the Citadel in Charleston. The elder Bagwell thought the experience could mature the boy. At the very least, it might offer him a chance at a career apart from the plantation, for Benjamin was determined not to let Archie join in the family enterprise. So nearly everyone was happy: the father, the older brothers, certainly Archie, and even his mother, although she wept for days at having to watch her lifeblood ride away. Everyone was happy, except General Beauregard.

Archie carefully cleared his throat and said, "Uh, sir, did you call for me?"

"I called for a courier, Lieutenant. All the real ones must have been busy. And now there would appear to be no need of one." The General turned back to the fort and murmured, "Oh, Robert, my dear Robert. Why did it have to come to this?"

Lieutenant Bagwell knew better than to interrupt the General's apparent grief. He stood in silence, uncomfortably waiting for it to pass. But then he could not help it. He blurted like an eager pup, "Sir! Sir! Their flag just went down! I don't see it anymore!"

"What? Let me look." He raised his field glass. "Praise the saints. I think you may be right. The Stars and Stripes are down. But they have yet to hoist the white flag."

Cheers were rising from the Battery and the rooftops; the citizenry had seen the lowering. Beauregard withheld expression. He kept scanning for the white flag. "It should have been up by now. The capitulation is not yet confirmed. I cannot order our guns to cease firing until it is. Damnation!"

Then he saw it at exactly the same time that young Bagwell did. "Look, General! The white flag! It's coming up!"

Beauregard let out a deep sigh and looked heavenward. "Sweet Jesus and

Mother Mary. Finally. Thank you, Robert. Thank you Heavenly Father."

The crowd doubled its joy. Top hats and handkerchiefs flew into the air. But several siege guns kept firing. "Goddamn it!" Beauregard shouted at Lieutenant Bagwell. "Get down there and stop those guns!"

"Yes, sir!" Bagwell said, excited to have a mission. "Right away, sir!" He stepped back to give himself room for one of his finest salutes.

Before Lieutenant Bagwell could get his elbow cocked, Beauregard roared, "I said go, boy, go!"

The Lieutenant scrambled away, nearly tripping himself to all fours. "Yes, sir! Right away, sir!" And in a clatter, he was gone.

General Beauregard shook his head at the boy. He could not stay peeved long, though. Within seconds the crowd was calling his name and heaping plaudits upon him from down below. Instinctively, he assumed a grand pose and bowed.

CHAPTER TWO

Virginia Military Institute
Lexington, Virginia
April 17, 1861
Late Afternoon

GENERAL BEAUREGARD SPENT FOUR DAYS RADIATING IN THE GLORY OF HIS new title, the Hero of Fort Sumter. But an unknown professor at VMI, Thomas Jonathan Jackson, cared little about him or the wild celebration on his behalf four hundred miles to the south. His duty was here at the head of his class, waiting for this latest outbreak of horseplay to settle down. Tugging at the collar of his uniform, he restarted his lecture but stopped it again when a flurry of snickering waved through the room.

"Class," he droned. "Class..."

The cadets ignored him. They had been insufferably rambunctious since hearing that the Yankees had been blasted out of Fort Sumter. Many had already declared that they would be enlisting soon for the real fighting and that they no longer had any need of formal schooling.

But that excuse held no water with Major Jackson, "Ol' Tom Fool," they called him. His unyielding discipline demanded complete attention in the classroom regardless and he meant to have it.

"Class..." he said, his monotone rising, "class..."

The boys laughed at him, the thrill of war bursting in their eyes.

"Attention, class..." Major Jackson ordered, a tremor wavering his voice. "Attention."

The cadets ignored him, chattering on as if he were not in the room.

Full-bearded and funereal, Thomas Jackson was out of step with the masses. He sat, walked, and stood at braced attention and, in the ten years that he had been at VMI, no one had seen him smile. He sucked on peaches stashed in lint-filled pockets. He often walked about with his right arm raised. It balanced his blood and organs, he said, and pepper made his left leg ache.

The odd man had come a long way, though, in a Gentleman's world, from the mountains of western Virginia to West Point and beyond. He served with utter fearlessness in Mexico, but he could not endure garrison life. The lonely nights, the lice, the drone of duty drove Major Jackson out of the Army. He resigned in 1851 and accepted a professor's chair at VMI. Though he had spent ten years dedicated to the profession, he did not master it and, at thirty-six, his frustrations were rising.

"Attention, Cadets, attention," the Major said. "You will come to attention...immediately. We must return to the lecture." Finally, some of the boys glanced in his direction.

"But sir," said a straw-blond with a winning smile, "surely even your blood must be up by now. This is war we're talking about. War!" The rest of the boys yipped in behind him.

Jackson steadied himself. "Cadet Ashcroft, this is neither the time nor the place for such a discussion. The lecture...we must return to the lecture." He fumbled for his notes on the lectern but they fell, scattering about like so many leaves. Laughter broke out again.

Red face beaming, Cadet Ashcroft said. "So tell us, Major, while you prepare your lecture down there on the floor, just how do you stand on war and secession. What are you going to do if Lincoln calls out volunteers and invades?"

Lucas Ashcroft had long been a cocky young man. His father, William, had raised him to be just that on their tobacco plantation in southwestern Virginia, near Roanoke. Lucas' grandfather, Abram Ashcroft, had been pugnacious in his own right, moving away from what he had considered the stilted snobbery and aristocracy of the tidewater area, where old money and older families had kept him landless since arriving in America from England. Abram had shaken the dust from that closed society and moved to the frontier, where he killed enough Indians and cleared enough land to carve himself a sizable farm and reputation

In the years after Abram died, his son William expanded the land holdings and acquired some twenty slaves. He turned the Ashcroft farm into the

Ashcroft plantation and the pride in his name swelled, an air of superiority, many thought, and he passed it on to his son Lucas. William especially took pains to imbue Lucas with a disdain of mountain people, the crackers who so tainted the *better elements* of the white race. At least the Negroes could be kept in their place, he claimed. Nothing irked either of them as much as an uppity hillbilly.

This attitude had gotten Lucas into a great deal of trouble at the Virginia Military Institute in his four years there, particularly with Professor Jackson. More than once, he had his father attempt to get him out of a disciplinary scrape by having him show up at school to try to have Jackson dismissed from the Institute. He wrote several scathing letters to board members and influential state officials concerning the Major's unfitness for such an esteemed faculty position but, to William's frustration, Jackson always survived the reviews.

Now, months later, the Major stood motionless before this same boy with the irate father, visibly vexed by his class clowning. He had never faced such open insubordination from a cadet and he knew punishment was in order, but he did not want another confrontation with William Ashcroft. He turned from the grinning boy and stepped to the chalkboard.

"The lesson today concerns the angles of the sun and employing them to determine the time of day."

The class catcalled as one. A hail of paper-wads hurtled down around the professor's head and shoulders.

Jackson did not flinch. H continued drawing a compassed circle on the board.

Lucas said, "I ask you again, Major Fool, I mean Major Jackson. What should we do if Lincoln calls for volunteers? I mean, certainly, a fierce warrior such as yourself would not become a pacifist at such a time." The class tittered. Paper-wads whizzed by.

Professor Jackson turned slowly and cocked his arm. "I in no way want war, Cadet Ashcroft. I have seen what war does to hearts, minds, and bodies and no true Christian could ever wish for such a calamity. But that is not our concern today. Our concern is..."

"But, Major," Ashcroft said, "you must want war. Why, war is what makes men great. Just look what it did for you!" He got a round of titters for that one.

"I say again, sir, I desire to avoid war at all costs. It should always be the last remedy sought by governments and it should be employed only when all negotiation and diplomacy have failed."

"But the Yankees already started the war down at Fort Sumter," Ashcroft said, "and while, by some freak of nature no one was killed, we still ought to take the fight to them right now, up at Washington City, and wipe out that cracker Lincoln and his nest of abolitionists before they can make any more mischief!" He got a rousing round of applause and "here-heres" for that.

"I will say it just once more. We should always seek peace first. Now, turn in your text to page…"

"Why, that sounds like Unionist talk to me," Lucas said, "abolitionist talk even. You're not becoming some kind of Quaker in your old age are you, Major?"

"Cadet Ashcroft," the Major said, "I have heard quite enough from you today. Like so many times before, you are exhibiting a lack of respect for me, a superior officer, and I intend to see you punished for your offenses, father or no father. At the end of this lecture, you will accompany me to the office of the Superintendent to begin court-martial proceedings."

"Whoa," the students chimed in comic unison.

"I don't care what you try to do to me, Major. I am resigning from the Institute anyway as soon as Virginia secedes, which is going to be soon, and I am going to get my commission from General Beauregard himself, a real soldier and a real hero."

Jackson was dumbfounded, stammering. To his relief, a disturbance from out in the hallway echoed into the classroom. Feet were racing, voices shouting. Hurrahs were tumbling into cheers. Hands clapped and hoots hollered. The door exploded open.

"He's called for volunteers!" a panting boy yelled in. "Lincoln's called for volunteers! 75,000 of them! To invade the South! To invade Virginia! Praise God! This means war!"

Major Jackson's students let out a hullabaloo and scrambled for the door, knocking down desks and each other to be the first one out. Jackson listened to the tumult spread from classrooms to barracks to the parade ground and then set about slowly gathering his papers and books. After wiping the chalkboard clean and tidying up the experiment table, he straightened the chairs and started for the door.

He stopped and looked back at his room of ten years, feeling a dull yet strangely nostalgic ache. He buried his emotions in his usual numbness and shuffled out of the classroom, his arm cocked again. He found Cadet Ashcroft out in the hallway waiting for him.

Deadpanned, Jackson said, "Are you ready to go and see the Superintendent?"

"Hell, no, you damned fool. If anything I ought to call you out, gentleman to gentleman, but what's the point. You aren't a gentleman. You're a mountain cracker."

"Follow me, Cadet," Jackson said.

"You really don't fathom it, do you, Major? I'm not your student anymore. I'm not even a cadet anymore. I am a soldier. A man. And you no longer hold me in your sway."

Unmoved, Jackson said, "You are under arrest, Cadet Ashcroft. You will follow me at once to the office of the Superintendent."

Disbelieving, Lucas shook his head, too exasperated to express it. He turned, swearing, and stormed up a flight of stairs.

After a moment adrift, Jackson left the building, mumbling a prayer as he went. He did not notice a brick smashing into the sidewalk beside him.

CHAPTER THREE

Washington City, District of Columbia
April 25, 1861
Afternoon

PROFESSOR JACKSON SPENT EIGHT DAYS DRILLING HIS REMAINING CADETS, waiting for a call from Richmond to serve and praying that Union troops in the Federal capital were not growing so numerous that they would overwhelm Virginia before she could be properly defended. He could not know it but his prayers were being answered bountifully.

Washington looked like a ghost town with its doors and windows shuttered against the rumored threat of Confederate invasion. Discarded newspapers skittered up Pennsylvania Avenue beneath the gloomy gray sky. Not a clopping horse's hoof or even a human footstep broke the stillness along the wooden sidewalks and half-cobbled pavement. The only voices to penetrate the silence came from the handfuls of civilian-clad militiamen guarding various critical and deserted intersections.

Wild talk had abounded for the past ten days about hordes of demonized savages from Virginia and Maryland descending with bat wings upon the vulnerable city to either destroy it or return it to Southern control. Rickety wagons and barricading boxes served as the only defense against that threat at this particular intersection, wagons and boxes and a motley assortment of poorly armed townsmen.

A boom sounded through the reverberant city. A gust of wind swept the echo up the street. The sound originated blocks away but these would-be soldiers cowered at the noise. Dogs began yapping in another direction. The townsmen jerked their heads toward that threat.

"What's happenin,'" Billy Anderson asked. He was a chubby boy dressed in a red-checkered shirt and suspendered trousers. "Is the traitors finally here?"

Billy was scared. He had never been away from his hearty Swedish mother anymore than the length of a school day and that was the way he liked it. With his father and two older sisters long dead from a scarlet fever epidemic, his mother the washerwoman was the only one to dry his eyes and feed him cookies when the other children teased him about his weight.

"I'm askin' again," Billy said. "Is them the Rebels makin' them noises?"

The others did not answer. Some wiped their sweaty palms. Others tried to swallow back the dryness in their throats.

Two horsemen slowly rounded a corner a hundred yards down the street. The frightened pickets rattled their muskets to the ready.

"It is the Rebels?" Billy asked. "Good God Almighty! This is the big attack, ain't it?"

"Hush up, fat boy," a top-hatted man said. "There's a carriage roundin' the corner behind them. They ain't gonna attack us with no carriage." He looked around nervously at a man in a powder blue Mexican War uniform and asked, "Are they?"

Ol' Mex, as people called him, peered down the street, saying nothing. Raw and weathered for a man of thirty-three, he had always been taciturn, even morose with an air of independence that came from living by his wits since the age of twelve. It was then that the beatings his drunken father routinely savaged him with became too harsh to bear and he set out on his own, working his way around the state of Rhode Island as a stable boy, farm worker, fish cutter, and anything else it took to keep himself sheltered and fed.

The outbreak of the Mexican War offered him his most promising job opportunity and, at eighteen, he took it without a thought for what a war might really be like. He quickly found out, fighting in every major battle between Vera Cruz and Mexico City, and the experience toughened him to a depth even his joyless childhood had not. He found a home in the army, though, and something of a little brother in an Ohio boy with a corn-fed smile named Leland.

But the peacetime army proved too boring, the unnecessary discipline too severe, and his friend Leland proved unable to survive camp dysentery, so

Ol'Mex left the army and spent another decade drifting from job to state to town to city, spending the past year here in the capital unloading wagons at a warehouse. He had never thrown away his threadbare uniform, though, and he proudly wore it now as he watched the approaching carriage.

"There's more riders," Billy said, "comin' into view behind that there carriage. They's bound to be traitors. Who else would be out on these streets?"

The mysterious entourage lumbered closer. An aproned storekeeper said, "Them ain't Rebels. Them better not be Rebels? 'Cause I ain't stayin' if them's Rebels. I ain't no soldier. I told 'em when they give me this here gun that I weren't no soldier."

A white-bearded old man spoke up. "How's a feller to tell if they's Rebels or not? Word is that they's still wearin' Union blue."

The clopping hooves and creaking wheels grew nearer. A windblown can rattled in the cross street. The merchant spun. His gun discharged in the air. The white-bearded man and the one in the top hat fired, too.

"Hold your fire!" Ol' Mex said. "Hold your Goddamn fire!" The shooters lowered their smoking arms.

"But I thought..."

"Hush up, you old fool!" Ol' Mex said. "Leave it to a passel of amateurs to go off half-cocked at nothin'."

The top-hatted man said, "Ah, don't you go soldierin' down on us just 'cause you done a hitch in the army, and fifteen years ago it was at that."

Ol' Mex jabbed him with a finger. "You'd best know I was in for nigh on to two years and I spent 'em fightin' Mexicans the whole damn time."

The white-bearded man said, "Well, that don't mean you know enough about armyin' to lord over us like some damned general."

"I know enough to save my charge till I know my target," Ol'Mex said. "Now reload before them riders is on us." But it was too late. He turned and saw them towering above.

"Cease fire, you damned idiots!" a salty sergeant ordered down. "We've got the General of the Army here."

"The general of what army," Billy asked.

"The United States Army, you fool! What the hell army do you think?"

"Well, I don't know. I just..."

"Shut up and let us through," the sergeant said. "And get a hold of your Goddamned nerves, all of you, before you get General Scott killed."

"General Scott?" Ol' Mex said. "General Winfield Scott? From the Mexican War?"

"And the War of 1812 and the Indian Wars and practically every other damned war this country has ever been in. Now clear the way. We're coming through."

Instead, the militiamen gathered around the open carriage and gawked in at the obese general in gold braid.

"By God, it is him!"

"Howdy-do, General."

"Yeah, howdy-do, General Scott."

Billy flashed a smile and extended his hand for a shake.

The Sergeant bumped them back with his horse and said, "Stand down, you scarecrows. You will show the General the respect he is due. Get into formation and present arms."

The militiamen stumbled and fell back over themselves, attempting to obey the Sergeant. They jounced and shoved in an earnest effort to comply, but the result was a jumble of clowns and cussing that ended in a waving line as irregular as the clothes they were wearing.

The General peered out from under his plumed commodore's hat with an expression that was equal parts pomposity and repugnance. His mouth frowned in disgust; his blood-shot nose formed a hawkish beak.

The Sergeant said, "Now, you pack of rabble. Present! Arms!"

The civilians did so as snappily as they could but the effect was confusion. When the last of them finally had his rusty flintlock presented forward, muzzle up, they focused on the magnificent warrior, the hero of every age since the turn of the century, the most famous man in American military history save George Washington himself.

As a lieutenant colonel during the War of 1812, Scott cemented his reputation as a professional fighting man. Relying upon intense discipline and slavish protocol, "Ol' Fuss and Feathers" transformed 1,200 sloppy volunteers into masterful soldiers who went on to battle British regulars to a standstill along the Canadian front. His bravery and wounds earned him the rank of brigadier and then major general, the highest rank in the army at that time. As the war ended, Scott was twenty-eight years old, nationally renowned, and in search of even greater laurels.

Between 1818 and 1842, General Scott embroiled himself in the distasteful business of separating the Cherokee and Seminole Indians from their ancestral lands. Where required, he oversaw the killing of resisters. In other cases, he employed his considerable skills as a diplomat and negotiated the choice parcels out from under them. He helped move the southeastern tribes to the Oklahoma Territory and they never retook their homes. For his efforts, a grateful government named Scott General of the Army, the highest military position in the country.

His career scaled even higher peaks between 1846 and 1848, when a land-hungry United States asserted what it considered to be its God-ordained right to possess all of North America from sea to shining sea. Since Mexico then owned one quarter of that expanse, it fell upon the General to take it from them by force of arms, which he did with finesse, flanking, and rapid deployment of troops. America thereby gained all the territory that later became the states of California, Arizona, New Mexico, Colorado, Utah, Nevada, and parts of Texas, Kansas, and Wyoming.

Heady with success, Scott ran for President in 1852. The qualities that served him so well as a combat general, though—exaggerated self-confidence, single-mindedness, and the unwillingness to compromise—led to his destruction in the political arena. The General lost the election to Franklin Pierce, his subordinate in the Mexican campaign, and he never re-entered politics.

At seventy-five, he was now embarking on what might prove to be his last great hurrah: Abraham Lincoln calling upon him to put down the insurrection that was threatening to tear the country apart. But his faith in successfully carrying out that mission was diminishing with each glance at these so-called militiamen he was supposed to turn into soldiers.

"Clear a path for the General," the crusty sergeant said. "Let us through here!"

The militiamen broke like ten-pins from their line and bumbled to comply. When they had opened their barricade, they presented arms again and let the General pass. With the barricade back in place, the little troop watched the carriage creak on down the street.

"So that was Ol' Fuss an' Feathers," Billy said. "Damnation, I never knowed he was so damned big. Hell, he took up that whole carriage all by hisself."

The old man with the white beard said, "I wouldn't talk if I was you, lard ass, though I have heard tell that he can't even mount a horse no more. I wonder how he's figurin' on leadin' an army into battle."

"Don't you fret about the General none," Ol' Mex said. "He led us to victory down in Mexico and he'll do the same up here against the secesh."

"What do you reckon he thought of us?" Billy asked. "As soldiers, I mean?"

"What in the hell would you expect him to think," Ol' Mex said, "what with all of you firin' off your guns at nothin' and damn near killin' him."

"I didn't shoot off mine," one said.

"Me neither," said another.

"Neither did I," Billy added.

"Well, I reckon not," the aproned man said, "since you don't even know how to load yours."

Most everybody laughed or tried to. Billy did not utter a sound. He hung his head, knowing that what they said was true. They had just issued him this rusty flintlock musket the day before and no one had gotten around to showing him how it worked.

"Here, boy, come over here," Ol' Mex said, feigning annoyance. "Bring me that piece and let me teach loadin' it to you before you end up killin' yourself or somebody else."

Billy instantly grinned and hurried over to the veteran. The rest of the militiamen waved the boy off and went back to their vigil of waiting, watching, and worrying.

CHAPTER FOUR

The Executive Mansion
April 25, 1861
Afternoon

FIFTEEN MINUTES AFTER LEAVING THE SHAMBLING MILITIAMEN AT THE intersection, General Scott's entourage pulled up in front of the White House. The front door opened and President Abraham Lincoln emerged wearing a frock coat and no hat. Two frontiersmen serving as sentries came to a shaggy attention and then dipped into their chewing tobacco pouches after the loosely jointed chief executive strode passed them.

With the ambling grace of a circus giraffe, the President approached the open carriage, being careful to give a nod to the uniformed driver and surrounding horsemen. "Good afternoon, General," he said pleasantly. "It's good to see you. It's good to see any Virginian who hasn't gone South with all the rest."

The General remained seated and said, "Mr. President, I have defended my country under the flag of the Union for more than fifty years. And so long as God permits me, I will continue to do so, even if my own kinsmen revile me for it."

"And I, for one, thank you for that, General," the President said. "I just wish there were more loyal Unionists here to defend the capital."

The General nodded into his fleshy chins. "They will come, Mr. President, they will come. The North will rally. I understand that Boston and New York and Philadelphia are wild with parades and great jubilation, all in support of you and the cause of the Union."

A red squirrel hopped up and chattered over an acorn before shaking its tail and skittering off. Lincoln tried to smile but all he could manage was a shake of the head. "Well, you'd never know it to look around this frightened town, now would you?"

General Scott frowned in agreement.

"No matter," Lincoln said, resigning himself. "It is the hand that circumstance has dealt us and we shall play it. So how do the cards read today, General? Will the great capital of our nation remain free for another day?"

"Well, sir, we do have our challenges," Scott said and he told him of the thirty-five hundred or so untrained militia attempting to guard two hundred and fifty miles of hostile perimeter as well as every important intersection and edifice in the city. He added that the telegraph wires had been cut at Baltimore effectively eliminating all contact with the West and the Northeast. And he mentioned the 6th Massachusetts.

Lincoln paced in a small circle, hands behind his back, staring at the dusty ground. "Tell me again, General. Exactly what happened to those boys up there in Baltimore?"

Scott repeated what he thought he had made clear on at least two other occasions. On the previous Friday, the 6th Massachusetts, one thousand fresh-cheeked boys away from home for the first time, pulled into southern-leaning Baltimore by rail from Philadelphia. The cars had to be towed by mule teams through the center of the city to be re-railed for the journey on to Washington.

After letting eight cars pass without serious incident, a mob of secessionists stopped the ninth and began to hurl bricks at it, so the officers detrained the troops and tried to get them away on foot. Some among the southern mob began to fire pistols. A few Massachusetts boys fell, and the officers returned the fire. Scott mentioned that the troops were quartered up at the Capitol building.

"Yes, I know. I'm going up there today to talk with them."

"That is fine, Mr. President. Your visit will be good for their morale."

"I'm not doing it for their morale, General Scott," Lincoln said. "I'm doing it for my own."

The President stepped to the front of the carriage team and began stroking a chestnut horse's face, as if seeking a moment's solace.

"So what was the final casualty count, General?" the President asked, making his way back to the carriage.

"The 6th Massachusetts lost four men and another thirty-nine were wounded, sir.""And the civilians...the secessionist losses?"

" They claimed twelve citizens dead and dozens more wounded. And on top of that, they burned every railroad bridge into the city."

"I know...I know," Lincoln hung his head and said. "And with Baltimore our only rail link to the North, we are completely cut off, and ripe for the taking by anyone who wants to come in and take it."

"It could be viewed that way, sir," the General said grimly.

A long pause followed during which silence roared in their ears like the ocean in a conch shell. For those suspended moments, there were no birds chirping or squirrels rustling, no clopping horses or barking dogs. There was only heavy air and stifling heat and the dead calm upon which it all rested.

The escort sergeant's mount snorted. Lincoln refocused. "I have been considering who should lead our troops into battle, assuming we get them here and get them organized."

"Yes?" the General said, his interest piqued.

"Yes, I know you would have preferred your man Robert Lee for the job, but since he has gone South, we will have to find someone else."

"Do you have anyone in mind?" Scott asked.

"I know you favor Joseph Mansfield. And this political general Butler sounds like a hard-driver. But I have also been hearing much about a fellow by the name of Irvin McDowell, the major in charge of the Capitol building."

General Scott shifted uncomfortably. The driver steadied his two horses. "Treasury Secretary Chase has been lobbying you again, hasn't he?" Scott said.

"Well, General, as you know, Simon Chase and I talk regularly as do you and I. And like you, he is a man whose judgment I value and whose support I dearly need."

"Sir," Scott said, "you must remember that the Secretary and Major McDowell are both Ohioans and that Secretary Chase has taken it upon himself to sponsor the Major even though there are many higher ranking, more qualified officers in line ahead of him."

"But that isn't the first time that has been the case, is it?" Lincoln said. "Couldn't he still be the best man for the job? What do you know about him anyway?"

The General acknowledged that McDowell was a West Pointer with solid staff and organizational experience. He was forty-two years old and a robust physical specimen. He countered, though, that the Major had never commanded so much as a company in battle and had shown neither the aptitude nor the inclination to do so. Scott described him as an adequate, mid-level staff officer and nothing more and added that putting him in command of a campaigning army would be a grave error.

"But Secretary Chase says that McDowell has done a good job drilling the men here in the city."

"Perhaps, sir. But far more is required of an army commander."

"Well, at any rate, we don't need to decide on McDowell or anyone else quite yet. I will continue to consider any and all recommendations you make." Two of the frontier guards by the front door caught his eye. They were engaged in a tobacco juice spitting contest and missing the spittoon every time.

Lincoln almost smiled. He watched a single crow take to the hot, blue sky and rasp its caw. It made him think of Illinois, of circuit riding, of the long satisfying rides all alone with his thoughts, his books, and his friends up ahead. Those were simple, happy times before his dreams of grandeur and those of his wife had fooled him and come true.

He massaged the back of his neck, then his shoulders. He could feel his tired spot aching deep and black within him, the spot that no joy ever seemed to reach and no amount of rest ever seemed to alleviate. "I hear crowds of citizens have been gathering down at the station every day in the dim hope that a troop train will roll in and save them and that they break up each dusk to shuffle sadly home. My God, my constituency is becoming a population of pitiful zombies sleepwalking their way through a nightmare about which I can do nothing."

The General gazed down at the carriage floor and marveled at the depths of this strange man's pessimism. The cavalrymen sneaked their own concerned glances.

Unaware, the President said, "I just hope Jefferson Davis does not send his men across the Potomac before ours arrive."

"He most probably won't, sir," Scott said. "I imagine he intends to wait for us to make the first move."

"Well, General," Lincoln said, gazing southward, "we can pray for that eventuality and have the faith of our fathers that it will come to pass, but I, for one, would trade a little of that faith for a look inside that wily man's mind."

CHAPTER FIVE

---◆·◆---

Montgomery, Alabama
April 29, 1861
Evening

IT MIGHT HAVE BEEN REASSURING FOR ABRAHAM LINCOLN TO KNOW THAT Jefferson Davis had spent the past four days worrying about what he, Lincoln, was up to. Confederate spies in Washington had begun filing reports confirming the arrival of large numbers of Federal troops in that city. This torch lit night, however, Davis had already determined to let someone else worry about that for a change. He was in his element, at the zenith of his career if not his life, and as he sat on the stage waiting to speak, he took in the glory, the joy, the excitement, and the unabashed pleasure.

The assembly hall of the Alabama State Capitol was buzzing with excited chatter. Laughter belted out over layers of spoken words and shouts. The Provisional Government of the Confederate States of America, gathering in their top hats and tails, was airing their impassioned opinions and every member intended to be heard.

These were the rich, the politicians and planters, the statesmen and bankers, the diplomats and businessmen. They were generals and financiers, factory owners and war profiteers, the driving wheels burning and churning for Southern independence. Nearly all smoked cigars or spit tobacco juice and nipped at flasks of ambered whiskey. They slapped backs and shook hands, wagged fingers and twisted arms, pausing as required to bow before gracious ladies.

Except for the white-gloved black men who invisibly attended them, they were gentlemen all, men of substance and quality whose affronted honor could no longer permit them to remain citizens of the United States. They had renounced that citizenship and come here to Montgomery to form a new government, a new constitution, a new nation. And tonight they would hear from their President, the Honorable Jefferson Davis of Mississippi, the very ideal, the paragon, the embodied personification of all that was right and noble about their Cause.

Born poor in Kentucky in 1808, Davis had moved as a boy to Mississippi where his father (and after his death, his older brother) prospered enough to provide young Jeff with a first-rate education, although he never took his studies very seriously. He was nearly expelled from West Point for his adolescent antics but managed to graduate and serve for eight years in the Army.

Always the rebel, he eloped with the daughter of his commanding officer, Zachary Taylor, and absconded with her to his budding plantation in Mississippi where they both contracted malaria and she died. The loss of his bride sobered Davis as age and military service had not, sending him into a decade of self-imposed seclusion and study. He emerged as an expert in government, history, philosophy, and constitutional law and married an equally well-educated young woman, Varina Howell.

Entering politics as a Democrat, he served in the House of Representatives for two years before the Mexican War called him to what would be meritorious service and a severe foot wound as the colonel of the renowned Mississippi Rifles. He could have remained in the army as a general but preferred posts in the 1850s as a United States Senator, the Secretary of War, and again as a Senator. He used these platforms to espouse his utter belief in the right of any state to secede and his sincere desire that none do so. It was well past saving the Union now, though, and he was prepared to make his reasons for separation clear.

From his ornately carved chair on the podium stage, President Davis was dispensing nods and thin smiles to admiring onlookers but, despite his desire to do so, he did not appear to be sharing in the bustling joy down on the floor. He looked serious and perhaps a little anxious, especially when rubbing at the aching neuralgia that had plagued his face and right eye for so long. He squinted through his left, glancing away altogether whenever some admiring young lady's smile engaged him too boldly.

To be sure, he was a handsome man in a gaunt, taut-cheeked sort of way, though he bore a pallor from years of enduring malaria and the fevers that still tormented him. His features ran from ridged brow to hawkish eye to an eagle's beak and chiseled jaw, terminating at a chin that sported a twirled tuft of beard. Seated, he kept his small-boned physique as rigid as his face and, when standing, he stretched to nearly six feet in height.

Everything about the man suggested strength of will and integrity of character. He was clearly a man of honesty, purpose, and, beyond all else, honor. His entire adult life as a soldier, planter, and statesman had been a knight's crusade for chivalry and, at fifty-one years of age, he had rarely fallen short of those ideals.

The gavel sounded, once then twice. A short, fat politico cried out over the podium, "Come to order! Come to order!" And the noise began to subside. After a lengthy introduction, he announced, "Gentlemen of the Congress, allow me to present to you our President, the Honorable Jefferson Davis." Applause rose, swelled, and settled. Davis stood and approached the podium. Slowly scanning the crowd, he shuffled his papers, and began.

He spent the first portion of his oration speaking carefully, meticulously, the way he had learned from courtroom attorneys. He matched the work-a-day tone of his voice with the mundane, but necessary, orders of business. He spoke of governmental matters, housekeeping issues related to the proper functioning of state bureaucracy. Someone had to come down out of the exhilarating ether of freedom and independence and address such concerns. There were funds to be raised, expenses to be defrayed, and unpopular tax-talk to broach.

Knowing that he could never hold an audience long with fare such as that, President Davis raised the holy specter of the Revolutionary War: George Washington, the panoply of Southern patriots, and their views on the sanctity of the states. In 1783, he said, at the close of the first war for independence, the Treaty of Paris named and recognized each state as an independent sovereign, and he went on to invoke the United States Constitution with its nod to the inviolability of the state governments.

Expansively, he said, "Strange, indeed, must it appear to the impartial observer, but it is nonetheless true, that all these carefully worded clauses proved unavailing to prevent the rise and growth in the Northern states of a political school which has persistently claimed that the government thus formed was not a compact between States, but was in effect a national government set up above and over the States. An organization created by the States to secure the blessings of liberty and independence against foreign aggression, has been gradually perverted into a machine for their control in their domestic affairs."

He got a solid round of applause for that and a bigger one when he reminded the crowd of how the framers themselves had tacitly sanctioned slavery. Twelve out of thirteen states that ratified the Constitution, he said, permitted the institution at the time of ratification. Pausing for the increasing applause, Davis surged on. "The declaration of war," he said, "made against this Confederacy by Abraham Lincoln, President of the United States, in his proclamation of the fifteenth day of this month, rendered it necessary, in my judgment, that you should convene at the earliest practicable moment to devise the measures necessary for the defense of the country. This occasion is indeed an extraordinary one, " he said, gesticulating. The ovation grew, punctuated by shouts and whistles.

Davis had to wait for it to die down. "Scarcely had the President of the United States received intelligence of the failure of the scheme which he had devised for the re-enforcement of Fort Sumter, that he issued the declaration of war against this Confederacy. He terms sovereign states 'combinations too powerful to be suppressed by the ordinary course of judicial proceedings, or by the powers vested in the marshals by law,' He avows that 'the first service to be assigned to the forces called out' will be not to execute the process of courts, but to capture forts and strongholds situated within the admitted limits of this Confederacy, and garrisoned by its troops, and declares that this effort is intended to maintain the perpetuity of popular government. He concluded by commanding 'the persons composing the combinations aforesaid,' five million inhabitants of the seven States, 'to retire peaceably to their respective abodes within twenty days.' This is nothing short of tyranny! Tyranny, I say!" And the Confederate Congressmen roared to their feet in agreement.

Weaving his way through several more ovations, Davis finally hushed the audience with a return to his subtler tones.

"We protest solemnly in the face of mankind that we desire peace at any sacrifice, save that of honor. All we ask is to be let alone; that those who never held power over us shall not now attempt our subjugation by arms. This we will, we must, resist to the direst extremity. The moment that this pretension is abandoned, the sword shall drop away from our grasp, and we shall be ready to enter into treaties of amnesty and commerce that cannot but be mutually beneficial. So long as this pretension is maintained, however, we with a firm reliance on that Divine Power which covers with its protection the just cause, must continue to struggle for our inherent right to freedom, independence, and self-government!"

The audience shot up and thundering ovation rattled windows and hurt ears. Cheers, hurrahs, whistles, and wails stood hair up on the napes of necks and brought tears to determined faces. A lightning bolt seemed to have electrified the auditorium with the rarified air of righteousness.

President Davis accepted the accolades as any distinguished orator would. He stepped to one side of the podium and then the other, dipping his head with humility, grace, and dignity. The ovation continued and he bowed again and then again. He was clearly yielding to the joy now, the excitement, the headiness of the times. Lifting his gaze upward, he prayed, "Thank you, dear God, for the patriotism of our people, the holiness of our Cause, and the righteous Christian warriors poised in Virginia to defend it."

CHAPTER SIX

Harper's Ferry, Virginia
May 1, 1861
Dusk

FOR TWO FRIGHTFUL NIGHTS, RAUCOUS LAUGHTER AND MERRIMENT HAD spiced the air in this tiny village at the confluence of the Potomac and Shenandoah Rivers. Bottles had shattered and raw-throated shouts had echoed up and down the cobblestones. Above the hubbub of an over-flowing tavern, a piano still plinked out its honky-tonk melody and boisterous songs about Jeff Davis and the Southern Confederacy resounded from the doors and windows.

The locals, mostly employees at the United States Armory and Arsenal, had welcomed these liberators at first, even though they had caused the retreating Yankees to raze their workplace. In spite of the personal loss, men, women, and children had turned out with Virginia flags and lace handkerchiefs to cheer Captain Turner Ashby and his dashing Confederate riders as they drove the arsonists across the Potomac River to Maryland.

In the days that followed, however, hundreds of blue, gray, brown, and civilian-clad militiamen flooded in behind them with shotguns, squirrel rifles, and jugs of whiskey to occupy the town. Ashby left for other adventures and all that remained were these undisciplined, undrilled ruffians with no one among them able to instill anything resembling order.

There were enough plumed and braided militia officers to do the job if they were so inclined, but mostly they threw parties and parades to keep their men in liquor and ale. They were always mindful that the privates had elected them to their ranks and could similarly unelect them if their popularity waned. And nothing made an officer any less popular than drill and discipline. Besides, the commanders figured, the war would be over in a week or two and nearly all of them would be returning home to pursue their political aspirations, so why risk alienating voters with anything as distasteful as order? It would only take one good fight to bring the Yankees to their knees anyway, everyone said, and they were confident that their gun-wise constituents already possessed the requisite skills to do that.

As a result, these young Rebels were having the time of their lives at the expense of Harper's Ferry. They were binging on white lightning and cheap liquor, cigars and plug tobacco, driving most of the citizens behind locked doors and shuttered windows for refuge. A few of the townsfolk were bold enough to engage the rowdies roaming the streets and alleys but most avoided them altogether, leaving the Rebels to celebrate among themselves.

"Hey! Hey, you!" one of them, a freckled redhead, called to another. "Hey! You! Stop!"

A tall, gangly youth in a blue uniform turned unsteadily and answered, "Who? Me?"

"No, the damned ghost you're with. Hell yeah, you. You're the only one standin' there, ain't you?"

The tall boy gazed around and slurred, "I reckon maybe I am at that. So what d'ya wanna make of it?"

The redhead hurried up to him. "I don't wanna make nothin' of it. I just want some of whatever's put that there sway in your step. Can you spare me a mouthful?"

The lanky one took a bottle out of his haversack and squinted at it. "I figure maybe I got enough left to let out a swallow. It ain't no fun drinkin' alone no-ways, I don't reckon."

The redhead grabbed the bottle and toasted, "To Jeff Davis then. And the Southern Confederacy!" He took a grimacing gulp and passed it back. Wiping his mouth, he said, "The name's O'Riley. Red O'Riley." He extended his hand for a shake. "What's yours?"

"Slim. Slim Cochran." He took Red's hand and shook it.

"So what outfit are you with, Slim, all dressed up in Yankee blue that a'ways?"

Slim straightened his shoulders and said, "The Potomac Guard. From up

Hampshire County way. God's country. How 'bout yourself?"

Red assumed an equally grandiose pose and announced, "Alabama. And it's as much God's country as any damned place you come from."

"Well, I don't know about that."

"I do," Red said emphatically. "There's a passel of us Alabam boys up here. An' didn't we have a hoot of a time getting' here on the train what with all them flags, and cakes, and pies, and kisses from purty gals."

"It's been the same 'round here, too," Slim said.

'Yeah," Red said. "But since we got here they's been slow puttin' us together into regiments. It looks like we're gonna get our own brigade, though, led by some Florida fellow named Kirby Smith or the like."

Watching the other drunkards staggering up and down the street, Slim forced down a mouthful and handed the bottle back over. "Well, Red, I reckon, us Virginians can use a few good Yankee-killers, if'n you can ante up, that is."

"Don't you worry none 'bout me anteing up. Nor none of my kind. I just hope there's enough of a war up here so's I can kill me a Yankee before it's all over. That's all I want to do is to kill one, up close, so's I can watch that son of a bitch die. I want to kill me one so bad I can taste it."

"Yeah, I reckon we's all hopin' to get a slice of the glory 'fore the whole shootin' match is over."

"I just hope to have at them Yanks before they give up. Damn, I can't tell you how I'm burnin' to gut one."

The boys watched a runaway wagon banging up the street without a driver and slouched down in front of a shuttered storefront with a sign that read "furniture/undertaker."

They were about to swap another drink when the thunder of horses clattered onto the cobblestones from the opposite direction. The noise swelled like a breaking wave and crashed beside them in a blurred flurry of hoots and hollers, straining haunches and spur-maddened eyes. The gray riders swung sabers and shot pistols; their beards and long hair flapped in the wind. When the quaking passed, Slim sagged back against the wall and said, "Holy hell! Who in God's name was that?"

"You don't know?" Red said, watching the end of the stampede pass. "Hell, boy, that was Turner Ashby hisself."

"You don't say," Slim said. "The feller what captured this here town?"

"He'd be the one," Red said. "And that ain't the half of it. I read in a newspaper how he's been spyin' behind enemy lines all the way up through Maryland and Pennsylvania."

"Spyin'?"

"Hell, yeah spyin'. I done read how he dressed hisself up in civilian clothes and walked right into a slew of Yankee camps claiming to be a horse doctor. And while he was pretendin' to be givin' exams, he was really countin' up how many men and cannons and mounts them square-heads had, right under their damn noses."

"You're goshin'," Slim said.

"I ain't. And they would've hung him, too, if'n they was smart enough to catch him. That spyin's a serious business, you know."

"Do tell?" Slim said, his eyelids drooping. "Well, it sounds like that Ashby feller's some kind of hellion all right."

"Well, I should say so," said Red. "And there's plenty more like him right here in this town."

"Yeah? Who's that?"

"Hells bells, boy, I'm talkin' about you and me and all these other patriots. All two thousand of us."

"Two thousand? Is that how many we got here now?"

Disgusted, Red shook his head. "Look around you, boy. Don't it look it? Hell, alls you gotta do is count 'em. Or read the papers."

"Shitfire, there's nothin' in them news rags that's worth a damn to me."

"Have it your way then." He pulled a tattered copy of the *Richmond Daily Inquirer* out of his inside jacket pocket. "But, boy, readin' is what separates us from the beasts of the field."

"O'Riley was it?" Slim smirked.

"Yeah. Same as my mama and my daddy and my eight brothers and sisters. All Irish and hard workers. Hard drinkers, too, after quittin' time."

"Well, O'Riley, you're full of shit." Slim turned away in time to catch an old drunk urinating on the storefront next to him. Feeling the warm wetness coming up through his trousers, he jumped up swearing and tossed the man out into the street. "Goddamn you, you'd best get up and run while you still can, you son of a bitch!" He examined the stain on the seat of his pants and cried, "Shit fire and save matches! Look what you done to me!"

Watching the old man stumbling away on all fours, Red laughed hard before trying to divert his new friend. "Here, Cochran, let him go and take a look at this. There's a piece on the front page of this paper that you oughta read."

Pulling at the seat of his trousers, Slim scoffed. "I told you I ain't interested."

"Well, you oughta be. It says here that a feller by the name of Lee has done took over all the Virginia forces. That's you, brother."

"So? One damned general's the same as the next, judgin' by the ones I've seen around here. They're all a set of worthless peacocks." He sat back down on the wooden sidewalk and grimaced at the spongy wetness touching his skin.

"This one ain't, it don't look. It says here that he was one of the best officers there was in the whole United States Army before he come South."

"That don't prove nothin'. That rag still can't tell me nothin' I need knowin'." But after letting a crowd of rowdies stumble past on the boardwalk, he said, "So what the hell else is in there?"

Red smiled. "Well, let me see. It says over here that they's thinkin' on movin' Jeff Davis and the whole entire Confederate government up to Richmond from Montgomery."

"Is that a fact?"

"Yep. And one I ain't too happy about neither, me bein' from Alabam an' all."

Slim nodded and yawned. He caught a whiff of horse apples and enjoyed the scent. It made him think of the time his little brother actually ate one on his dare. He missed his brother already and his widowed mother. He wondered how they would get along without him there to take care of the farm. But he would only be gone for a few weeks, he knew, and he'd be back in time for the harvest.

"Down here," Red continued, "it talks about what that gorilla Abe Lincoln has went and done now, takin' away the rights from his own damned people in Baltimore."

"Rights to what?"

Red squinted at the print and said, "Somethin' about the right of a feller to know why he's gettin' throwed into jail or the like. But that damned Lincoln's the one that oughta get throwed into jail, for startin' all this trouble in the first place. I'd like to make him the Yankee I gut up close."

"Well, I'm with you on that one," Slim said, leaning toward the paper. "What else does that thing say?"

"Here. Read it for yourself. My eyes is gettin' kinda fuzzy anyways."

Slim drew back as if from a hot stove. "Get that damn thing away from me. I don't want it."

"What's the matter with you anyways, boy, can't you read or somethin'?"

"Hell, yes, I can read! I can read as good as you can."

"Then read this. Read this part right there."

"You go to hell. I don't want to. And you're a Goddamn liar if'n you say I don't know how."

"Fine then. I don't give a damn. But you don't have to be so touchy about it. I know plenty of folks what can't read."

"By God, I told you..."

"Don't fret it none. It ain't no sin. As long as you know how to fight an' shoot and kill Yankees. That's all that matters now."

"And you best believe that I can shoot! I was shootin' before I was walkin'. And I can out-shoot you any damn day of the week, book-learnin' or no book-learnin'."

"What in the hell are you goin' on about, Slim? I never said nothin' about me shootin' better than you."

"An' you damn well best not neither."

"Get a hold of yourself, soldier. Hell, you're gettin' all worked up over nothin'."

Slim crumpled back into his slouch and folded his arms tightly around his knees. "Aw, you just go to hell."

Red grinned. "Hey, listen to this one. It says that Southern merchants is stoppin' payment to Yankee banks on debts still out. Now, that's more like it. Them Yank bankers and factory owners has been gougin' us long enough. If'n I done heard my daddy say that once, I heard him say it a thousand times. Ain't that what your daddy done told you? I mean, before he passed on?"

Slim said. "My Daddy worked hisself to death on our little hard scrabble farm long before he was able to learn me about nothin', before I was even old enough to go to school. That's why, well, that's why I had to stay home and help my Ma get by. But I've done heard all that palaverin' 'bout taxes and tariffs and banks and slaves and all that. And I don't give a good Goddamn about none of it. It's enough for me that them Yankee bastards is threatenin' to invade my farm and trample on my Ma and my little brother and every damn thing in this world that I hold dear."

"Well, I'm with you on that one, Slim ol' boy. But I'm lucky, I reckon. Me and my bothers and sisters got to go to school three or four months out of the year, you know, during the fallow time. I went all the way through to graduation. Eighth grade it was. And I reckon I'm even luckier because my Daddy and my Mama and all the children ever born to 'em is still alive and strong and doin' well. Yes, indeedy, I got the luck of the Irish all right."

Slim finger-drew on the dusty plank between his legs and grunted.

Red continued. "And there was always a heady amount of laughin' around our supper table every evening 'cause of Daddy mostly. He knew how to make us laugh and I reckon we done a fair job on him, too. Here. Let's have us another snort. To our folk we's here protectin'."

After toasting, they traded swigs and drifted into a thickening haze.

Eventually, Red went back to his newspaper. "You know, Slim, out of all the things in here, what worries me the most is the part on how Maryland is most likely gonna get forced to stay in the Union after all. You know what that means, don't you?"

"Sure, I do...yeah...of course I do..."

"It means that that mountain right up there, Maryland Heights they call it, is gonna be enemy territory. And we had, by God, better get some guns and men up there right quick or the Yankees is gonna beat us to it. And if'n they do, they's gonna blow us right the hell out of this soup bowl we's in down here."

Slim craned his neck toward the silhouette of looming Maryland Heights and said, "Yeah, I reckon I see what you mean." He took a pull on the bottle, his eyes drooping.

"Hey, save me some of that," Red said. He was beginning to slur. "The home folk need 'em another toast. To all our homefolk and all our kin. May we never fail in protectin' them from the heathen invaders." He finished off the whiskey, his eyes growing heavy, and slumped into a heap against the storefront. He mumbled a mushy sentence about a train whistle and more patriots answering the call but there was no one awake to hear it. Slim Cochran was already out. And with the singing and shouting and wild piano-playing fading to a distant gray, Red O'Riley nodded off, too, completely unaware that the newly-appointed commander of the Harper's Ferry garrison was getting off the hissing train.

CHAPTER SEVEN

Harper's Ferry

COLONEL THOMAS JONATHAN JACKSON EMERGED FROM THE LOCOMOTIVE
steam and surveyed the little town. He had marched out of Lexington,
Virginia on April 21 at the head of the Virginia Military Institute's cadet
cadre: 176 young men schooled in the science and application of modern
warfare. At that time, Jackson and the cadets were responding to Governor
John Letcher's call to report to Richmond immediately for duty as drill
instructors for the thousands of eager recruits flooding into the city.

After joyous receptions along the way, the cadets reached the state capital
where they were quickly put to work training some uniformity into the rambunctious mob of would-be soldiers. Jackson himself, never one to promote
his own talents, accepted a menial desk job as a mapmaker, a post for which
he had neither aptitude, training, nor interest. He, no doubt, would have
sunk into oblivion there and accepted his circumstances as being an expression of God's mysterious will, had God not intervened or, at least, a few of
his old acquaintances from Lexington.

These political men remembered tales of Jackson's one shining success in
life, his fearless performances as an artillerist during the Mexican War, and

they decided that he might be the one to whip the Harper's Ferry garrison into shape. They knew, too, that it would be a coup for Lexington to have a native son in command along the critical northern Virginia frontier.

Harper's Ferry's strategic importance, Jackson knew, was two-fold. First, it anchored the left flank of the Alexandria line, stretching from Washington, D.C. to the Blue Ridge Mountains. That line represented the first defense against Unionist thrusts into the Virginia piedmont. Second, it stood as the gatekeeper of the Shenandoah Valley and its natural north-south invasion routes. Whoever controlled it could either launch attacks southward to the back door of the state or plunge northward into the heart of the Union.

General Robert Lee met with the new colonel and laid out the mission before him. It was a cordial encounter but a formal one, giving no hint of the bond to come. Jackson had already told his wife that he considered General Lee to be a better choice for commander of Virginia's forces than even the legendary Winfield Scott. Lee, for his part, respected Jackson's dedication to God and his commitment to military discipline.

Briefed on his orders and braced by his faith, Colonel Jackson boarded a northbound train. He took along two V.M.I. cadets as aides and set out for his new command. He could not have been happier for he had been given the post which he preferred above all others.

The zigzagging trip through Gordonsville, Manassas Junction, and Strasburg gave the Colonel of Virginia forces a first-hand look at one of the state's most pressing military shortcomings: an inadequate rail system. He had to get off the train altogether at Strasburg and take a stage coach the twenty-five miles up to Winchester where he boarded another train for the final leg up to Harper's Ferry.

He made a note to contact General Lee about building a railway to eliminate the need for the stage. The General had already given him orders to send any captured locomotives and cars south. Rapid communications, supply, and troop movements, they both knew, would soon depend upon the iron horse, an invention as yet untried in warfare, and, from his previous personal travels, Jackson was aware that the Northern railroads out-distanced those in the South three times over.

The two-day trip from Richmond to Harper's Ferry gave the Colonel a chance to reflect on his circumstances. He was being made responsible for one of the most sensitive areas in all the Confederacy, and he knew if he failed, so too might his state and his new nation.

Not only was Harper's Ferry strategically located, the Shenandoah Valley it guarded had long been recognized as the breadbasket of Virginia with grain

fields and livestock that fed the state and several others as well. The Baltimore
and Ohio Railroad coursed through the sleepy village, connecting the boun-
tiful western states with the East, and barge traffic still traversed the
Chesapeake and Ohio Canal across the rippling river. It was the armory hard-
ware, though, and the amorphous body of Confederate militiamen supposedly guarding it that most concerned Jackson. Lee had ordered him to ship
the rifle-making machinery south and at the same time drill some discipline
into the drunken boys reported to be carousing about.

It was with the latter in mind that Colonel Jackson emerged from the hissing steam and proceeded down the main street of Harper's Ferry with his two
former cadets in tow. What he saw along the way distressed him. It would have
distressed any commanding officer to see so critical a position in such disarray.
But it especially distressed this devotee to a wrathful God. For he believed that
the Creator would only help those who walked in the light. And all around
him he saw nothing but darkness and boys too drunk to walk at all.

Sighing tiredly, he rubbed at his eyes. It was already dark and there were
no disciplinary actions that he could effectively set in motion at that hour.
Hell, it seemed, would have to reign here another night. He needed sleep now
anyway, many hours of luscious, seductive sleep and he plodded down the
street with his aides to find a room. It was then that he glimpsed a pair of
passed-out boys whose public condition he could not ignore.

Jackson strode over to the two boys. "Get up," he said, prodding them
with his big boot. "Get up and come to attention."

Groggy and confused, Red O'Riley squinted and said, "Hey, stop kickin'
me, Goddamn it. Who in the hell do you think you are anyways?"

The two cadets jerked Red and Slim to their feet and pinned them against
the storefront. "He is your new commanding officer," one said. "And you will
do as he says."

The other added, "That's right, and it's Colonel Jackson to the both of you
swine."

"Is that a fact?" Red said. "Well, I've seen plenty of so-called colonels
around here and not a one of 'em is worth his own piss."

"That's right," Slim slurred, pressed to the wall, "what'd you fellers do, run
outta whiskey or somethin' and come lookin' to us poor privates for a taste?
What in the hell gives you the right to go rough on us?"

Jackson stepped closer and said slumberously, "I have the right to instill
discipline because you are soldiers under my command. I am a colonel and
you are privates."

Red retorted, "Well, you sure as hell don't look like no colonel to me.

Why, you ain't got no gold braid or fancy patches or a sash or big hat or nothin'. Hell, you look like a damned bluecoat Yankee."

The first cadet flashed anger and tightened his clutch on the mouthy boy. "Do you want us to arrest these miscreants, Colonel? For insubordination?"

"And drunkenness?" the second added.

"No. Let them down," Jackson said.

"But, sir..."

"Let them down."

The cadets reluctantly obeyed their orders and the boys indignantly brushed at the musses in their clothing.

Jackson suddenly raised his arm up over his head. Red flinched, as if about to be slapped.

"Are you sure you don't want these *soldiers* taken into custody, Colonel? A public flogging might do them good?"

Slim's eyes widened.

Jackson pondered the suggestion and said, "No. The drill at dawn should prove sufficiently redemptive. Let them go. There are too many sinners here tonight to make an example of just two."

He turned without demanding a salute and started slowly on down the street.

Red called after the Colonel, "So you think you're gonna be the one to get us boys out on the drill field, do you? Hell, there h'ain't been even no generals able to do that. Especially at dawn!"

Jackson plodded on, seemingly oblivious to the challenge.

Slim and Red, for their part, stumbled away laughing about meaningless rules and the worthless officers who tried to enforce them.

CHAPTER EIGHT

Washington City, District of Columbia
May 23, 1861
Afternoon

"Go back to the woods, you nigger-lovin' baboon," came a cry from a group of laughing soldiers. The voice had a heavy Irish brogue. President Lincoln casually looked out in the direction of the insult but shrugged it off.

"Do you want me to stop the carriage," General Scott said, "and have the escorts flush out that insubordinate coward?" They had the canopy up, shielding them from the withering sun and making identification of the scoundrel all the more difficult.

"No, General, I've grown accustomed to such sentiments." He tried to smile.

Lincoln and Scott were heading toward the grounds of the Government Insane Asylum outside of town. Several regiments were bivouacked there and the two leaders were on their way to review them. On the rutted road in front of the carriage yet another newly arrived regiment of a thousand or so men was slogging its way through the yellow dust.

"I never thought I'd say this, General, but we've got more soldiers than this city can handle. True enough, they've made us feel safer from the secessionists, but they are becoming a threat to the citizenry in and of themselves."

Facing opposite the President, the General mopped his face with a hand-kerchief and said, "I would still contend that these men are the lesser of the evils but your point is well taken, sir. This town was never designed to accommodate a sudden influx of 35,000 visitors."

"I should say not," Lincoln said, grimacing, as he expounded on such problems as sanitation, disease, lack of food, theft, fire, and drunkenness.

General Scott folded his arms and silently reddened. He turned his face away from Lincoln and watched a company of sloppily marching men.

The President eased back in his seat. "Let me make it clear to you, General, that I in no way hold you personally responsible for the current condition of our troops. I understand that these are extraordinary circumstances but we must all, myself included, exert extraordinary efforts in our attempts to remedy them."

The General loosened his arms but there was still a pout on his sagging face. "Yes, sir," he said.

Lincoln gazed off in the direction of Virginia. "What we really need to do is get these boys out there and on the road to Richmond. That would get them out of the city, give them some on-the-job military training, and get some use out of them before their 90-day enlistments run out."

"Your points are well taken, sir," Scott said, returning the salutes of several boys in over-sized uniforms.

"I hope that they are, General. Do you have a timetable yet for when you intend to head them south?"

"As you know, I am sending some troops across the Potomac in the morning under the command of your *protégé* Elmer Ellsworth." He made no effort to mask his disdain for the famous parade ground drillmaster.

"Yes, but that will be only a limited operation, just crossing to secure Arlington Heights and Alexandria. I am talking about the big push. The advance on Richmond itself."

The gold-braided General said nothing. He shifted his weight, protesting volumes without words.

"What is it, General? Do you still disapprove of such an advance?"

"Mr. President, you are the Commander-in-Chief."

Lincoln nodded. "Of course, of course. And I will take full responsibility for the actions of our army, but war is your business, General, not mine. So please, tell me what you think."

Scott narrowed his eyes against a dusty wind and said that he believed an overland, "On To Richmond" drive would result in horrendous casualties for the Northern soldiers; that sealing off the rivers and coastline surrounding the

Southern states would achieve the same results with far fewer lives and property lost.

Lincoln crossed his legs and said, "I don't know, General Scott. I respect your military judgment greatly, but I will have to take this up further with the cabinet before I can make a final determination."

"Well, sir, please rely heavily upon your own counsel when doing so. There are, as you know, opponents to my plan in the Cabinet. Some are even calling it the 'Anaconda Plan' or some such rubbish."

Lincoln smiled weakly at the image of the sluggish constrictor. "I will continue to give your plan my thorough consideration, General. But I must tell you that I am leaning more and more toward the overland invasion perhaps with a simultaneous invasion of western Virginia from Ohio. I trust you are working up contingency plans along those lines."

General Scott mopped the sweat from his face again and sighed, "Yes, sir. I am."

"Good," Lincoln said. "And what of Baltimore? Anymore trouble up there?"

"Do you mean since that political general Butler disobeyed my direct orders and seized the place? No. No trouble since then and that is exceedingly fortunate for him."

"And for the country, I must add, General. Butler's establishment of martial law there is what allowed these troops to pass through the city unhindered. And I did communicate to him the impropriety of his insubordination against you."

The carriage came to another stop, a longer one this time. The President stuck his head outside and took a look around. The aging red brick asylum dominated the hilltop they had reached, a sprawling hilltop white with mushrooming dog tents. The flat across from the asylum was the only piece of open ground and it was crowded with row upon row of marching, drilling soldiers. Dozens of gowned inmates clung to the bars, grunting and watching.

"It looks like we're here, General," Lincoln said, a touch of cheer in his voice. "I must admit that I've been growing tired of these reviews, but I am looking forward to this one."

General Scott said, "I supposed as much when I heard that Colonel Ellsworth would be *performing*. I know that he is a particular favorite of yours."

"Of the entire country's, General. I would guess that he is the most popular and renowned soldier in this army just about now. Besides you, of course."

"Oh, Mr. President, I am certain that he is far better regarded by the present citizenry of this nation than I, though I fail to appreciate the reasons why."

Scanning the ocean of colorful uniforms, Lincoln said, "Fame is a fickle thing, I know, but he is famous and he is a military hero and this country needs every famous, military hero it can get just now."

"But a military hero who has never fought in a battle? Or served in an army? Or ever done more than entertain audiences with fancy drill?"

"I grant you, General, the boy's military qualifications read slim and I can understand the War Department's hesitation to commission him. But you must admit, his parades and drills and demonstrations have done wonders for the national morale and my own, I might add. He might only put on shows with his drill teams but he puts on the kind of shows that stir men's hearts to patriotism...and enlistment."

General Scott held his tongue and crossed his arms as the heat of the ground waved up outside his window.

Suddenly, the President blurted, "Look! There's Elmer now on his mount. And he's coming this way. My God, what a majestic figure that lad cuts." More sprightly than he had felt all day, he stepped down out of the carriage to await the parade-ground soldier, now the colonel of the 11th New York Fire Zouaves.

Colonel Ellsworth dismounted his shiny, black charger and saluted. "Welcome, Mr. President," he said, smiling a confident smile from beneath his bright-red kepi.

"Elmer, it's so good to see you again, my boy." Lincoln started to shake the young man's hand but caught himself and awkwardly returned the salutes.

"And a good afternoon to you, too, General Scott," Ellsworth said saluting into the carriage. "You honor me with your presence."

Scott grumbled, "We did not come all the way out here just to see you, Colonel. Your regiment is but one of many we will be reviewing today."

"Of course, sir," Ellsworth said, absolutely unrattled by the General's tone. "And a fine day it is for reviewing, sir."

"Yes, yes," Scott scoffed. "Let's get on with it, Colonel. Is your regiment ready?"

"Why, yes it is, sir. The men are just up ahead of you, sir, lined up in formation. You can't miss them."

"I should say not," Scott said. "They stand out like organ-grinder monkeys in those ridiculous Zouave suits."

"Uh, yes, sir," Ellsworth said, still unflapped. "Perhaps you could turn your carriage sideways, sir, thereby affording a better view."

"Don't you worry about my view, Colonel. You just prove to me that you have drilled these ruffian firefighters of yours in the standard soldier's school. I gave you the honor of spear-heading the penetration into Virginia tomorrow morning and I want assurances that your men will conduct themselves properly."

"Yes, sir," the little officer said. "You will be so assured."

"Tell me, Colonel," Lincoln said. "Just how do your men feel about crossing the river and occupying Alexandria? This could be a very dangerous assignment for them, you know. The disunionists could still be over there in force."

"My men are ready, sir," Ellsworth said. "We don't care how many secessionists are over there. We intend to rout them all and nip this treason of theirs in the bud and bring back to you every Rebel flag now flying over that treasonous town."

Lincoln smiled and said, "Here-here, Elmer! But please, son, do be careful. Your loss would be an unbearable burden to me and all my family."

"Do not worry about me, sir. But you might want to say prayers for those secesh over there."

Lincoln nodded, General Scott shook his head, and the young Colonel swung himself up and into his saddle. "Give my regards to Mrs. Lincoln," he said, saluting. "And to Tad and Willie. Tell them that I shall return with trophies for them all."

Lincoln said proudly. "I'll do that, Elmer."

"Good day to you then, sir. And good day to you, General." Receiving a wave from the President and nothing from Scott, he trotted his horse off in the direction of his baggy-trousered troops. He shouted out his orders to strike up the drums and bugles. And as the snappy commands began to devolve down through the Moroccan-clad firemen, the inmates behind the asylum bars broke out in a howl of crazy laughter.

CHAPTER NINE

Harper's Ferry, Virginia
June 15
Afternoon

BRIGADIER GENERAL JOSEPH EGGLESTON JOHNSTON STOOD ON THE RAIL-
way station platform and looked down on the bustling main street. Scores of
burgeoning wagons and hundreds of men were crowding the cobblestones on
their push out of town. Since relieving Colonel Thomas Jackson of command
some three weeks earlier, Johnston had determined that the town was inde-
fensible, surrounded as it was by heights, and now that two Unionist armies
were pushing toward him, Robert Patterson's from the north and George
McClellan's from the west, he had more cause than ever to fall back.

Standing beside the one train that had been shuttling his men down to
Strasburg all day long, he coughed out the thick locomotive soot. He was
finally becoming somewhat inured to the steam hissing around him, but the
sharp whistle blasts startled him each time they blew.

But overall, General Johnston felt gratified. In just a few weeks, these raw
recruits had metamorphosed from a drunken, disrespectful, and unruly mob
into the nucleus of an army, the Army of the Shenandoah. And he had been
quick from the start to give the credit to Colonel Jackson for the hours of
incessant drilling he had imposed upon the men to effect the transformation.

He knew that it had been Jackson alone who had trained these farmers for the three weeks prior to his arrival and Jackson who had sacrificed his popularity to make something like soldiers out of them. And the strict colonel's popularity was definitely lagging.

The results, however, were undeniable. The men were clearly developing a sense of pride about themselves as a fighting force. A high-spirited morale pervaded the ranks. General Johnston could hear it in the laughter, the cocky banter, the crackling chatter of excitement running back through the columns and files. These were men eager to fight with bold hearts for the battle to come. Hearts so bold, in fact, that he overheard some grousing from time to time about his having given up Harper's Ferry without even a bullet's worth of blood being shed.

More disturbing to him than the grousers in the Army of the Shenandoah were the commanders in Richmond. General Robert E. Lee and President Jefferson Davis had opposed the withdrawal all along. But with the recent Confederate defeat at Philippi only a few ranges to the west, he had been able to convince them that his left flank was threatened. Lee and Davis knew him well, having gone through West Point and the Old Army together, and they ultimately gave into his will.

And why would they not have? He had always carried himself with an unmistakable air of success, not arrogance or pretension, simply a proper erectness that suggested the generations of Virginia gentility that were his heritage. Always conscious of that heritage while striving to maintain his humility regarding it, he had, for all his fifty-four years, borne his position with admirable restraint.

His ascension to the rank of brigadier general in the newly formed Confederate Army had come easily since he had been the highest-ranking Federal officer to cast his lot with the Southern forces.

The whistle shrilled. The General jumped. The doors to the cars slid shut. No more men could squeeze on board, not even on top, so he ordered those left standing outside to exit the platform and sit down below it to wait for the train to return. He heard grumbling as always and understood. He would not have wanted to sit in the Virginia sun playing poker without money, reading the same letters over and over, or trying to sleep with his nose pressed into some wretch's unwashed body for four more hours. The grumbling audibly increased, though, when the slumberous Jackson joined him on the platform and began vacantly stroking his beard.

The General smiled and offered his gloved hand. "Ah, Colonel Jackson, I am pleased to see you. How is the withdrawal progressing with your brigade?"

Jackson shook Johnston's hand limply without meeting his gaze. "Tolerably, sir, tolerably."

"Any recent word from the companies you have covering our withdrawal?"

"No, sir," Jackson said flatly.

"Where did they last report Patterson's force? Have the Federals crossed the Potomac yet?"

"Yes, sir," Jackson said.

"Well, are they advancing on us?"

"Yes, sir," Jackson said, suddenly raising his right arm in the air.

Ignoring the gesture to which he had become accustomed, the General pressed, "Do you know where they are now, Colonel?"

"No, sir," Jackson said.

Johnston took off his kepi and mopped his baldhead with a handkerchief. "Well, sir, please do find out. Patterson's movements are a serious threat to us here. I hope you fully realize that."

"Yes, sir," Jackson said, staring blankly into the throng of sweating soldiers below him.

"What about Lew Wallace's raid on Romney yesterday? Do you still have men posted out that way?"

"Yes, sir."

"Good, because you know what that new force means, do you not?"

"Sir?" Jackson asked.

General Johnston was becoming a bit exasperated at having to coax the words out of Jackson. "Colonel, it means that we are now not only threatened by Patterson's army from the north and McClellan's from the west, but also Wallace's from just over the mountains at Romney."

"Yes, sir," Jackson said, lowering his right arm and bending to massage his left leg.

General Johnston shook his head and forced a mirthless chuckle. "Colonel Jackson, I suppose I should admire and welcome your calm amid circumstances such as these, but I must know, sir. Are you not the least bit concerned by any of this?"

"Concerned, sir?" He was now preoccupied with an infantry column tramping out of town. They were marching sloppily and it displeased him

"Yes, concerned, Colonel. Just what is your...secret?"

"Secret, sir?"

"Yes. How can you remain so detached in the face of danger?"

"I trust in the Lord, sir. And the bayonet."

Shaking his head, Johnston said, "Is it really that simple for you, Colonel."

"Sir?"

The General gave up. "Oh, never mind, Colonel, never mind."

Jackson's gaze returned for a moment to the column that was peeving him before saying, "May I, sir?"

"May you what, Colonel?"

Jackson reached into his inside tunic pocket and pulled out a half-eaten peach speckled with pocket lint. "For my dyspepsia, sir."

General Johnston shrugged and looked away. Jackson took that as an affirmative and began to suck on the fruit. A rivulet of juice ran down his beard. He sighed pleasantly.

The General studied Jackson for a moment. "Colonel, have you been listening carefully to all I have been telling you?"

"Yes, sir."

"Well, see that you listen very attentively now, sir, for I just received word from Richmond concerning the overall plans for the upcoming campaign and I want you to fully understand them."

Jackson lowered his peach and looked directly into Johnston's eyes for the first time. "You have the plans, sir?"

"Yes," the General said, clearly pleased to at last have the colonel's complete attention.

He told Jackson that the Army of the Shenandoah, some 10,000 men, would be operating in concert with General Beauregard along the Alexandria line. If the main Unionist attack were to come against him as expected, then they would feint Patterson's Federals into remaining fixed in the Valley and speed by rail over to Manassas Junction. Johnston said that such use of a railroad during battle had never been attempted but, if successful, it would offer the most efficient exploitation of their interior lines. General Beauregard had about 27,000 men, he explained, behind a little creek called Bull Run. With their 10,000 joining him, they would be able to even the odds against the 35 to 40,000 Federals sure to be invading from Washington.

Jackson let his gaze drift over the eastern mountains. "Washington," he murmured mystically.

"Yes, Colonel, Washington."

Sniffing the sweet aroma of Jackson's peach, Johnston re-directed the conversation. "You know, Colonel Jackson, I probably have not been as forthcoming as I should have been with my praise of your performance here at Harper's Ferry, both before my arrival and after it."

"Sir?"

"The way you whipped the rabble you found here into the beginnings of an army."

Jackson paused, apparently not understanding the need for a compliment. "Those were my orders, sir."

"And I am impressed with the efficiency you displayed in dismantling the rifle-making machinery at the arsenal and sending it south."

"Those, too, were my orders, sir."

Johnston nodded, "Yes, but you do not give yourself enough credit, Colonel."

"The credit goes to Our Heavenly Father, sir."

"Perhaps, but what about the way you captured those locomotives and all that rolling stock in one bloodless raid?"

"Our Heavenly Father was good to us that day. The glory goes..."

"To Our Heavenly Father, yes, yes, I know, but I just want to commend you for your part in it. And also for the way you put troops up on Maryland Heights, against the direct orders of General Lee and President Davis. That took a great deal of personal courage to invade undecided Maryland on your own authority."

Looking up at the tallest of the mountains glowering down on Harper's Ferry, Jackson said, "The men would have been threatened from those heights, sir. And I am in no way proud or pleased that I disobeyed a direct order from General Lee or the President."

"Well, Colonel, I must say, your ability to do so is part of the reason that I felt able to challenge their orders for us to strategically withdraw. Time will be our judge and time will tell if our standing with the high command has been adversely affected."

Jackson said nothing. He went back to sucking on his peach and stared into the mass of seated men. He raised his right arm in the air and focused in on someone to his front.

General Johnston traced his path of vision to two young privates, one with bright red hair, the other tall and lanky. They had unmistakably defiant looks on their faces. "Do you know those boys, Colonel?" he asked. "You could have them arrested for insubordinate stares like those."

Colonel Jackson did not answer. He shifted eyes between them both and kept on sucking his peach.

"Colonel Jackson," Johnston repeated. "Colonel Jackson?"

Jackson took the peach from his lips and looked at Johnston. "Sir?"

"I was saying, do you know those two boys."

He gave the redhead another glance, then the skinny one, and said, "Yes, sir. I believe I do."

"Well, I can have them arrested, if you would like. No enlisted man should..."

"That will not be necessary, sir. If we arrested every man in this army who presently holds me in contempt, I fear we would have no army at all."

"Very well then. Come with me to my headquarters. I want you to demonstrate toward Martinsburg tomorrow. To more thoroughly cover our withdrawal, Colonel Stuart will take part, and I want to go over the maps with you." The General strode across the platform and down the steps. Colonel Jackson shuffled along behind him, averting his eyes from the offending boys.

"Ha!" Red O'Riley cried. "I stared that sonuvabitch down."

"Yeah," Slim Cochran said, "an' he'll most likely come back on the both of us for it, too." The two shifted uncomfortably in the dirt, packed into a gray-brown mass as tightly as forty rounds in a cartridge box.

"Shit, he can't do nothin' to us that he ain't already did," Red said. "He's been drillin' us eight goddamned hours a day, ain't he, and keepin' us up all night on picket duty after that." He was speaking loudly to be heard over the chatter.

"Oh, I reckon he could think of somethin' worse to do to us, if'n he put his mind to it, like shovelin' the shit outta them damned latrines or some-thin'."

"Naw, he's already got them Kentucky boys doin' that," Red said, "and, truth be told, them animals deserve it."

"That's a fact," Slim said. "Hell, some of them toughs was about to beat me toothless the other night 'cause they claimed I was holdin' whiskey from 'em." He wiped the hot sweat from his face and squinted for a moment into the summer sun.

"You wasn't was you?" Red asked. "I mean, if'n you was you never shared none of it with me."

"Hell no, I didn't have none. You know as good as me that Jackson dumped the whole town's supply in the river."

"And what a goddamn waste of good whiskey that was. And all on account of his religionizin'."

Grinning, Slim re-told how he and a few others had out-foxed Ol' Tom Fool and managed to catch some of the precious amber in pots as it sluiced down the steep, grassy banks. He let out a hoot and bragged about what a rol-licking time they had that night.

"Yeah, yeah," Red said, "an' I didn't get none of it 'cause the bastard had me doin' extra picket duty that night for talkin' a little in the ranks." He jerked around at the sound of a boy vomiting nearby, the chunks and soured stench splattering backs and fouling the air.

Slim barely noticed. "What kinda damned man would deny a soldier his whiskey anyways?"

"I'll tell you what kind of man," Red said. "The kind of man who'd steal the horses and wagons from all the farmers around here and half the crops in their fields. The same farmers I come up here from Alabam to protect. An' all 'cause he don't have the sense to know how to supply his army."

"The same way we gotta pour our own damn bullets," Slim said, "and the cannon boys gotta build home-made caisson wagons for their guns."

Red scoffed. "But the best one on that stupid sonuvabitch has got to be the way he done refused to turn the command over to General Johnston for a whole damned day just 'cause some 'i' weren't dotted or some 't' weren't crossed on the orders. I'm just glad I got put in that Kirby Smith's brigade. Now there's a fightin' man for you, one that's bound for glory, not bound to be laughed at."

"That's a fact," Slim said. "Ol' Tom Fool sure as hell ain't gonna win my regiment no laurels."

"I don't reckon."

"Red," Slim said at length, sounding strangely distant. "You've come to be quite a friend to me over the past few weeks."

Red smiled and said, "Yeah, and you to me."

"Then, Red, you've got to promise me somethin'. I know we's in different outfits now but you've got to promise me anyways."

"Promise you what, Slim?"

Slim paused. Tears came to his eyes. "Promise me that you'll find me after the battle. The big battle. Promise me that you'll find me after and check and see if I'm hurt and help me if I am."

Red grinned. "You ain't gonna get hurt. The only ones that's gonna get hurt is gonna be the Yankees."

"But will you check on me anyways just to make sure?" He took Red's hand and squeezed it. "Please."

Red pulled his hand away, glancing around to make sure that no one had seen the offense. "Why hell, yes, Slim, I'll find you, if that's what you want. And I'll bet you shit to a shoe shine that you'll be fine and I'll be fine and we'll be getting' drunker 'an hell to celebrate our victory. And then we'll be heroes. Real heroes. The kind that go home to hankies and sweet cakes, and the arms of pretty girls."

"You promise? I mean, you really promise on your God-swore word to come lookin' for me?"

"Hell yes, I promise. Now pull yourself together, boy, before you make a damn fool of yourself." Red took off Slim's hat and mussed his sweaty hair. Their laughter dissolved in the whistle of the departing train.

CHAPTER TEN

Near Martinsburg, Virginia
June 16, 1861
Mid-morning

Rifles blasted and bullets sucked air overhead as Lieutenant Colonel James Ewell Brown Stuart's cavalry column accordioned to a sloppy halt in the middle of a meadow road.

"My word," Private Jacob Sebastian said, hunkering down. He was a bookish young man with wire-rimmed spectacles, unmilitary looking even in his gray-braided waist jacket. "What on Earth has that showboat gotten us into this time?"

"He knows what he's doing," said Private John S. Mosby, the bantamweight beside him. "I would wager that he has one of his little 'training exercises' up his sleeve and that's fine by me."

Another crackling of gunfire puffed out of the tree lines on either side of the road and spit bullets across the clearing. The one hundred cavalrymen and their mounts ducked and skittered as one.

Pushing his spectacles up the bridge of his nose, Jacob said, "This is the third time this morning that Colonel Stuart has intentionally put us in harms way. And now look back there. There are Yankee horsemen closing in behind us."

"That means that the only way out of here is straight ahead," Mosby said.

"Unless he turns us back into those riders."

"Well, count on us turning back then," Jacob said angrily. "That's what he's had us doing all morning. I swear, that Stuart still thinks he is out West fighting Indians."

Sounding like the lawyer he was, Mosby said, "You are in contempt, school marm. You will hereby cease and desist your open disrespect of the Colonel. He, unlike you, is simply a fighter."

And indeed he was. Ever since his early childhood in southwestern Virginia, J.E.B. Stuart had been quick to beat up bigger boys than himself, especially when those boys teased him about his big nose and short stature.

Nature's worst had not even frightened young Stuart. When barely old enough to climb big trees, he took on a hornets' nest at the end of a high limb. The hornets attacked with their hundreds of stingers, and Jeb nearly fell to his death. But he did not leave that limb until he had knocked down the nest and sunk it in a nearby pond.

Several years later, Stuart graduated from West Point in spite of his demerits for brawling and went out West with the cavalry to take on the Comanche and Apache Indians. He took a bullet in his chest while still managing to cut the guts out of the Indian rifleman with his saber. And in 1859, he made his first national impression when he helped capture John Brown at Harper's Ferry.

Jacob Sebastian, for his part, was unimpressed by any of that, having a disposition that was considerably less belligerent than that of his commander. Although he had been born Southern, or Southern enough, in Baltimore to non-slave holding parents, a moderately successful physician father and a mother dedicated to endless charities, Jacob was neither combative nor had military inclinations. He was a scholar with a deep, coursing love of history, literature, Greek, and Latin. His father had managed to see that Jacob was as well-schooled early on as his income would allow, but it soon became clear that any hope of university study would be dependent upon scholarships which the hard-studying son had little difficulty in winning.

After four rich years of pure academic pleasure at the University of Pennsylvania in Philadelphia, Jacob graduated with a degree in the classics and went forth into the world in search of the only type of work for which such a degree prepared him: teaching. He began his career in rural Virginia, near Richmond, as a schoolmaster in a one-room schoolhouse, attempting to teach upwards of twenty students at a time in grades ranging from one to eight. Abysmally low pay, having to live with students' families, and an over-riding sense that his life at this station was going nowhere made him quickly begin questioning whether teaching was truly his calling. But worse than that was the realization that he could barely touch on the classics which he found so personally fulfilling and even the basic reading, writing, and arithmetic which he did teach were daily thrown back in his face by unappreciative students, many of whom mocked him and his love of academia.

Dreary months passed into a year and then two and the gnawing emptiness deepened. Dissatisfaction with his students' lack of interest and their dissatisfaction with him seemed to have him locked in a prison without words. He longed for a change, perhaps for post-graduate study, perhaps to write a book like Melville, a book that would land him a professorial chair at an esteemed university like Penn. He knew he had it in him. He knew he could write a novel about some grand adventure, some test of man against nature or man against man. He was sure he had the talent. All he needed was the grist, the material. And in April of 1861, he thought he had found it but now, just one month later, he was not so sure.

"Well, I may not be a fighter," Jacob told Mosby, "but I will surely never have the chance to find out if the good Colonel does not get us out of this field before we are all massacred." He had a momentary pang for the disrespectful children who had driven him to enlist in the first place.

"He'll do something," Mosby said. "He didn't lead us out here to be offered up as lambs for the slaughter."

A few of the other troopers drew their revolvers and began shooting into the black forest on either side of the meadow. The schoolmaster grappled at his own holster to do the same.

Before he could free his pistol, the caped and plumed Stuart rode down the line, ordering like a trumpet, "Company! Hold your fire! Hold your fire! Dress up your column! Dress it up!"

"Hold our fire? Dress it up?" Jacob protested. Three or four enemy slugs burnt the air overhead. He ducked instinctively.

The twenty-eight-year-old commander drew rein near Jacob and John. He was practically singing his orders through his full, wavy beard. "Company! Left! Face!" In a clumsy, bumping, rattling jumble, the column attempted to turn their fidgeting mounts to the left.

"Attention!" Stuart rang out. "Now I want to talk to you men."

"My Lord," Jacob said. "He can't be serious. He's not going to give us one of his esprit talks? Not here. Not now." More bullets whined by.

Mosby shushed him quiet. "Shut up, you fool, and learn something from this man about bravery."

The Colonel's laughing voice arose into the wind. "Ignore the gunfire from the trees. Those are only pickets and pickets who cannot shoot straight. You are brave fellows and patriotic, too. But you are ignorant of this kind of war and I am teaching you. I want you to observe that a good man and a good horse can never be caught."

Flinching from another scattering of bullets, the schoolmaster whispered, "The devil with him! He thinks this is all some sort of game. A game, I tell you."

The wiry lawyer shook his head. "Why in the hell did I have to get paired up with the likes of you?"

But John Singleton Mosby knew exactly why they had wound up together. In fact, it was Mosby himself who had chosen Jacob as a messmate upon learning of Jacob's academic credentials and propensities. For his were quite similar. He had his own love of the classics: great books, natural philosophy, Greek, history, and Latin. Mosby's education had been just as thorough as Jacob's, having attended the University of Virginia until being expelled for shooting another student. The wounded student, an avowed bully who had already knifed another student, survived so John's prison term had been limited to less than a year and, in typical Mosby style, he taught himself the law during his confinement and emerged from prison a professional man.

The similarities between Privates Sebastian and Mosby had their limits, however, as each day in the field further revealed. Mosby believed wholeheartedly in slavery, having grown up on a Richmond area plantation surrounded by slaves and his father's constant defense of the institution. He had attended the kinds of school where Jacob had taught and bedeviled the schoolmaster as Jacob had been bedeviled. Young John Mosby fist fought every chance he got even though he was the smallest boy in his class, and he was better-rounded than Jacob, dividing his time equally between his passion for books and his equal passion for hunting, fishing, riding, and shooting. In these ways, he was far more like his mentor Jeb Stuart than Jacob Sebastian, and he strained to ignore the latter's grousing now and turn his full attention back to the Colonel.

"And another thing," Stuart announced. "Cavalry can trot away from anything. A gallop is unbecoming to a soldier, unless he going toward the enemy. Remember that. We gallop toward the enemy, and trot away, always. And be steady. Never break ranks." Higher-pitched pistol bullets now zinged in from the closing Federal cavalrymen.

"Damnation!" Jacob said, hiding behind his horse's neck. "Damnation to hell!"

"You should go home, school marm. You are not fit for this. War is meant for the likes of Colonel Stuart...and me."

Stuart's voice cut the clear morning. "Prepare to receive your instruction!

Left face! Front into line! Quickly, boys, quickly!" Each pair of horsemen fell in to the left of the pair in front of them and attempted to line up on the guidon pennant to the far right. The effort was ragged but the company managed to struggle into a zigzagging battle formation facing the Federal riders.

"Dress it up! Dress it up!" Stuart ordered. "Tighter! Tighter!"

The sweating men and horses sidled together until boots were touching boots. Colonel Stuart called, "Draw!" The riders gripped their hilts and withdrew six inches of the blades from their scabbards, "Sabers!" And in a rattling slide, one hundred shining swords came the rest of the way out and went to shoulder, hilts at the waist and blades straight up.

"My God, my God!" the schoolmaster said, the pit of his stomach shifting like sand through a sieve. "He is really going to do it. He is really going to charge us right into those Yankees."

"I believe you are correct," the barrister said, licking his taut lips. "Finally, we are about to taste the saber charge."

"God help us," Jacob said. "God help us all."

Stuart bellowed, "Forward! March!"

The horses lurched out to a nervous walk.

"Dress it up! Dress it up!"

Turning his blanched face upward, Jacob prayed, "Heavenly Father, into thine hands I commend my spirit."

"At the trot! March!"

The gray riders spurred their mounts to a dirt-splattering trot.

"Dress it up! Dress it up!"

The line tightened.

Colonel Stuart cried out with glee, "Advance! Sabers!"

The blades flashed to the front, the hooves rumbling beneath them. The horses sped up into a canter.

And then the Colonel gave it, the most dreaded and craved of all commands: "Chaaarge!!"

Reacting, not thinking, fearing not aggressing, Jacob spurred his mount to a surging, wildly whipping tumble of leather and steel, hooves and horseflesh, pounding thunder and a galloping gait. He could hear Stuart laughing, "Charge, boys! To glory! To glory!"

With an impulse, not a thought, Jacob sensed he would be dead in the next instant. He screamed out in the vague, numbing hope that his straining, bursting throat would somehow blunt the pain of death. He quaked and trembled, shook and shuddered. Shock ripped through every nerve. His hat flew off. His scabbard clanged. His ganglia burned red-hot.

"Chaarge! Chaarge!" Stuart cried out.

Jacob clenched every muscle to stay on his horse, to keep on screaming. "Chaarge! Chaarge!" He almost fell off. Trampling hooves flashed up in his face. "Chaarge! Chaarge! Chaarge!!"

Chaos roared in his ears. A gray-green murk mired his mind. Half blind with sweat and panic, he saw nothing beyond his horse's pumping head. The field blurred beneath him. The trees flashed by him like a kaleidoscope. He smelled grass, dirt, sweat, and fear. He tasted blood in his mouth. He heard himself shout, "Chaarge!"

He did not slow down. He could not slow down. He spurred his terrified horse to full speed. Flecks of fire sparked in the murk up ahead. A mount somersaulted down beside him. "Chaarge!" he yelled. "Chaarge!"

Horses appeared through his fogged spectacles. Blue smeared in. "My God! My God! Yankees! Yankees!" A wave of blue rushed toward him like ground to a falling man. He cringed to receive the blow and smashed into them, colliding, nearly ejecting into their solid wall of men and horsemeat, Yankee men and Yankee horsemeat, all screaming and neighing and straining.

Jacob went mad, whirling his sword in every direction. He hit something here, something there, but what it was he had no clue. He heard clanging and thudding, yelling and cursing. He swung and slashed and thrust. He kicked and parried, lunged and ducked. He choked and gagged and cried.

Jack O'lantern faces swarmed around him like ghouls. He fought one away, then two and three. "Yee-iiiiiiiiiiii!" he screamed, driven and driving. He lashed out and slashed out at anything he could reach, anything close enough to reach him. He rasped and scratched to kill the killers who were trying to kill him. "Yee-iiiiiiiiii," he cried again and again and again.

The clangorous fight might have lasted a minute; it might have lasted a day. But it finally ended. The darkness around him faded. The sun reappeared. He was panting, amazed to be alive. He heard a voice that was not his own. It was the bantam lawyer loosing a celebratory shout.

"We did it! We did it! We sent them running! Look at them go!"

Jacob wiped the sweaty fog from his spectacles and looked. All he saw were Confederates, happily jeering at the retreating Yankees. "We won?" he said. "We won? And I'm all right?"

Mosby smiled. "Yeah, I don't see any red badges on you."

Jacob groped himself, feeling for wounds but found none. "I...I'm all right...I'm still alive."

"Hell, yes," the lawyer said, slapping his shoulder. "We just survived our first battle. And we won it. We have seen the elephant and lived to tell the tale."

Jacob clasped Mosby's arm, tears edging his eyes. "Praise God...praise God in Heaven. How about the others?"

"No one is dead that I can tell," Mosby said, "though one or two came unhorsed. It appears that we didn't kill any Yankees either. But they ran. They did do that. We can claim an undisputed victory here."

Jacob gazed around the battlefield, his eyes pinched, his nerves raw. There were a few hats and accoutrements lying about and the meadow grass was torn up but little else appeared disturbed.

"But how can this be?" he said numbly.

"How can what be?" John said.

"Nothing is different. Everything is the same."

"What do you mean?"

"I...I don't know exactly. It's just that something should be changed, that's all. I mean, how can we go through what we just went through and have nothing be different."

"I'll tell you what's different, marm." Mosby smiled. "The damned blue-bellies no longer occupy this ground. That is what is different."

Jacob nodded vacantly. "Of course...I understand that. It's just that...oh, never mind."

A call came from the far end of the company, "Them Yankee pickets is a'movin' in them woods again. They's tryin' to flank us!"

Colonel Stuart came riding to the front, his grin broader, his eyes twinkling more brightly. "Well done, men, though they didn't offer you much of a scrape. But I think you're getting the idea of it. A few more lessons and I'll make cavalrymen out of you yet! So let's see what other mischief I can stir up for you this morning."

A cheer went up. Stuart called over it, "Company! Form up in column of twos!"

A smattering of rifle shots puffed out of the tree lines on either side of the field as the men got their mounts back onto the road. The bullets sucked air overhead as before and Jacob ducked as before, but not quite so far or so quickly. In spite of his frizzing nerves, he thought perhaps he was beginning to feel different about rifles and Colonel Stuart and himself. Maybe he really had been right to flee the exasperation of teaching the dullards around Richmond. But when another scatter of Minie balls sprayed closer, he ducked as low as ever and reconsidered.

CHAPTER ELEVEN

Williamsport, Maryland
June 16, 1861

MAJOR GENERAL ROBERT "GRANNY" PATTERSON PACED IN HIS HOTEL room, wringing his hands behind his back. He was tall, fit, and handsome for a man of sixty-nine though worry had him looking his age at the moment. And his worries were significant. As a mere militia officer, he knew that he had been promoted well beyond his level of competence due to his having served with General of the Army Scott during the War of 1812 and the Mexican War. He recognized his inadequacies as a commander and realized that everyone around him was beginning to as well.

He had never claimed to be a professional soldier. Since arriving in Pennsylvania as an impoverished Irish immigrant, he had turned his attentions to business, amassing fortunes in planting, textile mills, railroads, and steamship lines. He was an undisputed master of commerce but not of war and now that the lives of 18,000 young men depended upon his every decision, he was doing the only thing he could think to do: pace, worry, and wring his hands.

"For God's sake, General," a cadaverous officer said from his chair. "Sit down before you wear out the floor. I swear, you are as nervous as a long-

tailed cat in a room full of rocking chairs. General Scott did not send me up
here to judge you but to assist you." The man ran his hand over his close-
cropped, red hair, his hard eyes skittering.

"Sit down? Sit down?" General Patterson said in his Irish brogue. "How
could I possibly sit down, Colonel Sherman? General Johnston's entire secessionist army is right across the river waiting to destroy me, for the love of
Mary!"

"You don't know that for a certainty, General," Sherman said. "The scouting reports are inconclusive." His hands trembled as he lit a cigar.

"Well, if you will forgive my saying so, Colonel, you don't look any too
calm yourself and you are a West Point man used to this sort of thing."

"I've been out of the army a while," Sherman said. He spoke rapidly, dis-
jointedly, a glint of erratic genius darting about in his eyes. "I resigned my
commission in '50, got married, took up banking, lawyering, real estate. You
name it, I did it. I was running a military school down in Louisiana when the
war broke out. Don't you own a cotton plantation down there yourself, complete with slave labor? Don't misunderstand me. I don't give a damn about
slavery one way or the other. I just . . . I heard that about you."

General Patterson paused his pacing long enough to consider this runaway
talking machine. He began to speak but stopped when Sherman started up
again.

"The whole point is that I, too, am out of practice myself when it comes
to soldiering. And it will take me some time to get settled back into it, too,
I'm sure. But as far as my nerves go, don't let them deceive you. That is just
the way God made me. So don't you worry any about me and my bravery, if
that is what you are getting at. I am at my bravest when my tremors are at
their worst."

The aging general shrugged and said, "Be that as it may, Colonel, I care
little about your nerves. I care only that you understand my situation here
and tell General Scott that my apprehensions are justified."

Sherman scratched his scruffy beard and puffed on his cigar. "But General,
you seem to forget. You have 18,000 men under your command. That must
certainly be an advantage over the secessionist numbers."

"Ah, but you are wrong there. General Scott just pulled out my best regiments, the regulars, and ordered them back to Washington."

Sherman crossed his long legs. "He ordered them to Washington? For what?"

"He said something about the President fearing a secessionist uprising
from within the city, but I cannot imagine any situation down there that
could be any worse than the one up here."

"When are the regulars pulling out?" Sherman said. "I thought they were already across the Potomac, moving on Harper's Ferry."

"Hell, boy-o, I sent them across all right. Some of them. They were the only ones who had any training or experience at spearheading a move like that. And now they are on their way back, leaving the green boys who went with them on their own. General Scott kept pushing for me to advance, advance, and when I finally did, he called back the best of my men and took them from me."

"Well, I suppose that does change things," Colonel Sherman said, shifting in his seat. "I can understand your frustration. I'll make certain that General Scott gets a full accounting of your position on that issue. But the question remains, when are you going to be able to get your men, the ones you have left, over into Virginia to engage the enemy, so they cannot pull out and reinforce Beauregard down at Manassas?"

General Patterson stormed to a stop. "Sweet Mother of God, Colonel! If I knew that I would not be pacing like a damned caged animal, now would I?"

Sherman puffed his cigar and said nothing, a scattering of tics twitching across his face.

Patterson pressed on, sounding more Irish as his excitement rose. "If I order them into Virginia with their diminished numbers, they could be destroyed altogether. And I can't allow that, now can I, Colonel."

Sherman re-crossed his legs and said, "Well, General my advice…"

"I don't need your advice, Colonel! I need more men and I need to keep the men that I have! I am not going to sacrifice my boys in driblets like they are so many swine being led to the slaughter. That may be the way of you cold-blooded West Pointers, boy-o, but I am made of better stuff than that!"

Sherman's face reddened but his voice projected firmly. "Please be careful how you address me, sir. I am a colonel in the United States Army and I expect to be treated with the respect incumbent upon that rank. I was sent here on a fact-finding mission by the General of the Army himself to determine whether you understand and are carrying out his orders. Can you illuminate me in that regard?"

General Patterson resumed his pacing and said, "Well, young sir, therein lays the very crux of the matter, doesn't it. General Scott has not been the least bit clear in his orders to me. He has told me to advance, to withdraw, to hold my position, and to do it all boldly and cautiously at the same time. To tell you the truth, I do not think General Scott himself knows what he wants me to do."

"But what about engaging the Rebels and preventing them from slipping away to join Beauregard. You do understand that part, do you not?"

"Yes, yes. I understand all that."

Sherman paused to draw on his cigar and said, "How do you stand with regard to the 90-day volunteers, the ones who signed up right after Sumter? Are you making any effort to re-enlist them for three-year terms?"

"Oh, hell, Colonel, we don't need to do that. This whole mess will be over long before that."

Colonel Sherman shook his head and went into the little oration he had been sharing with any and all who would listen concerning his predictions for a long war. It was going to be a drawn out affair, a conflict with thousands, perhaps hundreds of thousands killed and millions wounded, captured, and missing. Cities would be destroyed along with farms and factories. Entire regions of the country would be rent asunder.

Half the politicians and army officers in the North were already calling him crazy for his pessimistic views. But he felt compelled to alert the nation that the current unpleasantries showed every sign to him of developing into a bloodbath the likes of which the modern world had never seen. And as for the victor, he would never venture a guess.

General Patterson had stopped his pace somewhere in the middle of Sherman's prophecy and he now stood, mouth ajar, at a loss for words. A rap on the door shook him out of it.

"Enter," Patterson said.

The door swung open and an aide announced, "A courier to see your, sir. He just got back over the river from the Virginia side."

"Does he have any news regarding Johnston's Rebels?"

"Yes, sir."

Motioning impatiently, the General said, "Then send him in, Lieutenant, send him in."

A fatigued cavalry corporal stepped into the room, his knee-high boots splattered with mud. He saluted. "Sir, begging to report?"

"Yes, yes, go on, Corporal. What can you tell me of the Rebels and their position?"

"They're closin' in, sir. Lots of them, judging on the fight their cavalry is puttin' up."

"What do you mean, Corporal? What are they doing? Where are they? Whose cavalry is it?"

"Well, sir, they appear to belong to that fellow Stuart. He's got 'em attacking our patrols and pickets down Martinsburg way."

"Martinsburg? Why, that is only fifteen miles from here."

"Yes, sir, I just made the ride."

"And they were definitely on the offensive?"

"Yes, sir, I got into a scrape with some of 'em just this morning. And them boys wasn't just on no reconnaissance. They was fightin' like hellions. Like they had infantry support right close behind 'em."

"You are sure of that, Corporal? That they were spearheading an attack and not just making their usual scouting probes?"

"Yes, sir, I was there, sir. And they was bold, real bold."

"Do you have any idea who was commanding the Rebel infantry? Was it General Johnston himself?"

"I can't say for certain, sir, but I done heard from a Reb prisoner that it was a man by the name of Jackson."

Patterson reflected for a moment and said, "Indeed. Very well, Corporal, get back down there and keep me informed. If the secessionists are massing to attack, and it would appear that they are, then I am going to need all the warning I can get." He saluted.

"Yes, sir," the Corporal replied. Returning the salute, he left the room.

"Damn it! Wouldn't you know! As soon as General Scott takes away my best troops, Johnston's entire force goes on the attack."

Sherman folded his arms tightly against his chest and said, "That was no doubt by design, General. The damned Rebels know our every move."

The Irishman turned and said, "How? Spies?"

"Washington is full of spies but the traitors don't need them. Hell, General, the Northern newspapers tell them every damn thing they would ever need to know. If I ever get the chance, I am going to shoot all those Goddamned reporters and editors as traitors to the Union."

Patterson collapsed into a chair, appearing to care little about spies and reporters just then. "Good God. What am I going to do? If I attack without my full complement, I might be driven from the field. If I pull back across the river, I will be disgraced."

After a silence, someone rapped on the door again. "Yes, enter," Patterson said tiredly.

The aide stepped in, "Sir, you have a telegram from General Scott."

"Spare me the formalities, Lieutenant. I know you have already read it. Tell me the gist."

The aide replied, "Well, sir, I want you to know that I have not..."

"What does the message say, Lieutenant?"

The aide came to attention and burned his gazed into infinity. "He wants to know what you are going to do, sir."

Patterson said nothing. The Lieutenant waited at full attention. Colonel Sherman waited, too, tapping his fingers nervously on his knee.

The General wrung his hands and sighed deeply, achingly, straining to get the leaden words off of his chest.

"Tell General Scott that…that I am withdrawing my men from the Virginia side. Tell him that without the troops he has ordered back to Washington, I am in no position to advance."

"Are you certain, sir?" the aide asked.

The old man snarled to life. "Yes, damn it! And it is not your place to ask me such a thing!"

"Yes, sir, I just thought…"

"And it is not your place to think either!"

Snapping to attention, the aide said, "Yes, sir. Sorry, sir." He saluted and started to leave but stopped. "Oh, I almost forgot. I also have a message for Colonel Sherman. You have been ordered by General Scott to return to Washington. Back to your brigade, sir."

The Colonel nodded, the General stood up, and the aide left the room.

Patterson said, "So that is it then. You will return to your brigade, after reporting on me, of course. What will you say, Colonel? How will you summarize my performance here?"

Sherman stood, revealing his long, lean frame. He picked up his hat and kneaded it between his fingers. "I will say, sir, that command decisions can be desperately difficult. And that the gravity and implications of yours are considerable."

Patterson faced him. "Have you ever been in command, Colonel, before receiving your present brigade? Have you ever been responsible for men's lives?"

"No, sir, I have not. And I would be lying if I told you that my thoughts and feelings have not been disturbed of late whenever I consider what it means. I, sir, have no great faith in my ability to lead men in battle and I in no way judge you for the manner in which you choose to lead yours. We are all beginners, sir, when it comes to waging the kind of war which lies ahead of us, and I do not think it wise to make grand predictions of how we shall measure up. Only time will tell that, General, and that is what I will be reporting to General Scott."

Patterson straightened and nodded. "Fair enough, Colonel Sherman. Your brother, John, the Senator, has been a great encouragement to me. He said you were a fair man, an honest man. And I have found that to be the case. Good luck to you in your first command. God knows you will need it."

"Indeed I will," Sherman said. "Indeed I will. Oh, and I will recommend to General Scott that he keep you well-informed as to the date of the invasion. That is when you will need to engage Johnston up here most aggressively to prevent him from joining up with Beauregard down at Mannasas. The date is being kept locked away for obvious reasons, and the spies in Washington will be working overtime to find it out. Let us just hope that the politicians can keep it a secret." He squeezed the tremor out of his hand and saluted but, before he could snap it down, his fingers began trembling again.

CHAPTER TWELVE

The Executive Mansion
Washington, D.C.
June 29, 1861

PRESIDENT LINCOLN WAS STANDING BEFORE HIS MOST IMPORTANT ADVI-
sors waiting for their bickering to die down. They were the heavyweights,
some literally, all figuratively, and they were gathered in this smoky, high-ceil-
ing room to do what they had been chosen to do: give advice. Secretary of
War Simon Cameron, Treasury Secretary Salmon P. Chase, and Secretary of
State William Seward were seated around a table. General-of-the-Army Scott
was splayed out across a sagging chaise lounge. Two young lieutenants stood
at his head and feet to shift the General as needed.

Several other officers and politicos had seats throughout the room, but it
was clear that the men at the table were the ones with the most influence. It
was equally clear from the arguments and posturing between them that they
were vying with each other for the power associated with it.

"Gentlemen, please, "Lincoln said, "we must stop fighting among ourselves if we are to get anything done. I want the benefit of all your minds but
when their combined brilliance is revealed to me all at once, I fear I shall
become blinded. We must remain focused."

"Well spoken, Mr. President," Seward said, grandly projecting his prominent nose. "And, Mr. President, our focus must be on slavery and its utter abolition. Until that wretched institution is expunged from our land, we shall never be fully admitted into the fraternity of modern nations. Slavery is a scourge, a stain, a chancre on our..."

"Oh, spare us the grand-standing, Seward," pointy-faced Secretary Cameron said. "You're not running for President anymore. Mr. Lincoln here already beat you out for the job, remember? Isn't that how you got your present position?" He grinned maliciously like a ferret hoarding a berry.

"What I remember," Seward said, "is you ascending to your position in exactly the same manner, and being forced out of the nomination race well before me." He returned the needling smile but with a bit more panache.

"Gentlemen, gentlemen," Lincoln said. "Please. We must forget what brought us together and focus."

"Of course, we must," Cameron replied. "And we must focus away from slavery and onto the execution of the war."

Seward would not relent. "Are you saying, sir, that slavery is not an issue in this war?"

"I am saying, sir, that you are completely out of touch with the people of this country, North as well as South, if you think that they would stand for the immediate freeing of six million Negroes."

"Gentlemen, please," Lincoln insisted. "You must moderate yourselves and your rivalries. This bickering reminds me of the story about three boys who found the one penny. It seems that..."

Bald-headed Salmon Chase interrupted, "Mr. President, we all enjoy your stories but I must interrupt to concur with Secretary Seward's views on abolition, though I concur with him on little else, and I must share my own concerns about Mr. Cameron's less-than-legal political practices."

Cameron shot to his feet and shouted, "Are you accusing me of criminal behavior, Chase? Why if your blood wasn't still boiling to be President...and yours too, Seward, you would understand that..."

"Stop it!" Lincoln said. "Stop it, right now! All three of you. I will hear no more talk of schemes and corruption today. My God, we are at war and we must unite ourselves before we can fight the enemy."

The room hushed. Cameron eased back down. The Cabinet members exchanged venomous glances at each other.

Tugging at the bottom of his vest, Lincoln lowered his voice and said, "Now. General Scott has been kind enough to make what was, for him, an arduous and painful journey here and I, for one, appreciate it." He bowed slightly to the reclined general. "And just how is the gout today, General Scott?"

The General nodded. "Tolerable, Mr. President, tolerable, thank you."

Lincoln attempted a smile and turned to the others. "So. Gentlemen. I asked General Scott to join us today for a couple of pretty fair reasons, I think. One, to catch us up on the overall military situation and, two, to introduce General Irvin McDowell, the man who I have chosen to lead our troops into Virginia. And General McDowell will, in his turn, share with us his plans for doing so."

With his most unctuous tone, Secretary Chase said, "Mr. President, while I am aware that some here actively campaigned against General McDowell's appointment, either because he was promoted over more senior officers or simply because I sponsored him, I have no doubt but that you will be as impressed with my fellow Ohioan as I am. He graduated from..."

"Your man's appointment has already been confirmed, Mr. Chase," Seward, a New Yorker, said. "There will be no more need of another of your self-serving endorsements."

The President heaved a tired sigh. "Mr. Seward, please. Let us move on. Allow General Scott to bring us up to date on recent military developments."

The general grunted as he tried to sit up. His aides hurried to help. "Thank you, Mr. President," he managed. "As you know, the telegraph over at the War Department has been hot for weeks now with reports from every state and territory in the Union. Where would you have me begin?"

"Anywhere but Alexandria," Lincoln bowed his head and said. "I simply cannot bear to think on the death of Elmer Ellsworth anymore. My heart simply aches every time I do." No one broke into the President's personal moment of grief but everyone knew what had caused it. The parade-ground colonel had led his Zouaves across the Potomac to seize Alexandria, Virginia. He and his men met almost no resistance but they did notice the Confederate Stars and Bars flying defiantly atop a hotel (one that had offended Lincoln's eye and sensibilities from the second floor of the White House for weeks).

Little Elmer Ellsworth took it upon himself to storm up to the roof of the hotel and cut down the Southern banner. On his way back down, the proprietor stepped out of the shadows and blew Lincoln's favorite soldier nearly in half with both barrels of his shotgun. For his act of patriotism, the owner took a long, nastily curved bayonet completely through his gut that left him stuck and hanging on the wall. But the damage was done to this charismatic young man who Lincoln had once called a son. The most popular soldier in the United States Army was dead and he soon became a national hero.

General Scott broke the silence. "But, sir, his death, tragic as it was, has been enormously beneficial to the morale of our troops. I get reports daily of regiments chomping at the bit to attack the secessionists. Their battle cry is 'Remember Ellsworth'."

"Yes, yes. But say no more of it. Tell me about the state of the country."

Happy to move on, Scott started by reporting on Missouri. He said that the secessionists out there had murdered a group of German home guardsmen at an outpost called Cole Camp. None of them were real soldiers, he said. Most had just gotten here from the old country and did not even speak English. There was gunfire and the Germans started to run. Some attempted to surrender but the secessionists ran down at least fifteen and murdered them in cold blood.

An angry murmur rippled through the room. Mr. Lincoln raised his hand to his temple and muttered, "Welcome to America...the promised land."

State Secretary Seward, his tone imperious and condescending, asked, "General Scott, what about that traitorous governor out there, Claiborne Jackson? Haven't your men taken care of him yet?"

Defensive and simmering, the General said that Nathaniel Lyon's force had chased him and the disunionists out of St. Louis and then out of Jefferson City. He went on to report that Unionist casualties in the campaign had not been too severe although there had been a rather sharp action at Boonville on the 17th costing General Lyon some thirty dead. He emphasized that the losses had been well worth the strategic gains.

Lincoln turned his back to the group and stepped over to the fireplace. Leaning his long arms out against the mantle, he murmured, "Lord Almighty, am I ready for this, this trading of young men's lives for 'strategic gains'? And just what were these 'strategic gains', General. I trust that they were of at least comparable value to the thirty lives sacrificed to achieve them."

"They were, sir," Scott said. "And in the end, they will save lives."

He explained that by Lyon taking Boonville on the Missouri River, he took the river itself and cut the Rebels off from the northern half of the state. Governor Jackson took his loss there to mean that he could not hold onto the central and northern parts of the state and he withdrew to the south, presumably to re-group and await reinforcements from Texas and Arkansas according to accounts. The disunionists would be back, Scott informed the President. Missouri was simply too important to let go of without a fight. It was a maxim of the day that whoever controlled the state of Missouri controlled the Ohio, Missouri, and upper Mississippi Rivers. Scott said that the greater part of Missouri was presently secure for the Union but that ultimate victory there would take far more of a commitment from the government in men and materiel.

At that, Scott's breathing faltered. He began to gasp. The two aides quickly shifted him on the chaise but the move did not stop the wheezing.

Lincoln bent down and asked, "Are you all right, General? Should I summon a doctor?"

The General went into a spasm of coughing but he waved the offer off. After a few moments, he regained control of his lungs and the normal, lesser shade of red returned to his face. "Forgive me, Mr. President. I am fine. Now, what was it we were discussing?"

"We were discussing a greater governmental commitment to Missouri," Treasury Secretary Chase said, "But where is all of this money going to come from? There are not enough funds in the Treasury to pay for a 1,000 mile front; not under our current monetary system."

Secretary Seward said, "Oh, please, Chase, don't rehash that same old diatribe. We all know you favor mass printing those inflationary greenbacks, with your picture on them no doubt."

Chase leaned across the table and shook his finger at Seward. "Now you listen here, Seward. I will have you know that..."

"Stop it!" Lincoln cried. "I cannot and I will not allow this country to suffer because of the pettiness of its brightest minds. You will learn to work together."

Sufficiently scolded, they both sat down. Cameron sniggered at seeing his rivals dressed down. Lincoln looked his way.

"And I must address myself similarly to you, Mr. Cameron. You, too, could be considerably less antagonistic during these proceedings."

The smirk wilted from Cameron's face but he still emanated an unrepentant mien.

Lincoln ignored it and began to pace, his hand behind his back. "Now, what about the other border states? What is their status?"

Secretary Chase spoke up. "Well, sir, my Ohio boys, under General McClellan, are showing steady progress in securing western Virginia for the Union."

Seward could not resist. "Mr. Chase, are not 'your' Ohio boys in the company of sizable numbers of boys from Indiana and Illinois?"

Lincoln scowled at Seward.

The Secretary of State quickly presented his palms in mock surrender and said, "Sorry, sir. My apologies. Please continue, Mr. Chase."

Irritated, Chase said that events seemed to going well for the Unionist forces in western Virginia. Statesmen from the area were setting up a pro-unionist government in Wheeling called the Restored Government of

Virginia. They had already elected legislative representatives from the north-western counties as well as a provisional governor named Francis Pierpont. Secretary Chase mentioned that they hoped to secede from the rest of Virginia and form their own loyal state.

"That is all well and good," Lincoln said, "but the military question must be settled first. Can you illuminate us in that regard, General Scott?"

Scott cleared the rattle from his throat and said that there was still skir-mishing taking place in the rugged mountains, mostly of little consequence thus far, but that McClellan had telegraphed him that matters would be com-ing to a head soon. The Rebels had been concentrating, General Scott explained, and he had ordered General McClellan to move against them as soon as practicable.

Seward said, "Well, he certainly seems to be taking his time."

"The mountains are dense and the roads are few over there," Scott said with an angry eye. "But McClellan will be attacking soon. He has assured me of that."

"What about you, Mr. Seward?" Lincoln said. "Do you have anything to add? What can you tell us politically, say about California?"

Seward took his turn and said that California was so long, north and south, that it reflected the rest of the country as a whole. In the north around San Francisco, loyalist sentiment was prevailing, but to the south represented by Los Angeles, there was considerable talk of secession.

"We must not neglect California," Lincoln said, "though she is a full month away by ship. We need her gold and her ports and her men."

Everyone concurred except Chase whose rolling eyes belied his fear of a diminishing Treasury.

"What about Delaware?" Lincoln asked.

Chase fielded that one, saying that just the day before some Deleware Democrats had held a peace conference urging the recognition of the Confederacy. He assured the President that no expenditures would be spared to prevent such a debacle. The country needed Monsieur du Pont's gunpow-der and he said he would support any measures necessary to maintain its uninterrupted flow to the Federal armies and the Federal armies alone.

There was a chorus of hearty "here-heres" for that, even from Seward and Cameron.

"And what of Maryland?" the President asked. How are events unfolding there?"

General Scott heaved a heavy breath and said that the Unionist occupation troops there were holding Baltimore and other secessionist strongholds in the state in a virtual state of martial law. Just two days earlier, he explained, General Banks had had to arrest Baltimore's chief of police, George Kane, for his flagrant Confederate bias and now the Rebels were up there demanding their habeas corpus rights.

"The men are lawbreakers and seditionists," Lincoln said, "and they shall not find refuge in the finer points of the law. Especially in Maryland. For if we lose her, the capital of this nation instantly becomes surrounded by enemy territory. And I will not allow that to happen."

There was a murmur of agreement.

Lincoln took a few long-legged steps before saying, "And always I must come back to Kentucky, the lynch-pin of the Union. God knows I pray to have Him on my side but I simply must have Kentucky."

"I agree, Mr. President," Cameron said, not wanting to be left out of the discussion. "If the Southerners control Kentucky, then they control the Ohio River and they will sever the Union geographically as well as politically."

"Yes, yes, Mr. Cameron," Seward said with an affected yawn. "We all know that."

"But Secretary Cameron is right and we cannot hear it enough," Lincoln said. "Kentucky is worth all the attention we can give her. What is the current status there, General Scott?"

He said that there was no change of which he was aware; that the critical border state still hung in the balance, claiming neutrality while the various factions maneuvered for control. They might end up, he ventured, establishing two separate capitals, like in Virginia. He said that Robert Anderson, the hero of Fort Sumter and a native of the Bluegrass State, was having less than complete success recruiting for the Union but that he was still out-recruiting the Rebels approximately two-to-one.

Lincoln stepped over to the mantle and leaned against it again. "Good, good. I was born down there, you know. I lived there until I was seven years old. It's a lovely place, Kentucky." He drifted for a moment in what seemed a pleasant memory.

"I feel compelled at this juncture," General Scott said, "to mention once again that we could eliminate so many of these troubles by giving my plan a chance."

Cameron quickly said, "Please don't pitch that anaconda scheme of yours again, General. It would not work and, even if it did, it would take too long. Our people would not tolerate the wait. Hell man, Horace Greeley and his *New York Tribune* have gotten this whole country chanting 'On to Richmond! On to Richmond!' And that means an overland invasion of Virginia."

"I fear, General," Lincoln said, "that for all the invaluable advice and coun-sel you have given me, I must concur with Secretary Cameron on this one. I, too, believe that we must first deal a blow against General Beauregard's force at Manassas before we attempt to surround and cut off the South. And that being the case, let me get General McDowell right now and let him explain his plans for such an invasion."

The President ambled over to the door and opened it. He motioned out-side with a soft smile. Ushering the man in with polite deference, he announced to the room, "Gentlemen, I give you General Irvin McDowell, the man who will be leading our army to Richmond."

CHAPTER THIRTEEN

Lee-Custiss Mansion
Arlington, Virginia
June 29, 1861

COLONEL WILLIAM TECUMSEH SHERMAN STOOD BESIDE THE PILLARS OF THE
hilltop manor a requisite distance from three of McDowell's new generals, men
now in charge of a full division each in the newly formed Union Army of
Virginia. He ignored the exclusive clique and gazed out across the Potomac at
Washington City, District of Columbia. Straight ahead, he glimpsed the
Presidential Mansion, beyond that to the right, the unfinished Capitol dome
with its construction derrick of angled lumber. And in the middle, surrounded by dozens of indolent cattle, he saw the beginnings of the cut-stone obelisk
that was supposed to someday honor the namesake of the city.

On westward breezes, he could smell the cattle, or was it the fetid canal
running alongside them? It might have been the stench from the Army butch-
ery set up alongside General Washington's would-be monument. In any
event, he in no way perceived the miasmal cow town before him as worthy of
the title 'national capital.' The rows of dingy slum houses alone insured that.

The squalid scene served to increase his natural distaste for politics and
politicians, his own little brother, Senator John Sherman of Ohio, notwith-
standing. He wondered how they could have allowed the center of Federal

power, the supposed showplace for foreign visitors and dignitaries, to degenerate into such a national embarrassment. He shook his head, knowing that the city, the politics, and the politicians had been the ruination of so many previously untarnished men.

In spite of his long-standing disgust with politicos, Colonel Sherman did respect his brother and he readily acknowledged the debt he owed to one other Senator in particular: the late Thomas Ewing of Ohio. It had been Senator Ewing who had taken him in as a nine-year-old orphan and raised him as his own. Sherman knew that, had it not been for the Senator Ewing's influence, the U.S. Military Academy would have never accepted him.

Perhaps, though, his foster father had most richly blessed him by consenting to the union between his daughter Ellen and himself upon his graduation from West Point in 1840. For she had turned out to be the much-needed grounding for Sherman's erratic and often troubled genius.

Through twenty years of marriage, Ellen had seen him through an endless series of highs and lows, nervous exhaustions and recurring bouts of melancholia. She had endured his passovers in promotion, his difficulties with superiors, and the grinding drudgery of peacetime garrison duty. She had even supported his decision to leave the Army in 1853 and had dutifully weathered the disappointments and failures of his civilian life, which eventually drove him back into the military.

It was the eight-year hiatus from the Officer Corps that had caused Colonel Sherman to refuse President Lincoln's personal offer of a brigadier's star and perhaps a division of his own. But since that refusal, he had struggled with second thoughts, and he now found himself surrounded by superiors whom he considered to be his inferiors.

One of them, David Hunter, a 59-year-old native of Washington, D.C. with a habit of twiddling the ends of his greasy, catfish mustache, had also resigned from the Army for five years and failed as a real estate agent in Chicago. His relocation to Illinois had proven advantageous to him in one regard, however, for there he had met and befriended Abraham Lincoln. Sherman knew that connection had gotten Hunter his stars.

Sherman viewed Samuel P. Heintzelman, a fifty-six year old with a scraggly gray beard and long thinning hair, as a scarred scrapper given to frontier manners and blunt talk. He did not doubt Heintzelman's personal bravery. The brusque man had proven that through thirty years of battling Indians, Mexicans, and anyone else who dared cross him, but he wondered whether he possessed the initiative and strategic sense necessary to command any unit larger than a squad or a company.

White-haired, stately, and trim, sixty-two year old Daniel Tyler carried himself with obvious distinction and character, and Sherman was glad to have him as his immediate superior officer. No one had ever doubted Tyler's honor, but corrupt military suppliers whom he had rigorously prosecuted as a young officer saw to it that he was punished. He remained a lieutenant for fifteen years despite his U.S. and French military academy training and his infantry, artillery, and ordnance experience. He resigned from the Army in 1834 and applied his code of ethics to the business world where he became wealthy and trusted in various canal and railroad companies. Although West Point trained, Tyler's leadership skills had never truly been tested.

Colonel Sherman was chagrined at being out-ranked by these lesser men, but that was how it would have to remain for the time being. It was too late to seek out a brigadier's star now. But, battle casualties, he knew, had a way of shaking up command hierarchies and creating vacancies to be filled by the next man in line. He would bide his time, do his duty, and be ready to move up when his turn came.

Sherman was contemplating that move when General Hunter approached him and said, "It is rather ironic, don't you think, Sherman, that we have gathered here on Robert Lee's front porch to plan for the traitor's demise?" He twisted the ends of his mustache and huffed a haughty laugh.

Cigar hand trembling at his lips, Sherman said, "Oh, I don't know, General. I wouldn't go counting the chicks just yet. I believe that we are going to have to win a few bloody battles to keep Colonel Lee from coming back to re-claim his estate."

Hunter's face pinched. "I heard that you always looked on the sour side of things, Colonel, that you were one given to foolish exaggerations and fears about this war and how long it would last."

Sherman, restraining his anger, said, "Would I be any less foolish, General Hunter, if I exaggerated how short it would be?"

Hunter waved him off with a 'bah' and turned away.

The Indian fighter Heintzelman approached and said glumly. "Well, I'll tell you this much, Hunter, we're not ready enough to move today, or tomorrow and that damned Horace Greeley is gonna get a passel of poor, untrained boys killed by all his shoutin' of "On to Richmond! On to Richmond!" He spit tobacco juice on the marble floor and rubbed it in with the sole of his boot.

"You are correct, General Heintzelman," Sherman said. "Most of the volunteers can barely figure out how to get their brogans on, let alone march 25 miles and maneuver under fire."

Hunter said, "Well, I am ready and willing to take my men down there to

Manassas whenever ordered to do so. I am not afraid to give the traitors battle."

"I did not say that I was afraid either," Heinzelman protested. "I just don't want the startin' time of it to be forced on us by them goddamned newspaper editors and fat politicians that never so much as farted foul air in anger."

"Well," Hunter said, "I don't give a damn who makes the call. When they tell me, I go. I am not afraid of any damned Rebels." He turned to Sherman. "Can you say the same, Colonel? I have been watching you and I must say that I have never witnessed a West Pointer as nervous as you."

Colonel Sherman's anger simmered but he held it back.

General Tyler stepped over and said, "General Hunter, I do not believe that Colonel Sherman's personal bravery is in question here. And may I remind you, words do not a brave soldier make. I think you would do well to refrain from any proclamations regarding your own courage until you have proven it."

"Now that is some fancy remark," Hunter said, "coming from a man who has never even been in a battle. And I am telling you, Tyler, waging war is nothing like running a railroad."

Those two were glowering at each other when the front door swung open and a uniformed aide appeared. "General McDowell will see you now," he said. "If you would please follow me." Tossing out cigars and chewing tobacco, the three brigadier generals filed into the mansion. Colonel Sherman brought up the rear, his face hot with anger.

The aide showed them to the dining room where they found Major General McDowell finishing up what appeared to have been a one-man feast. The thick man was slurping up the remnants of his dessert, an entire watermelon, surrounded by dozens of empty serving dishes. Wiping his mouth, he belched and said, "Now that was monstrous fine! Monstrous fine indeed. Have a seat, gentlemen. I assume you have already eaten."

They all nodded. General Hunter added a hearty 'yessir'.

"Good, good," McDowell said. "It is always best that commanders eat with their men, the same food and surroundings and what not. Good for morale, you know."

Sherman glanced knowingly at the elegant dining room, the china, and the silver setting.

McDowell noticed and said, "Oh, the only reason you find me here amidst these trappings is that I feel personally responsible for preventing this lovely home from being vandalized. I have made it my headquarters. Temporarily. It belonged to George Washington's adopted son, I think, a man named Custiss, I am told, before Robert Lee married his daughter and inherited the place."

"A fine decision, General," Hunter said. "To make this your headquarters. A fine decision indeed."

Heintzelman and Sherman exchanged glances. Tyler sat erect and stared straight ahead.

"Yes, well," McDowell said, "in any case, I will be offering you no refreshments. I neither smoke nor drink, not even coffee or tea. I consider them all to be vices and suggest that you do the same." He belched again.

Not even Hunter, an avid drinker, could agree with that but he nodded obsequiously nonetheless.

McDowell continued. "The reason that I called you here this evening is to review what was discussed at the Cabinet meeting today, at the Presidential mansion, with the President and his cabinet, my plans for the invasion of Virginia, for July 8th."

"July 8th?" Sherman said. "Why that is just a little over a week from now. There is no way that this army will be ready to fight by then."

"We will move on the 8th, Colonel," McDowell said. "Those are President Lincoln's orders to me and they are mine to you."

"But, sir," Heintzelman said, "the Rebels must have 25,000 men over there by now. And they are dug in, behind a river no less."

"It is not a river, Hinkleman. It is a run, Bull Run."

"Heintzelman, sir."

"Of course, of course," McDowell said, dismissing the mistake.

"I, too, must add my reservations," the stately Tyler said. "While I fully understand the pressures being put upon President Lincoln and General Scott and, accordingly, upon you, I believe a marching date of the 8th is premature."

"Hogwash, Taylor," General McDowell said. "Have you heard the spirit, the enthusiasm that our boys have for this upcoming battle? They are ready even if they can't do the damned manual of arms."

Hunter tweaked his mustache ends and said, "I could not agree with you more, General. And as for my division and me, we will be ready to advance the moment you order it. The sooner the better, I say."

"Good, Hunter, good. That is the kind of talk I like to hear."

Hunter gave the others a self-important look.

"Now," McDowell said, "if you would all join me in the parlor, I would like to reveal what we know of the secessionists' positions and how I intend to destroy them."

"Here-here," Hunter said, his words bathed in oil.

And they headed out of the room, leaving behind the devastation of General McDowell's supper.

CHAPTER FOURTEEN

Along Bull Run
July 1
7:00 a.m.

LIEUTENANT ARCHIE BAGWELL ROLLED UP HIS MAP AND POINTED FROM atop his horse at an expanse of rolling fields and wood lots. "According to this, General Beauregard, the Orange & Alexandria Railroad should be right over there. Just down from McLean's Ford. You can make out Jones' tents just this side of it."

"That is General Jones to you, boy," Beauregard said, "and don't you forget it. And don't go thinking that my opinion of your work has raised any just because I tapped you to come on this inspection tour with me. The rest of the staff was already engaged."

"Yes, sir. Of course, sir," Archie said, dropping his eyes. "But I just wanted to point out that General Jones is down there, sir. He is holding the end of the Alexandria Line. Our extreme right flank"

"Do you actually think that I do not know that, boy?" General Beauregard shook his head at him disbelievingly. "There are some low hills just east of the railroad. They will have to be defended."

"By who, sir?" Archie said, more carefully this time. "I heard you say that we were stretched as thin as we could stretch already."

"When I pull the troops back from our forward positions at Fairfax Court House, I will post another brigade down there, commanding the railroad. That is a natural invasion route and I must not ignore it. Make a note of it."

The boy stuffed the map inside his triple-buttoned jacket and began groping for something else.

"Did you lose your pencil again?" Beauregard said. "Damn, boy, sometimes I think you are working for the enemy."

"Oh no, sir," Archie said, flustered. "Here it is." He took out the pencil and hurriedly scribbled on a pad. "Will you want entrenchments dug there, sir?"

"Of course. And abatis. The trees on top of the hills can be cut down and faced toward the enemy."

"Yes, sir. I will ride a dispatch to General Jones as soon as your inspection is finished."

"See that you do. And give him my warmest regards. Neighbor Jones is just about the friendliest gentleman I have ever encountered in my military service and he is a very able commander."

"Yes, sir."

"Now it is time to pay a visit to one of the most ornery."

"Early, sir? I mean, Colonel Early?"

"You may call him what you wish. The cantankerous coot has yet to earn my respect. Now come along and maintain two lengths distance behind me at all times."

"Yes, sir."

Beauregard and the white-trousered cadet were riding north toward Blackburn's Ford when they spotted a stoop-shouldered man approaching on horseback. Beauregard could see that the man was bearded and balding and wore rumpled civilian clothing. He would have thought that he was asleep in the saddle had he not been chugging on a bottle of whiskey.

"Good Lord," Archie said. "There he is now."

Beauregard strained his eyes. "So it would seem. The man is trouble, West Point or not, and I am going to nip him in the bud." He brought his majestic mount to a stop beside Early's swayback nag and said, "Salute me, damn it. I am your commanding officer."

Early smiled and offered a half-salute. "Oh, yes, sir. I know, sir. You're the Goddamned Duke of York." His voice was high and whiny like a hillbilly grand-pappy. At forty-five, he looked sixty-five with his gray beard and stringy side hair and his bent posture seemed to add another ten years.

"Straighten up, Colonel Early. You will maintain the proper bearing with me. I made you a brigade commander and I can just as easily unmake you one. And if I find that you are drinking on duty, especially at this hour, I am going to..."

"Oh, this." He held up the bottle and grunted a sarcastic laugh. "Why, General Beauregard, this is medicine, prescribed to me by a doctor, for my rheumatism. I've suffered with it all my life and it flairs up something fierce on these damp mornings, don't you know."

"Do not toy with me, Colonel. I will not tolerate unprofessional behavior in this army's officer corps."

"Neither will I, General," Early said. "As a matter of fact, I've had to confiscate more than one bottle from some wayward lieutenants under my care."

"Yes, I have no doubt," Beauregard said. "And what about your uniform, Colonel, or lack thereof. I told you to properly attire yourself before taking the field. How do you expect to earn the respect of your men looking like that?"

"But this is all I have to my name, General. I wanted to dress up all spit-and-polish like you, sir, but I couldn't find a damned Yankee-blue uniform like yours."

Beauregard leaned toward him, his lip quivering, and said, "Well, at least I am in uniform, Colonel, a neat and tidy uniform befitting a real officer."

"General," Early said, "in 25 years as a soldier and a prosecutor and a Virginia legislator, I've learned one thing real damned good. You can't judge a book by its cover. And while you've got a real pretty cover..." He broke off in caustic laugh.

"Silence, Colonel," Beauregard ordered. "And if I ever again catch you inebriated or being insubordinate in any way, I will relieve you of your command and immediately initiate court-martial proceedings against you. Do I make myself clear?"

Early's laughter quickly mulched over into anger and he said, "Oh, yes, sir. Yes, you do, General, sir. And let me make myself just as clear. I am not a man to be trifled with, by you or anyone else. And I believe that you will find me a worthy foeman if that's what you've a mind to do."

General Beauregard clenched his jaw. He uttered low and slowly, "Colonel Early, are you threatening me?"

Just as low and just as slowly, Early replied, "Oh, no, sir. I wouldn't think of such rank insubordination, especially not with this witness of yours tagging along behind you. But I think we understand one another." His mouth curled up into a nasty smirk.

Archie blurted, "You *are* making a threat, Colonel Early. And you will be held accountable for it. For the good of the Cause. Why, I..."

"Pipe down, boy!" Early snarled. "Mind your rank. If you cared anything about the 'Cause,' you'd let me pass so I could get on with my efforts to promote it."

"You are beneath contempt, sir," Beauregard said. "And it is well known that you have never promoted our Cause. I happen to know that at the Virginia Convention, you voted against secession at every opportunity."

"Well, *sir*, if you know that much about me then you ought to know that I have supported my State to the hilt ever since she took her stand."

"Cease and desist immediately, Colonel Early," Beauregard ordered. "I want to hear no more of this. Report on the condition and disposition of your brigade. That is why I am here, not to listen to your heathen rantings." When Early did not respond quickly enough to suit him, the General shouted, "I said report!"

Early drew back, stunned a little by the Creole's sudden intensity. "All right, all right. What do you want to know?"

"Their position. Where are they?"

"They're just where you told me to put them, scattered out as thin as paper from McLean's Ford to Blackburn's Ford. And in my opinion they couldn't do a lick of good if the Yankees attacked anywhere along here today. They're nothing more than skirmishers strung out as some sort of reconnaissance force or something."

"And that is exactly why I have them so deployed, Colonel. What about the smaller fords? Do you have them all adequately defended?"

Early said, "My boys have cut down trees for abatis there and dug in where I felt best."

"What about their morale?"

"It's good, I reckon. They want to fight, the way all fools want to fight before they ever have."

Beauregard frowned at that remark but let it pass. "Do you have many sick?"

"A fair share, down with the measles mostly. A few deaths from it."

"Keep a close eye on your command, Colonel, spread out or not."

"That's just what I was doing out here, General, before you and your lap boy here stopped me." He needled Archie with a leer.

Archie puffed up his chest but clamped his mouth shut before any more anger could come out.

"That will be enough, Colonel Early," Beauregard said. "You are excused. And keep me informed about what is happening here. Twice daily. Even if nothing is happening, I want to hear about it."

"I'll be sure that you do, *General.*" And he offered a sloppy salute with the same cocky glint in his eye.

Grinding his teeth, Beauregard returned the salute briskly and let Early through on his nag.

The colonel grinned at the cadet as he passed.

The boy tried to glare back but nervousness averted his glance.

General Beauregard turned in his saddle in time to see Early uncork his bottle and drink down another taunting draw.

CHAPTER FIFTEEN

Blackburn's Ford
8:15 a.m.

SILENT AND FUMING, GENERAL BEAUREGARD LED LIEUTENANT BAGWELL A half mile up the trail where they came upon Blackburn's Ford and the sound of axes chopping wood. This shallow, stone-rippled spot in the run was the camp of Brigadier General James Longstreet's Virginians, and they were hacking down trees along the waterline like beavers.

Taking it all in, Archie could no longer resist his impulse to speak. "So what can you tell me about this General Longstreet fellow, sir. He is a South Carolinian like me, I know, but he hasn't been up here long enough for me to get an impression."

"And since when did your impressions of my brigadiers amount to a pile of mule dung, Lieutenant?"

"Well, sir, I don't know. I just..."

"Oh, never mind," the Creole said. "I can tell you this much. He is the complete antithesis of that miscreant Early. He is a proven professional. West Point. Mexico. The Seminoles. You could learn a great deal from him about real soldiering."

"Why was he so late getting here? Was he hesitant to resign from the Old

Army?"

"Perhaps, I do not know. Somebody found him buried behind a desk load of papers at the Paymaster's office in Richmond and had sense enough to get him out in the field where he belongs. That is him over there. The big man with the big hat and big beard."

"Lord, he looks like a mountain man."

"He does indeed."

They slowly weaved their horses through the dog-tent village, returning salutes from eager lads along the way. Some were stripped down to suspenders and bare chests, trying to accommodate the waving heat. Others, prostrate in their tents, appeared ill and only had undergarments on. Most of the remainder were either chopping wood or drilling in a nearby field. There were, however, a number of healthy looking youths doing little or nothing at all.

Several of them approached General Beauregard and assailed him with a barrage of rapid-fire complaints.

"General Beauregard! Thank God you have come."

"Yes. General Longstreet has been treating us unfairly, little better than field hands."

"That's right. We are gentlemen, from the oldest tidewater families and we deserve to be respectfully handled, not worked like servants and white trash until our hands and feet blister."

"Yes, yes," General Beauregard assured them. "I have heard from your fathers and I am looking into the matter. I am certain that some accommodation can be reached, but for now you should carry on with your assigned duties without complaint."

Grumbling, the crowd of gentlemen dispersed and Beauregard passed the rest of the way through the camp, flaring his nostrils at the wafting smells of mud, vomit, urine, and feces. When he and Archie emerged near General Longstreet, the robust man approached and helped Beauregard dismount.

"Good morning, General Beauregard," he said flatly. "Welcome to Blackburn's Ford." He saluted but did not smile.

Beauregard stretched out the stiffness in his legs and said, "Good morning to you, General Longstreet."

"What brings you out this morning, General?" Longstreet asked. There was suspicion in his tone.

"Just the duties of being the commander, General." He scanned the topography of the place, the cleared hillside on the opposite side of the run with the rutted road coursing down to the foliated creek banks, through the camp and up the cleared hillside behind him. Nodding, he said, "I am pleased with what I see here, General."

"Thank you, sir," Longstreet said, still without an ember of enthusiasm.

"And might I add, General Longstreet, that it is refreshing to see a brigade commander who looks and comports himself like a professional soldier."

"You've been to see Early, I take it?"

"I have."

"He is a trouble-maker. I am sorry that he is here. And on my flank no less."

"Yes, well, perhaps this is not the best place to discuss another brigade commander. Morale and all, you know."

"Well, I say morale be damned," Archie broke in from atop his mount, "that man is a rogue and he..."

"Silence, Lieutenant," Beauregard snapped. "You are once again out of line."

He hung his head and sighed. "Sorry, sir."

Turning back to Longstreet, Beauregard said, "General, I must say, those men drilling in the field right now are manuevering like a clock. Splendid work. You have them looking like regulars."

"Thank you, sir."

"Yes, splendid, indeed. It must be due to the regimen you put your men through, the drilling, the inspections, policing the camp, and all the physical labor you require of them."

"I suppose so, sir."

"Yes, well, that brings me to another reason I wanted to speak with you."

Longstreet stared fearlessly into his commanding officer's eyes and said, "Yes?"

"Yes. General Longstreet, I have recently heard from several of the fathers of some of your volunteers. They are some of the most prominent men in Richmond with powerful ties to members of our government officials, including President Davis himself."

"Is that a fact?" he said skeptically.

Archie looked on, sensing the tension build.

"Yes, General," Beauregard said, "and these men are concerned that perhaps their sons' spirits might be dampened if they continue to be required to do the menial heavy-labor tasks that your more common men perform."

"I treat my men equally, sir. They are all soldiers. I require all of them to do the necessary work that soldiers have always done. Would you like it better if the defenses weren't completed or that resentments cropped up over the special treatment of a few?"

"No, no, of course not, General."

"Then let me have a free hand with those spoiled little rich boys. God knows they need it."

"I understand completely how you feel, General, and I am loathe to interfere with the discipline of your troops, but I am being pressured from the very top regarding this."

"What would you have me do then, General Beauregard? Let the sons of bitches lay around in the shade all the goddamned day, sipping lemonade and watching the real men do all the work?"

Beauregard wagged his finger at Longstreet. "Please mind your tone, General. I need not remind you that you are addressing your commanding officer."

"Well, what am I supposed to do then to get the work done if I can't order my men to do it?"

General Beauregard took an unconscious step backward to avoid the man's hot breath. "Well, General Longstreet, down in Charleston we used slaves."

Longstreet balked, "Slaves?"

"Yes. They are seasoned workers whose efforts could save your men's strength for when they will really need it, during the battle. There are hundreds of slaves in this area and I am certain that their owners can be persuaded to hire them out, at least until the heavy work is finished."

Longstreet folded his muscled arms tightly across his chest. Archie thought steam might come blasting out of his ears.

"So what do you think?" General Beauregard asked carefully. "About the slaves. Share your thoughts with me."

Longstreet gazed down at the ground and stirred the dust with the toe of his boot. "General Beauregard, I am a soldier. That is all I have ever been or ever will be. And all I can say is that this goes against every instinct I have about what makes for good soldiers and good soldiering."

"You really think so?"

"Yes, sir, I do."

"But why?"

"Napoleon," Longstreet said.

"Napoleon?"

"Napoleon said the second most important quality to develop in a soldier is bravery in battle."

"And refresh me, what is the first?"

"Developing their ability to endure hardship."

"By chopping wood and digging earthworks, I presume."

Longstreet nodded gravely.

"So you would resist using slave labor then?"

"Yes, sir, but like I said, I am a soldier. I follow orders. All orders. Even if I think they are cock-eyed. And I will obey this cock-eyed order if you give it."

"Fair enough," the Creole said, quickly grasping for closure. "Then I will send you the slaves as they are gathered up. Please see that they are not mistreated. I will be promising their owners that. You may want to scour your ranks for any former overseers. It takes a rare talent to get the maximum effort out of a Negro without damaging him, and you will need all the expertise you can get."

"I'll see to it, sir." But it clearly burned him to say it.

"Good. Now, about your orders here. Keep your scouts out and your eyes on that hill over there. For I believe yours will be one of the first brigades engaged in this fight."

"Do you have any idea when any of that might happen?"

"I do not know anything with certainty yet, but I have a man up at Bonham's right now who is coordinating our efforts to find out. That is all I am able to say at this point. But, with any luck at all, I will be able to give you ample warning."

"I'll be ready for them," Longstreet said. "Whenever they come." He saluted smartly, but his eyes belied a vague disrespect for the gentleman general.

Beauregard knew that Longstreet was a renowned poker player. Perhaps this was all part of some kind of poker face. Whatever it was, it unsettled him as he re-mounted his horse. "Guard this ford and this road with your very life, General. For if the enemy should break through here, in the middle of our line, then they will most assuredly divide and conquer us all in detail."

"Don't you worry about me. I'll get the job done."

"Fine, fine. Good day to you then, General."

"Good day to you, too," Longstreet said.

And Beauregard splashed across the ford with Archie Bagwell a dutiful two lengths behind him.

CHAPTER SIXTEEN

———————•———————

Fairfax Court House
12:30 p.m.

GENERAL BEAUREGARD AND ARCHIE BAGWELL CRESTED A RISE AND LOOKED down on the village in the flat below. It was surrounded by its dirty-white dog tents like all the other camps and similarly smelled of human waste. "There it is," Beauregard said. "Bonham's fiefdom. I swear, that man has been out here on his own so long, he thinks he has an independent command."

"Well, that is Milledge Bonham for you, sir. My father has been trying to deal with him for the past ten years. He works with people in Congress, you know."

"Do tell," Beauregard said sarcastically.

"Yes, sir. My father said he was always over-sensitive about seniority and rank and whatnot. He squawked pretty loudly if someone with less time in the House got some plum committee appointment instead of him."

"He was none too gracious when I replaced him here as commander of the Army of the Potomac either. I could tell all the way back in Charleston that Bonham would be trouble. He was complaining there to anyone who would listen that he deserved my command due to his militia rank. State officers. Bah! They are nothing but a collection of lawyers and politicians pretending to be soldiers."

Archie nodded, pleased that his general was mad at someone else and not him for a change.

"What is that dust cloud all about?" General Beauregard said. "Over there. It must be an entire regiment, heading south. I did not issue any such orders." He took out his field glass and studied the flags of the distant men for a moment.

"Can you identify them, sir?"

"Oh, yes," he said beneath the glass. "I know who they are and where they are going. They are the 1st South Carolina and they are going home."

"Home, sir?"

"They enlisted for ninety days and they have served them, such as they were. They got their parades and kisses and now they are running home before the real shooting starts."

Archie asked, "How many more such enlistments do we have just marking time until they can leave?"

"Too many. And the Federals are faced with the same dilemma which is why I know that they will be launching their attack soon."

"You know when the Yankees will attack, sir?"

"Not exactly. Not yet. But I will."

"I'm afraid I don't understand, sir."

"That is because you have no business understanding, Lieutenant." And he spurred his horse ahead in preparation for a Napoleonic entrance to the camp.

They found General Bonham outside his tent flailing his arms and shouting profane orders at his staff. With his turned up mustache and white beard, he looked and sounded like an old Prussian commander. Even his soup-bowl haircut and Dutch boy bangs could not soften his countenance as he upbraided every subordinate officer within range of his booming voice.

A group of enlisted men passing by called happily to him, and he interrupted his tirade long enough to answer them back with smiles and waves. And as soon as they passed, he resumed the denigration of his staff. "I heard about this," Archie said, "how he loves his men and hates his officers."

"That is easy enough to understand. The enlisted men are not a threat to his rank. They will never be in a position to challenge his precious seniority. But silence. Here he is now."

"Ah, General Beauregard," Bonham called out in an amiable tone. "Dismount, please, and come along. Let's get you some shade inside my tent."

"You wait out here, boy," Bonham said brusquely to Archie.

"I will give the orders to my staff people, General Bonham," Beauregard said and then he repeated Bonham's command.

General Beauregard stepped into the canvas-scented darkness and took a seat opposite Bonham. Another man, a farmer, stood in the shadows.

"Do you know Colonel Jordan, General," Bonham said, as if showing off a prize pig. "He is one of my best men."

"Of course, I know him," Beauregard said. "And he is not your man, he is mine. It is I who attached him to you, if you will recall."

Bonham laughed coarsely, "Of course, General, of course. It's just that he has been in and out of my headquarters so much lately that it seems like he…"

"Well, he isn't," Beauregard said. "And I have not come up here to discuss whose man he is. What I want is a report on his activities and what they have revealed to us thus far."

"Certainly, sir," Bonham said, seemingly pleased to be an irritant to his commanding officer.

Beauregard eyed Bonham suspiciously before turning to the farmer. "So Jordan, what can you tell me?"

Steady and unsmiling, the colonel said, "I am afraid I don't have much to report just yet, General Beauregard, although I have been working on the manner in which the intelligence gathered in Washington can be safely passed through the lines to us."

"And just how do you propose to do that, Colonel?"

"By arranging for civilian traffic, farm wagons and buggies and the like, to smuggle the masquerading messengers across one of the bridges crossing into Virginia."

"But wagons could take too long to get here," Beauregard said.

"Exactly, sir. Which is why I have arranged for various Virginia patriots on this side of the Potomac to lend their homes, clothing, food, and fastest horses to my couriers for the second leg of the passage."

"Which will lead them to me here at my headquarters," Bonham said, "my camp being the closest to enemy lines and all."

Beauregard ignored Bonham and said, "Is that it, Colonel Jordan? You just smuggle them across the river, give them a horse, and wish them well?'

"Well, sir, that is not exactly how I would put it, but yes, a great deal of individual resourcefulness will be required on the part of the couriers to evade Federal pickets and patrols."

"And to avoid being shot by our own pickets and patrols, it would seem."

"That, too, sir."

The Creole crossed his arms and sighed heavily. "Are you confident that this network of yours will work?"

"Yes, sir, I am."

Beauregard reflected for a moment and said, "How do you propose to keep the content of the messages secret, if the messengers should be seized by the enemy?"

"With a code, sir, one that I devised. All messages coming from and going to Washington will be written and translated only by those in possession of the key."

"And who will be in possession of the key?"

"Well I, of course, will need one," Bonham spoke up. "To translate the messages as they are brought here to me."

"You, General, will not need one," Beauregard said emphatically. "Your only function in all of this will be to send the messages that you receive, still in code, to my headquarters by your fastest rider."

"But what if the message states that I am about to be attacked? My brigade is the most vulnerable one in the army, the closest one to Washington. I will need every precious second of advance warning time if I am to deploy against the enemy and defeat him."

Beauregard reddened. "General Bonham, you will send all messages to me. Colonel Jordan will decode them at my headquarters, and I will issue you any orders pertaining to the deployment of your troops. Is that clear?"

"But, General, don't you think that..."

"The matter is settled, General Bonham. The fewer people in possession of the key the better." General Beauregard composed himself with a deep breath and said, "Now, Colonel Jordan. Just how reliable are these sources of yours, the ones getting the information in the first place?"

"Quite reliable, sir."

"Anyone in the War Department?"

"No, sir, but one has established a contact with someone with access to sensitive War Department documents."

"Indeed? And will this man be able to find out what day the Federals will advance? I need to know that so I can have General Johnston give Patterson the slip up in the Valley and make it down here in time for the fight."

"That is what we are working on, sir. That is the prime objective of our entire operation at this point."

"As well it should be."

"Yes, sir."

"As intriguing as all of this is to me," Beauregard said, "I will probe no more deeply into the details of your mission, the men involved, and the methods. I know all I need to for now, and I can appreciate your need to keep identities secret, even from me. I will trust that you and your men have everything well in hand."

"We do, sir."

"But General Beauregard," Bonham said, "don't you think that I ought to know the identity of the agents so as to identify them when they appear before me?"

"No, General Bonham, I do not. This meeting is adjourned. I want to check the defenses here and review some of the troops."

The two generals exchanged salutes and filed out of the tent, wincing their eyes at the blinding-blue sky. They passed Archie who was waiting dutifully. Colonel Jordan, for his part, followed behind gazing pensively toward Washington. It was almost as if the farmer could see someone there, Archie thought, someone special, someone, perhaps, he loved. But Archie's romantic notions vanished when he saw the man's face go dark.

CHAPTER SEVENTEEN

Washington City
July 6, 1861
Midnight

THE WIDOW ROSE O'NEAL GREENHOW SAT IN THE BACK OF A BOUNCING carriage and caressed the hand of its owner: the Honorable Senator from Massachusetts, Henry Wilson. Not only was Wilson a ranking Republican on the Senate floor, he was the Chairman of the Senate Military Affairs Committee which encouraged her to stroke him all the more sensually. For the mature brunette was, in addition to being the most admired hostess in Washington, a Confederate spy willing to do nearly anything to obtain the kind of information that a man like Henry Wilson was bound to have.

Her dedication to the Confederate cause was neither new nor shallow. It had its inception in early childhood on a tobacco plantation in southeastern Maryland, where the high-spirited girl, Wild Rose everyone called her, lived with her parents, pampered by slave mammies, maids, cooks, playmates, dressmakers, and darkies of every role. It was not until her mother and father both died of the same malarial fever that she realized the immense debts they had incurred to support their extravagant lifestyle and the effect that those debts would have on her.

She was forced to watch auctioneers selling off her Negro friends, breaking up families. She wept for their plight and her own, swearing to someday regain her wealth and position, her servants and her slaves. It appeared that she would never get that chance, however, that she would instead sink into the hopeless degradation of an orphanage never to own anything or anyone again.

Before that fate could befall her, though, her mother's sister showed up to take her back to her Washington boarding house to live and work. For the first time in her tender, uncalloused life, Rose O'Neal scrubbed floors, washed dishes, laundered clothing, cooked and served meals to the boarding house guests. Remarkably, she did not complain. Every day she thanked her aunt for rescuing her from destitution.

By the time she was sixteen, Wild Rose had blossomed into such a stunning, articulate beauty that the gentlemen guests invited her to join them in their after dinner conversations which invariably gravitated toward the pressing issues of the day: expansionism, the Texas question, the border dispute with English Canada, tariffs, the spread of slavery into the territories, and, of course, secession. The discussions were usually one-sided because they were regularly attended by the likes of Jefferson Davis, James Buchanan, and a cabal of other Southern politicians seeking good food, good drink, and good company.

Rose particularly fell under the spell of the elder statesman who would later be called "The Father of Secession": South Carolina Senator John C. Calhoun. Night after night, year after year, Rose sat adoringly at the wild-eyed, wild-haired rebel's side, absorbing his rhetoric and dramatic intellect. If she was not a true believer in the Southern cause when she arrived at her aunt's boarding house, she no doubt was when she left. So inspired, she accepted the marriage proposal of a wealthy Calhoun protégé named Greenhow and was soon on her way to becoming the doyenne of Washington society.

The death of her husband and the ample inheritance he left behind allowed the widow Greenhow to entertain Washington's elite exquisitely for several years. With her natural grace and fluid language, she endeared women and intoxicated men. And on this sweaty Washington City night, horses clopping and wheels creaking, the well-breasted Mrs. Greenhow was definitely intoxicating Henry Wilson.

"Go on, Henry," she cooed. "What were you saying about General Scott?"

"Oh, nothing that would interest anyone as delicate as you, my dear," he said, slurring his words due to the whiskey she had been providing him from her flask.

"Oh, I'm just silly, I guess," she said. "Imagine it, a lady who actually enjoys hearing about war and armies and politics. But coming from a man as wise and well placed as you, Henry, it just seems to take on an excitement, a drama even that I don't find in anything else. It is unrefined of me, I know, but please, indulge my eccentric ways."

"Well, my dear, if it will not bore you."

"Oh, nothing you say could ever bore me, Henry." And she rested her fragrant head upon his shoulder.

The frock-coated Senator said, "Well, I believe I was saying that Scott and all the rest of the goddamned West Pointers in this army are nothing but a passel of whiners. They keep complaining that their little babes-in-arms aren't yet ready to fight. But damn it, the people want the slave-mongers' blood and so do I."

Mrs. Greenhow stroked the man's sagging jowls and purred, "Of course, you do, Henry, and I'll bet it takes a man of your strength of will and character to hold them to a deadline to advance, doesn't it. Here, take another sip."

Drinking from her flask, the Senator tried to focus his eyes. "You're right, of course. And now it is obvious to anyone with a brain that Scott will never meet the first deadline my committee sent over."

The widow whispered, "And what date might that be, Henry?"

"The 8th," he said. "But that tree-ape Lincoln let Scott push it back again. But enough of all that. On to more pressing matters." He grinned and squeezed her thigh.

"No, no, no, you naughty boy," she teased, redirecting his stubby fingers. "First tell me the exciting part. When will the army move now? What is the new deadline?"

"Later, my rose petal, later." He slipped his hand back onto her thigh.

"Will it be the ninth, or the tenth, Henry darling?"

"No, not then. But who could care about such trifles at a moment like this?" He raised his hand to her bodiced breast, but she turned it away.

"When, Henry, when?"

Frustrated, Wilson sagged back into his seat with his gut protruding and took another drink. "I can't tell you that, Rose, I can't tell anyone that."

She worked her fingers between his legs and tantalized him with a few probes. "But I simply must know, Henry, to plan my social calendar, don't you see."

He moaned, "...oh, yes...yes...I mean no. no...please...it's..."

"It's what, Henry," she drawled softly. "Is it next week? The week after?" She brought her massage to a stop.

He squirmed, trying to get her to continue. "No...no...don't stop...don't stop...not now..."

"Is it next week, Henry? Are the boys advancing next week?" She remained still, offering no further stimulation.

"No, not next week, it's...it's...no, Rose, I cannot say. Now, please, touch me...touch me..."

Glancing at the opposite seat, she saw his brief case. The information had to be in there among his papers, and she finally resigned herself to the sacrifice she would have to offer up in order to get it.

"For God's sakes, please, Rose, please, you have brought me too far to stop now."

"All right, Henry," she said flatly. "I will share my favors with you, but not here

in this carriage like some soiled dove. Have your coachman take us to my home." She folded her arms tightly against her chest and gazed bitterly out the window, revolted by his chortling glee.

An hour later, Rose pushed with all of her strength to get the naked man off of her, but he was passed out drunk and felt like a sack of manure. She was sweating enough, though, to slide out from under his belly and free herself to the side of the bed.

Sitting there naked for a moment, she gazed down scornfully at this supposedly great man and had an overwhelming urge to pinch him. But she knew that the pain might awaken him even in his drunken stupor, and she settled for a few muttered curses about obnoxious Yankee politicians and their selfish ways in bed.

She wondered why men with access to the truly important information always had to be so boorish, why they all had to grind back and forth against her in their sloppy ecstasy, oblivious to any pleasures but their own. Whether possessing such insensitivity was a requirement for attaining power or the natural result of having done so, she did not know nor long consider. All that mattered to her now was making her sacrifice worth the cheapening it made her feel.

She felt a chill and shuddered, suddenly aware of her nudity. She slipped into a frilly robe and gave herself a warming squeeze. "His papers," she muttered.

She started to get up but froze when a twig snapped beneath her open, second-story window. She heard leaves rustling outside and crept to the window. Peering down, she did not see anyone. She strained to listen but heard only her own heartbeat. Tiptoeing away from the window, Rose then heard a scuffling, like someone jumping over her garden wall. She rushed back to the window and nearly called out a challenge but caught herself when the Honorable Senator began to stir in bed.

After he had resettled, she cocked an ear toward her garden but, hearing nothing more, she padded barefoot to the mirrored dresser where the man's briefcase lay.

"The papers must be in here," she whispered to herself, "with the date."

Tossing back her freed hair, she glanced at Wilson again. She detected no further signs of consciousness and returned to her search. "Marching orders...the advance...it must be in here somewhere." She rifled through the papers until she found something that looked promising.

"What's this," she said, licking perspiration from her upper lip. "Regiments...battalions...batteries...dear God...here it is...the 16th...the 16th...they are advancing on the 16th!"

She clasped her mouth to conceal her excitement and heard another sound outside. She hurriedly stashed the paper in her dresser drawer and returned the others to the leather case. Then she put on slippers and a shawl and glided down the staircase to the front door.

On the way, she met her white-haired house servant. The dignified black man held a lantern, revealing his formal attire. "What are you still doing up, Oscar?"

"I thought there might be trouble, Ma'am. I heard something outside."

"Yes, yes, I did, too. But I can handle it. Just get me the revolver."

"But, ma'am," he said, "shouldn't I be the one to..."

"No, just get me the gun." And the servant slowly did as he was told.

Carefully opening the front door, Rose scanned up and down the street. Everything appeared quiet enough, but the shadows of the trees across the way were too dark to penetrate.

Oscar appeared with his lantern and said, "Is there trouble, Ma'am? May I summon the constable?"

Rose smiled. "No, Oscar, that will not be necessary. But you could brew me a cup of tea please. I may be up for a while."

The man bowed gracefully and said, "Of course, Mrs. Greenhow."

"And please try not to awaken the other servants. There is no need to tire out the entire household over this."

"As you wish, Ma'am." He faded to the back of the house.

Oscar returned with the hot tea and said, "Ma'am, would it be all right if I sat up with you a while, just in case you need me for anything?"

Rose started to refuse the offer but reconsidered and said, "Why, yes, Oscar, I would appreciate the company. Pull up a chair."

Together, they sat that way until dawn, saying little but feeling much. Only in the revealing light did the street seem truly empty and only then did she get up. The Senator was rattling around upstairs, moaning about a headache and crying for coffee.

"If you will excuse me, ma'am," Oscar said, creaking to his feet. "I will attend to the gentleman."

"Don't bother, Oscar, that man is no gentleman and I have no further use of him. I will see him out. You go get some sleep. And thank you for staying up with me."

"Of course, ma'am. But are you certain?"

"Yes. I have a letter to write, to a true gentleman."

"To Colonel Jordan, Ma'am?" He tensed for a moment thinking he should not have asked.

Without a thought of that, Rose said, "Yes. He is one of your favorites, isn't he, Oscar."

"Why, yes, ma'am, he is."

"Mine, too."

He nodded. "Would you like me to deliver your letter to Colonel Jordan over at the office of the Quartermaster, Ma'am?"

"No, that won't be necessary, Oscar. He is not there any longer. I am going to ask Bettie Duval to deliver it. You know her, the young beauty with the raven hair."

"Yes, Ma'am."

At that, Henry Wilson stumbled down the stairs, swearing at Oscar, "Where in the hell is my coffee, boy? I am an important man with important appointments to keep, and I will not be kept waiting by a simple darkie."

Simmering imperceptibly, Oscar bowed and left the room. Simmering more visibly, the Widow Greenhow got up and unceremoniously escorted the politician out her front door without farewells, a kiss, or his morning coffee.

CHAPTER EIGHTEEN

The Confederate White House
Richmond, Virginia
July 14, 1861

EIGHT DAYS LATER, A GRAYING, MUSTACHED MAN KNOCKED GENTLY ON A bedroom door off of the war room and waited to be acknowledged.

"Is that you, General Lee?" came a weak voice from inside.

"Yes, Mr. President, it is I. May I enter?"

"Yes, by all means, come in. You do not need to stand on formality with me."

General Lee opened the door and stepped softly into the room. He glimpsed a tall window on the left draped with lace curtains, a large mirror on the wall ahead, two upholstered reclining chairs, clothing chests, a single hole chamber pot, and a wide, canopied bed on which the cadaverous president was lying prostrate.

"My prayers are with you for a speedy recovery, President Davis," Lee said earnestly. "Is it your neuralgia again?"

Davis fingered his face. "I fear so, General. It seems that the only relief I can obtain during these spells is when I lay this way. But this too shall pass."

"Yes, sir," Lee said. "God's grace is sufficient."

R.E. Lee believed that, even when his father, a Revolutionary War hero, deserted the family and his debts, leaving him to care for his invalid mother.

In need of a free education, the very serious Robert gained admittance to the United States Military Academy, graduating in 1828.

As General Winfield Scott's aide and scout during the Mexican War, he earned promotions for bravery and resourcefulness. He made full colonel after the war and fought Indians in Texas. After a term as superintendent of the Military Academy, he ascended into the public eye when he apprehended John Brown at Harper's Ferry. He resigned from the Old Army when his country seceded and accepted his present position as chief military advisor to the Commander-in-Chief of the Confederacy.

"What is the latest from the western counties," the President said. "Against McClellan? Is it as bad as the initial reports indicated?"

"I am afraid so, Mr. President. The circumstances are perhaps even worse than we had first thought."

"Worse? How could they be any worse?"

The immaculately tailored general said, "Well, sir, of the 8,000 men I sent up there to the mountains, it now appears that fully one quarter of them are casualties."

Davis covered his eyes with a shaking hand. "A quarter? 2,000 men? Lost?"

"It would appear so, sir."

"How many dead?" Davis asked.

The General shook his head. "No one seems to know for certain, sir, but most estimates are in the neighborhood of about one hundred."

Davis sagged. "One hundred men. My God."

"Yes, sir," Lee said, lowering his head as if to take responsibility for the loss.

"And the rest? The other casualties?"

"There were many wounded, some grievously, but our greatest losses came in the form of those captured and missing."

"Whatever became of Colonel Pegram? Wasn't he the one in charge where most of the fighting took place?"

"Yes, sir, he was. At Rich Mountain. He and perhaps six hundred men surrendered after unsuccessfully attempting to link up with General Garnett on nearby Laurel Hill."

"And the artillery chief, that Northerner, what was his name?"

"Julius de Lagnel, sir. His fate remains unknown. It is clear that he was wounded but he may have eluded capture. If he did, he is probably somewhere up in that wilderness right now suffering alone, without care."

"What about Robert Garnett? What is the last that we heard of him?"

General Lee sighed. "It seems that he was trying to lead his 5,000 men out, to the north somehow, the southern route at Beverly having been cut off by the Federals. He conducted himself with utmost valor, I am told, and died while personally conducting a rear guard defense. At a place called Corrick's Ford, I believe. Remnants of his command are still straggling into the lower Shenandoah Valley."

Davis studied his military advisor's face. "I am sorry about Garnett, General. I know that he was your adjutant and a personal favorite. I hope you do not blame yourself. The man volunteered for the assignment, as I recall."

Lee nodded vacantly. "Yes, but he was still grieving the recent death of his wife and child to fever. I should not have sent him up there like that."

Davis asked, "Are you all right, General? Have a seat there, in one of the reading chairs. You look a little peaked."

Suddenly aware of his unseemly self-pity, General Lee straightened and said, "No, sir. I am fine. Forgive me. How else may I be of service to you?"

The night-shirted President sat up. "All right. Tell me this, General. What do you predict will be the overall strategic effect of our losses in western Virginia? At Rich Mountain."

General Lee gazed thoughtfully out the second story window. "Mr. President," he said at length, "I must tell you that they may be serious, very serious indeed. The natural invasion route from Ohio is wide open over Rich Mountain."

The President shifted uncomfortably. "Perhaps you will have to take charge up there personally, General, once we get a little breathing room at Manassas."

"I have been thinking the same thing, sir. I would rather go myself than send another in my stead. But for now, we must watch General McClellan's army. It has been estimated at 20,000 men, and it is now free to cross the Alleghenies and attack General Johnston at Winchester, perhaps even General Beauregard at Manassas."

"Lord in Heaven," President Davis said. "Do you think he could really carry out such a campaign?"

Lee nodded. "Yes, sir, it is logistically possible. General McClellan is being supplied by the Baltimore and Ohio Railroad which he now controls nearly to Harper's Ferry."

Davis buried his face in his hands and said nothing.

"But, Mr. President, I have been observing General McClellan's movements for the past few weeks and, I believe, there is reason to be hopeful."

Davis looked up and said, "Hopeful? Please tell me why, General. God knows I could use a dose of hope just now."

"It would seem, sir, that General McClellan moves with undue caution, completely lacking in celerity. At Rich Mountain, he could have captured our entire force had he exhibited even a modicum of decisiveness."

"So you do not think that he will cross the mountains in time to affect the outcome at Manassas?"

General Lee softly drawled, "That would be my humble opinion, sir, but it would be best if General McDowell invaded at Manassas on the 16th like Mrs. Greenhow's young lady reported. General McClellan could never make it over by then."

"I suppose you are right. But I would bet that General Beauregard would assail me with such a scheme. I swear, that man's head is absolutely inflated with all the hero-worship he has received since Fort Sumter."

General Lee wanted no part of that developing feud. He said simply, "That reminds me, Mr. President, General Beauregard's aide, Colonel Chesnut is here to see you."

"With another of his general's Napoleonic strategies for me to endorse, no doubt. Well, I will not do it. I don't even want to hear this one."

"Colonel Chesnut has come all the way from the Alexandria line, sir."

After a moment to fume, Davis said, "Oh, all right then. Show him in."

A few moments later, General Lee returned with Colonel James Chesnut, a handsome, fortyish aristocrat from South Carolina who was second only to General Lee in gentility.

President Davis extended a trembling hand to greet him. "Good to see you again, James." He tried to smile but it clearly hurt his face to do so.

"I hope you are recovering, sir," Colonel Chesnut said. "The country needs you just as it did when we served together in the old Congress."

"I appreciate that, James, and I would like nothing more than to reminisce about those happier times but the current demands preclude that just now."

Chesnut bowed slightly. "Of course, sir."

"So," Davis said, "what word do you bring me from General Beauregard? A few days ago, he informed me that I needed to send him General Johnston's entire Army of the Shenandoah, immediately if not sooner. To be used in some grand sweep throughout the better part of the North."

Colonel Chesnut said, "General Beauregard has abandoned that plan, sir. He regrets that there is not enough time for an invasion of the North but stands upon his conviction that General Johnston should move down to Manassas as soon as practicable."

"Well, James, you inform your General that the decision as to when General Johnston will leave the valley is mine and mine alone."

"Yes, sir," Chesnut began diplomatically. "It is just that General

Beauregard would like to be informed as to your thoughts regarding the move. For even with the train, sir, it will take two days at least to transport appreciable numbers of General Johnston's men down to Manassas."

"I am aware of that, Colonel. I am aware of all operations and contingencies in northern Virginia. You forget, sir, that I am, at heart, a military man."

"Oh no, sir, not at all, sir." Chesnut said, bowing.

"You tell, General Beauregard that I will send him General Johnson as soon I have incontrovertible proof that the Unionists have left Washington and not before. Is that clear?"

"Yes, sir," Chesnut said and paused. "There is one other matter General Beauregard wanted me to discuss with you."

"Let me guess, another of his grand strategies."

"Well, yes, sir, he does have a plan which he wanted me to share with you."

"Dear God in Heaven," Davis said, "what is it now? Is he planning to take Canada from the British?

"No, sir, but he wishes me to advise you that he does not want to fight a defensive battle. He desires, as soon as the Unionists reach Centreville five miles to the north of our lines, to launch a wide-ranging flanking movement probably from our right and against the enemy's left and destroy them there before they have a chance to attack us."

The President thought for moment. His West Point training, years of fighting Indians, and his colonelcy in the Mexican War would not let him relinquish strategy development to any general. He was certain that he knew more about the military arts than most of them, certainly Beauregard, whom he already suspected of conspiring to take the credit for any successful strategy regardless of who conceived it.

"I will consider such a plan, Colonel Chesnut. But not without it being closely supervised by me. Tell General Beauregard to keep me well informed about any plan of his. He is to do nothing without my knowledge and approval. Do you understand me, James?"

"Yes, sir," Chesnut said, sensing accurately that the conversation was over.

"Good. Now, gentlemen please forgive me but I simply must rest. I fear my neuralgia is growing worse. Give my regards to Mary, Colonel. Tell her to write me one of those beautiful letters of hers. She has such a fine way with a pen."

Pleasantries were exchanged and General Lee held the door open for Colonel Chesnut. Standing there, the General glimpsed a painting on the wall. It was of Saint Michael casting Lucifer out of Heaven. He hoped that casting the Yankees out of the Confederacy would prove easier but, unlike everyone else in the South, he did not think that it would.

CHAPTER NINETEEN

———————◆•◆———————

Five Miles East of Fairfax Court House, Virginia
June 17, 1861
Mid-Morning

JULY 16TH DID PROVE TO BE THE STARTING DATE FOR THE UNION INVASION and, as far as General Irvin McDowell could determine, it was one of the most disorganized days in the history of the United States Army. Miscues abounded. Blunders prevailed. Even his few West Point-trained officers sprinkled through the ranks proved unable to wrangle the herd of 33,000 undisciplined volunteers toward its goal at Bull Run. It was, McDowell knew, an army three times the size of any which had ever tramped across the farmlands of North America, and it was tormenting him now that he could not control it.

Midway through the second day of the march, it was clear to him that the worst of his fears had been realized. He could not douse the mischief that consumed the Union ranks as they forayed toward Fairfax Court House. If any officers were trying to manage these rowdies, he could not see them. If his orders were descending the chain of command, they were not being obeyed. Nothing short of God's own hand, it seemed, had any chance of pushing these men down their assigned roads toward the easy victory they all expected.

McDowell's plan called for advancing his five divisions on three parallel roads leading westward out of Washington. General Daniel Tyler was to take the northernmost route and try to get in behind any of Bonham's Rebels in Fairfax Court House. David Hunter and Dixon Miles were to take the middle roads and advance on Fairfax frontally to hammer the secessionists against Tyler's anvil. Samuel Heintzelman was to march his division along the southerly route and turn northward to hit Fairfax on its southern flank. And bringing up the rear was O. O. Howard. His job, presumably, would be to bury the dead and care for the wounded, the Confederates' dead and wounded of course since the Northerners did not plan to have any.

Once the Rebels were cleared out of Fairfax, McDowell intended for General Tyler, the trim, white-haired gentleman who had spent most of his life running canals and railroads, to advance a reconnaissance-in-force at the center of the Confederate line at Blackburn's Ford of Bull Run, and draw just enough fire to assess the positions and strength of the Southerners there without bringing on a general engagement. The *coup de gras* was to follow the next day with a huge sweep around either the Confederate left or right flank, depending upon topography and enemy troop dispositions, while feinting a series of direct assaults on the Rebel front.

It was a strategy, he believed, that Napoleon himself would have been proud to devise, full of stealth, grand maneuvers, and midnight marches. But before McDowell could put his plan into operation, he knew he had to get his Army of Virginia to the battlefield. And he was pounding his saddle in a red-faced rage because of the delays.

"Goddamn it, Hunter!" he said. "Would you just look at this mess? These damned volunteers aren't soldiers on the march. They're a mob of sons-of-bitching frolickers at a Sunday social."

"It is dreadful, sir." General Hunter said, twisting at the frayed ends of his mustache.

"For two days now," McDowell said, "these so-called fighting men have been falling out at will for water or blackberries or whatever pleases them."

"You are right, sir," Hunter said, always eager to agree with superiors.

The beefy McDowell wiped the dust-blackened sweat from his face and said, "I understand that it is hotter than hell, Hunter, but still, your men have covered just twelve miles in two days. And they are the vanguard of the army, for god sakes. They are holding everyone else up. What can you do to pick up their pace?"

"Please be assured, General, that I am doing everything humanly possible. I have made arrests for looting, chastised them for falling out. All these ragamuffins do is laugh and go right along singing their ribald songs and horse playing."

"It makes me sick," McDowell said, coughing up brownish mucous and spitting it down to the dust. "And some of the so-called officers are worse than the men."

"Sir?" Hunter said, defensively.

"That's right. Did you hear about the captain of the 79th New York? Those damned Scots Highlanders?"

Hunter sighed relief that he was not to be the designated offender. "Uh, no, sir."

"The son of a bitch took off after a pig in his bare-assed kilt and brought on an avalanche of laughter. It stopped the entire column for a full thirty minutes. And the brother of their colonel is none other than Secretary of War Simon Cameron."

The two mounted officers shook their heads disgustedly and fell silent. They watched the ragged procession inch by, the men lolly-gagging and playing their grab-ass games. Some fell out right in front of them to chase chickens or relieve themselves, usually upstream from where other men were filling their canteens. The smell of sweat, urine, dust, and feces was noxious. At regular intervals two or three carriages creaked by full of gowned ladies and top-hatted gentlemen. McDowell recognized one of the men as Senator Henry Wilson, the chairman of the Senate Committee on Military Affairs. The civilians were toasting the impending victory with champagne and nibbling on dainty finger sandwiches, cavorting as merrily as the soldiers themselves.

"What do you make of that, General?" Hunter asked, "Washington society's finest coming out to watch the battle as if it were no more than a dress parade?"

McDowell wrung the perspiration out of his goatee. "They are fools. I must have seen a couple of hundred of them out here over the past two days. Hell, I can barely keep the infantry moving at speed without those lunatics clogging the road."

The column lurched to a complete halt, collapsing into itself like an accordion. Men fell down and crawled off in the shade beside the road. Some singers, undaunted by the suffocating sun, struck up "John Brown's Body" with lyrics about hanging Jeff Davis to a sour apple tree. Others competed with a new song, a frisky little tune called "Dixie".

The column did not budge for several minutes. "Rebel sharpshooters again?" General Hunter said.

"I suppose. Or more goddamned abatis across the road. I swear, those traitors must have beavers in their pay. If I would have had some cavalry, I could have reconnoitered out there and had the roads cleared ahead of time."

"I am certain of it, sir. It is criminal that the President and General Scott sent you out here without eyes and ears. Why, they could not even provide you with so much as an accurate map of the area."

General McDowell harrumphed. He knew Hunter to be a sycophant who would slander him behind his back if it served his career. "There is plenty of blame to go around for everybody, Hunter. Including you."

"Me, sir? I am sure I don't understand."

"Was not your division to be drawn up before Fairfax Court House yesterday?"

"Well, yes, sir, but..."

"Was it not to trap the Rebel outposts there against Tyler's division behind them?"

"That is all true, sir, but..."

"Did you successfully carry out your orders, General Hunter?"

"Well, no sir but..."

"Then the first part of my strategy has failed and there is plenty of blame to go around for that, am I not correct, General?"

Hunter backed off and said, "You are correct, sir." After a pause to watch a few more knots of the herky-jerky column pass by, he added, "So what is your alternative plan, sir, if I may ask?"

"Hell, Hunter, I don't know. Nothing is going according to plan. Not here, not with Tyler above us, not with Heintzelman below us. Heintzelman says he has encountered more earthworks to the south than expected and that the terrain is badly broken."

"Good maps would have told us that, sir."

Ignoring another attempt at ingratiation, McDowell said, "I am going to have to ride down there and assess the situation for myself. I might have to scrap any plans for Heintzelman to sweep around the Rebel right flank, our left."

Hunter could not suppress a grin. "And attach his troops to my division up here, for a grand sweep around our right?"

"Perhaps," McDowell said flatly.

His grin broadening, Hunter said, "With those extra troops, perhaps I should also lead the preliminary advance against the Rebel center as well at Blackburn's Ford."

McDowell cut him off sharply. "General Hunter, how many times do I need to tell you, it is not an advance. It is a reconnaissance-in-force. And General Tyler will be leading it. You will be leading the main thrust if and only if General Heintzelman and I determine that the ground on the left is too broken."

Hunter wisely thought that he had better leave well enough alone and he said nothing more.

The column dragged to a rattling start again, still at its heel-stepping, back-bumping pace. "Well, thank God for small miracles," McDowell said. "We might make it to Fairfax by Christmas."

CHAPTER TWENTY

———◆•◆———

Fairfax Court House, Virginia
July 17, 1861
Night

GENERAL MCDOWELL AND THE VANGUARD OF HIS MEN FINALLY REACHED Fairfax Court House after dark. After eating the rations that were supposed to keep them fed for a week, some of the volunteers went into the village looking for real food. When they could find little in the abandoned homes, the Yankees loosed their frustrations. The two sweltering days it had taken them to reach Fairfax had obviously not exhausted them. Nor did they appear as ready as their divisional commander, David Hunter, had predicted to settle down to their sacred duty.

Bonfires of furniture burned in the streets, crackling sparks up into the darkness. Outbuildings and clapboard houses blazed away. Wild-eyed horses screamed out their panic and shrieking fools hooliganized in petty-coats while drunkards tug-of-warred over booty, usually destroying it in the process.

Rifles discharged in vicious, random blasts. Manic laughter rasped the air. Joyous shouts and hideous oaths mingled in what might have seemed a victory celebration had there been a victory to celebrate. But even without one, it was a celebration nonetheless; a devilish, dancing, unbridled spree and it disgusted Daniel Tyler, the silver gentleman, as he looked on from General McDowell's tent.

"Those boys are a sight, aren't they, General Tyler?" McDowell mumbled through a mouthful of potatoes and gravy.

Tyler arched an eyebrow and nodded.

"But don't you worry," McDowell said. "They'll be settling down soon enough."

"And what do you base that upon, sir?" Tyler grumbled.

"I have just issued orders to every regimental colonel requiring that he appoint an officer and ten of his best men as Provost Guards to police up the offenders." A rifle blasted off outside. Tyler flinched. McDowell went back to his dinner.

"And just what do you expect to do with the mass of men they will have to arrest?"

Stuffing a hunk of buttered bread into his mouth, McDowell chewed until he could manage to say, "I am going to send them to prison back in Alexandria for a start. And it won't be a 'mass' of men, General Tyler. As soon as I make an example out of a few, the rest will settle down."

A woman's scream turned Tyler's head. "Well, sir, if I may say so, those measures may be too little too late for some."

A flaming building collapsed outside in a fracas of sparks and snapping crashes, lighting the night sky like a swarm of fireflies. General McDowell wiped his mouth and belched. "Well, you just let me worry about that, General Tyler. There are other matters that I want you to direct your attention to tonight."

Tyler turned, his interest piqued. "My advance tomorrow on the secessionist center?"

"Goddamn it, Tyler, do you not yet understand my orders? It is not to be an advance but a reconnaissance-in-force."

Stiff and simmering, the elder general said, "I understand your orders perfectly, General McDowell, and I am entirely capable of carrying them out."

"Well, I will just have to trust you on that one, now won't I, for I will be down with Heintzelman on our left tonight and some part of tomorrow." Someone vomited outside, splattering a wretched stench that wafted into the tent.

Pinching his nose, Tyler said, "Have you heard anything from Rob Patterson, up in the Valley? Has he been successful in keeping Johnston tied up?"

"All I know is that Patterson has been playing a cat and mouse game with the Rebels for several weeks, but I wonder who is the cat and who is the mouse."

"Patterson will do all right," Tyler said. "He is a feisty old warrior. At least he used to be. He has plenty of battle experience under his belt."

"Yes. That is what worries me."

"What do you mean by that," Tyler said as laughter erupted outside.

"I mean that it has taken him many years to get all of that experience under his belt."

"And?"

"And, General Tyler, he is nearly seventy years old. The man responsible for keeping one of the most respected Generals on either side of this struggle tied-up in the Shenandoah Valley is an old man. He should have never been put in command of anything, and he would not have been had he not been a close personal friend of Winfield Scott."

Tyler stiffened, "While I may agree with you, sir, concerning Robert Patterson's patronage, I must disagree entirely that his age is an issue. For god's sake, he is only eight years older than I am."

"Calm down, General, calm down. Have I said anything whatsoever about your age?"

Tyler fiddled with his cravat. "Well, I suppose not but..."

"Then stand down, would you. I am talking about Patterson here, not you."

"Well, I suppose so, but it did sound as if..."

"General Tyler, I don't care how old you are as long as you carry out my orders tomorrow. Do you understand that?"

"Yes, sir, I suppose I do."

"Then you are dismissed. Leave me now and let me eat in peace. You will receive your written orders shortly."

Tyler saluted and stepped out of the tent. Feeling strangely unsettled, he turned back from the flaming melee and caught McDowell shaking his head and smirking.

CHAPTER TWENTY-ONE

Major General Joseph E. Johnston's Headquarters
Near Winchester, Virginia
July 18, 1861
Early Morning

THE NEXT MORNING IN THE SHENANDOAH VALLEY, THE PARLOR OF ONE well-kept gentry home smelled of fine cigars, half-burnt fireplace logs, and baking bread. The residents were obligingly upstairs out of the way, leaving their honored guests to their work. General Johnston sat upright with his brigade commanders gathered dutifully around him. They were General Thomas Jackson, Colonel Francis Bartow, General Edmund Kirby Smith, and General Barnard Bee, as well as the young colonel of his cavalry regiment, J.E.B. Stuart.

"Gentlemen," Johnston said quietly, "At 1:00 a.m. this morning, I received from Richmond a telegraph ordering me to move the entire Army of the Shenandoah down to Manassas Junction to reinforce General Beauregard 'if practicable'. That, of course meaning, if we can practicably deceive General Patterson's Yankees into remaining up here out of the fight after we have left."

The officers stirred, all except for Jackson whose dull eyes did not respond. Colonel Stuart leaned forward in his chair, percolating with enthusiasm in spite of the fact that he had been riding throughout the countryside all night long. "Why, of course it's practicable, General Johnston. Patterson is a doddering old fool. He'll never suspect anything."

The others murmured their support. Jackson stifled a yawn.

"So tell me then, Colonel Stuart," Johnston said. "What makes you so certain that Patterson won't just follow us down to Manassas with his 20,000 men and fall upon General Beauregard's flank there?"

"Why, it's as clear as the teats on a sow, General. His entire performance has proven him to be weak-willed and vacillating. He advances at a turtles pace and only when no enemy faces him. Then he runs like a rabbit when my patrols appear. My boys have been riding circles around him for weeks now with complete impunity."

General Johnston waved away a swirl of blue cigar smoke. "I must admit, it would seem a good opportunity to slip away. It would seem 'practicable'."

Stuart nodded his wavy beard, his eyes ablaze. "It would, General, it would. And I think we should waste no time in doing so."

General Johnston looked around at the others and said, "Do the rest of you share in Colonel Stuart's enthusiasm?"

Stout, proud Barnard Bee spoke up, saying, "Well, sir, since the bulk of the responsibility for screening our movement would devolve upon Colonel Stuart and his cavalry, I believe that we should rely heavily upon his recommendation. I concur with Colonel Stuart."

Bee's opinion had already come to be respected. Born in South Carolina, he had attended West Point, earned two field promotions and a wound in the Mexican War, and fought Indians on the frontier.

"And the rest of you?" General Johnston asked.

They nodded and muttered in agreement.

"Very well," Johnston said. "We move then."

Colonel Stuart slapped his knee-high boots and grinned. "When, sir?"

"When can you set up the screen?"

"We can have every road and pass between the Yankees and us covered by this afternoon. I will issue orders to attack every enemy patrol or scout that tries to get close enough to see what we are up to. The increased activity on our part alone will trick old Patterson into thinking that we are staying up here to fight him."

General Johnston gazed out the front window with a look of promise in his eyes. "Then do it. Immediately."

The murmuring grew louder. Excitement bubbled over into exclamations. Kirby Smith's second-in-command, Arnold Elzey, bolted up and exclaimed,

"Excellent, excellent."

Just before resigning his Union commission at the beginning of the war, Elzey, a West Pointer, surrendered the wealth of weaponry at the Augusta, Georgia arsenal he commanded to the Confederates whom he joined shortly thereafter. Those muskets helped arm the very men massing in northern Virginia.

"Excellent, indeed," Elzey said again.

"Just point us the way, General," Bee added.

"Who goes first?" Bartow said. He was a Yale Law School graduate, a member of the Provisional Confederate Congress and a persuasive orator, but a man with limited military experience. "Beauregard could have the battle won before the last of us ever get down there."

"That's right," Bee said.

"Please, sir, let me have the honor of leading our advance," Kirby Smith said. He was a hardened man, not usually given to pleading. A West Point graduate, Indian fighter, and hero during the war with Mexico, he was a devout Christian who dreamed of someday leaving the military to become a minister. But he did not want to miss the first and last great battle of the War for Southern Independence. "Please, sir, let me lead the way."

Only Jackson said nothing. Seeming not to care about who went first, he remained seated and perfectly erect.

"Please," Johnston said. "I appreciate your spirit but there is more we must consider. Be seated."

"Of course, sir," the scraggly-bearded Elzey said.

"Forgive the outburst, General," Bee added, bowing as if at a ball.

Bartow started a campaign speech. "Sir, I believe it to be in the best interest of the country for me to inform you that... "

"Please," Johnston said, raising his hand to silence him. "I have made my decision. Allow me to lay out the order of the march and explain the route."

"Oh, we know all about that, General," Elzey said. "We are going to take the train."

"Yes," Kirby Smith said. "And whoever goes first is going to make military history."

"That's right," said Congressman Bartow. "That man is going to be the first commander ever to lead men into battle in cars."

Excited chatter made its way around the parlor again but still, Jackson remained quiet

"Yes," Johnston said, "we will be using the railroad. But we must first march twenty-five miles overland in order to pick up the Manassas Gap line at Piedmont Station. We will have to march up and over the Blue Ridge in just twenty-four hours with no straggling."

All but the one eagerly nodded their understanding of the task and their willingness to undertake it.

"For that reason, I have chosen General Jackson and his 1st Virginia Brigade to lead the way. He has demonstrated to me an ability to rapidly march a column of men and to maintain strict adherence to military discipline along the way, not that I have found fault with any of the rest of you in that regard."

The parlor hushed, though Johnston could almost hear what his commanders were thinking.

Jackson?

Old Jack?

In the military history books?

My God, the man is barely literate.

He has the social graces of an ape.

Colonel Stuart spoke up, saying simply, "My boys will ride General Jackson's left flank, screening his movements from enemy eyes. I promise you that the Yankees will not see him leave."

"Yes," Johnston said. "You will have to do that. And you will have to create enough of a diversion to deceive Patterson into thinking that I am preparing to attack him up here."

"Of course, sir," Stuart said, rising excitedly and donning his redlined cape and ostrich-plumed hat. "Then if I might be dismissed, sir, to begin my preparations." He saluted on the move, his spurs jingling on the way out

Johnston hurried his return salute so as to avoid the appearance of any impertinence on the young man's part. "Yes, of course, Colonel Stuart, of course. And Colonel Stuart."

Stuart stopped at the door. "Sir?"

"You have already gained something of a reputation for, how shall I say, flamboyance in the field. Please remember, sir, over and above providing the army with an adequate screen, you are my eyes and ears when it comes to reconnaissance. You are far more important to me in that role than as an offensive arm."

Stuart smiled one of his sauciest smiles and said, "I will keep that foremost in my mind, sir, for as I am certain you know, the glory of battle means nothing to me." And he hurried from the house whistling a happy tune.

Suppressing a smile of his own, General Johnston turned and addressed the others, "Now, as far as the rest of you are concerned, here is the order of the march." He put on his spectacles and read from a sheet of paper, running each brigade commander through his place on the departure schedule. Elzey and Smith were last.

"But, sir," Elzey said, "the battle will surely be over by then. Can you not somehow see fit to squeeze us in sooner?"

"No, Colonel, the order is set. "You and General Smith will bring up the rear on the railroad."

Elzey hung his head. "But last? Dead last? Our boys are going to be sorely disappointed, sir."

"That is because they are good soldiers, Colonel, like yourself. But some brigade must go last and I have chosen General Smith's with you as his senior colonel."

Disappointed, Elzey nodded obediently.

"Besides," Johnston said, "the fortunes of war being what they are, who is to say that it won't be your brigade that will arrive at the most opportune of times. Perhaps just in time to sweep the enemy from the field like Blucher at Waterloo."

"I don't see how, sir," Elzey said. "But I have been a professional soldier all my adult life and I have never disobeyed an order. I will not start now."

"Fine," Johnston said. "Now, we do not have much time. I must let you get to your brigades to begin preparations. Are there any questions?"

General Jackson raised his hand.

"Yes, General. What is your question?"

"Question?" Jackson said woodenly.

"Yes. You raised your hand."

General Jackson looked at his upraised arm and said, "Oh, that. That is for my blood, sir, to balance my organs."

"Oh, yes, yes, of course. To balance your organs."

Jackson nodded. The other brigade commanders glanced at each other furtively.

With his other hand, Jackson reached into his pocket and took out a peach. "May I, sir?"

Johnston said, "Go right ahead. For your dyspepsia, as I recall."

Jackson nodded.

"Yes, yes. Proceed. We are finished here anyway."

The men rose. Jackson was closest to the door so he led the way out, limping noticeably.

"What ails your leg, General?" Johnston said.

"Oh, it is nothing, sir. I foolishly peppered my supper last night. That always gives me a leg-ache the next day."

The trailing officers exchanged more sidelong glances about this quirky mountaineer, the vanguard of their army, the man most likely to lead them into battle.

Jackson, for his part, shook his leg out, raised his arm higher, and began sucking on his peach.

CHAPTER TWENTY-TWO

General Beauregard's Headquarters
The McLean House
July 19, 1861
4:00 p.m.

A BURST OF LAUGHTER ROCKED THE PARLOR IN WHICH GENERAL Beauregard was holding court. It came from his generals who had gathered around him to celebrate his army's triumph at the Battle of Blackburn's Ford or the Battle of Bull Run, as they were calling it. Blue cigar smoke drifted in lazy swirls that accelerated with each slap of a back or boisterous gesture. Spittoons rung with brown, tarry bulls-eyes and whiskey glasses clinked in toasts.

What began as a skirmish between a few Federal soldiers and a handful of Rebel sharpshooters at Blackburn's Ford a day earlier had ended in a full-fledged battle—and a victory for Brigadier General James Longstreet and his brigade of Virginians.

It was to be a reconnaissance-in-force for the Union troops, to assess the positions and strength of the Southerners. The orders from General Irvin McDowell to General Daniel Tyler could not have been clearer. Do no engage the Rebels. But little did the white-haired general know that his adversary Longstreet had a different strategy up his sleeve.

And so it was that after a few skirmishes, and several fruitless attempts by his men to run screaming for the protection of the woods, Longstreet corralled his troops and carried out the ambush he had so carefully planned.

Tyler, for his part, was left with the difficult task of explaining to McDowell why the 12th New York regiment did not get the dispatch that all the other troops had—to pull back, that the fight was over and it was time to disengage—and so had walked unknowingly into Longstreet's trap, with their commander, Colonel Israel "Fighting Dick" Richardson cheering them on. More importantly, Tyler had to somehow explain to McDowell why the reconnaissance-in-force had turned out to be called the *Battle* of Blackburn's Ford.

The battle was not the pretty dress parade that Washington society's finest had envisioned, but rather it was an agonizingly bloody encounter with casualties on both sides. On top of that, Longstreet had had to deal with his own personal battles—the insubordinate, whiskey-sloshing Colonel Early, who provided the back-up brigade, and Beauregard's little messenger boy, Lieutenant Bagwell, who misinformed Early, so that his troops fired on their own men.

But, it was a victory nonetheless and a time for celebration, and the generals gathered at Beauregard's Headquarters were ready for it.

T hese spiritous men, the brigade commanders within Beauregard's inner sanctum, were the men who would execute the General's next master stroke: Dick Ewell, Shanks Evans, Neighbor Jones, Milledge Bonham, Theophilous Holmes, Philip Cocke, Jubal Early, and James "Pete" Longstreet. But in the amber light filtering into the room, they toasted Longstreet and Early for the win and heaped plaudits upon them like royal mantles. Longstreet nodded and remained humble. Early, on the other hand, wallowed in the praise and generated a good deal more of it for himself.

"So why do you think McDowell did not resume his attack today, General Beauregard?" Early said. "Do you think he was afraid to take me on again?" He laughed with a whiskey voice as did a couple of others.

"Let us not forget, sir," Beauregard said, "the role General Longstreet played at the ford. I fear that his native humility inhibits him from soliciting his ample share of the laurels."

Longstreet gave a polite nod. "Why thank you, General, I appreciate that. But I am well satisfied. I believe that duty fulfilled is reward enough for a soldier."

A murmuring of approval bubbled up.

"Well, said, Pete."

"My sentiments exactly."

Early's black, brooding eyes simmered behind his beard. He crossed his legs and re-crossed them impatiently.

"Jube makes a good enough point though," Shanks Evans said, emptying a bottle into his glass. "It was strange that McDowell did not move today. Do you think he'll do it tomorrow, General?"

"That is difficult to say, Colonel Evans. A man like McDowell is always hard to predict."

"But didn't you graduate with him at the Academy, sir?" asked Dick Ewell, *Ol' Baldy*, "Surely you must have formed some impression of him there."

"He was a hard man to fathom even then, General Ewell. The one thing I do remember about him was that it took him a long time to get started on something but, once he did, his resolve to finish it was considerable."

"So you think he's going to come strong tomorrow then, General?" Neighbor Jones asked, his trademark smile fading a bit.

Beauregard thought for a moment and said, "Yes, I believe he will attack first thing tomorrow with his full strength: 37,000 men."

"Where?" Jones asked.

"In the middle again, I suspect. I hope. Then, while I hold him there, I can swing my right around behind him at Centreville, cut him off, and capture his entire army. I just pray that Johnston's people will be here by then."

"To Joe Johnston then!" white-bearded Bonham announced, clearly warmed by the liquor.

"We don't need Joe Johnston," Early declared, "nor any of them in the Valley. We can whip these goddamned Yankees with our 25,000 if we have to." The men, or the whiskey, concurred.

"But, Jube," Nathan Evans slurred, "I, for one, would feel more certain of victory if my force on the left flank was stronger. I mean that is where they have access to the best bridges and roads."

"You need not worry about the left, Colonel Evans," Beauregard said. "My offensive on the right will keep the enemy from doing any damage to our left."

The conversation stopped when another man entered the room. He stood in the shadows, braced and silent, trying to wave the cigar smoke away from his face.

Beauregard challenged, "Que vive?"

The man lumbered into rays of light and said, "I am General Jackson, sir, from General Johnston's command. I just arrived by car with the first of the Shenandoah brigades."

Beauregard arose and beamed. "Well, come in, General, come in. You don't know how pleased I am to see you."

Jackson shuffled closer to the gathering of commanders and received their flurry of handshakes, happy curses, and slaps on the back. He lurched back at the smell of their breath.

General Beauregard stepped in and showed him to a seat. "Is General Johnston with you, General Jackson?"

"No, sir." Jackson said sleepily.

"When will he get here?"

"Perhaps tomorrow, sir, if God wills it." He waved at the smoke again.

"Tomorrow? Morning or afternoon?"

"I would say afternoon, sir, if God wills it."

"Good, good," Beauregard said. "Can you tell me, General Jackson, how are the cars working? Will they be able to move the entire Army of the Shenandoah down?"

"Yes, sir, I believe so. If the problems do not become any worse."

"Problems?"

"Yes," Jackson said, suddenly pre-occupied with the ache in his left leg.

"Yes what, General? What problems?"

"Well, sir, there is the very slow pace and shortage of cars and the sabotage by Unionist railroad workers."

"Sabotage? By railroad men?"

"Yes, sir, it would seem so."

"What proof do you have?"

"There were breakdowns all along the way, sir, and other suspicious delays. I had to personally restrain some of my men from bringing harm to the loco-motive crew. My men thought, perhaps correctly, that those people were intentionally trying to keep us from getting here."

Early said, "You should have thrown those Yankee-loving bastards under the wheels, Jackson. I sure as hell would have."

Jackson said numbly, "The Lord, sir, does not countenance murder in any of its guises nor will he bestow his blessings upon those who practice it. Whatever God wills regarding the movement of our troops will be done with or without human interference."

Early smirked and shook his head. He glanced at Evans for support and got it.

"Well, in that case," Beauregard said, "perhaps we must accept the possi-bility that not all of General Johnston's army will get here in time for my flanking action from our right. I must thus stretch our defenses on the left thinner for the time being."

Jackson cocked his head toward Beauregard, suddenly listening.

"Now more than ever," the Creole said, "remain alert for my orders to attack the Unionist left and be ready to move at a moments notice. I am still committed to that strategy."

It became clear that Beauregard was phasing back into his work mode now and directing the meeting to a polite close. Chairs creaked. Men stood up. They came to attention, some weaving slightly, and pleasantries were exchanged as they left.

Jackson was following up the rear when General Beauregard stopped him and said, "General, step over to the map, if you would, sir, and allow me to show you where I want you to place your brigade." The two men went to the map table. "Here, General. I want you in reserve behind Mitchell's Ford right here." He pointed.

"The position looks strong," Jackson said.

"Yes, the greater part of my force is there."

Jackson paused and said, "I do not understand why the enemy would even consider attacking such a strong point, especially when the best road and the only bridges are so lightly defended up here." He touched the Stone Bridge on the map.

Placing his hand on the much taller man's shoulder, Beauregard walked Jackson to the door. "You need not concern yourself with the deployment of troops, General. I have all of that well in hand."

"Yes, sir," Jackson said. "If you say so, sir." And he stepped exhaustedly toward the door. "I will see to my brigade now."

"Excellent," Beauregard said, forcing a smile. "And a good afternoon to you, General Jackson." He closed the door with a dismissive shake of the head.

Outside, Jackson stumbled upon someone he had not seen for two months: the straw-blonde lieutenant with the blue eyes and a bright red face. It was Lucas Ashcroft, the class clown from VMI. The former cadet shot him a bitter look and said, "That's right, Major or Colonel or General or whatever the hell you go by now. You'll always be Ol' Tom Fool to me and anybody who really knows you for what you are."

Jackson saw the enmity in the boy's eyes and said, "Be careful, son. You are risking punishable insubordination with your remarks."

"You can't touch me anymore, Jack. I am not your cadet. I am a commissioned officer now, a lieutenant in the Confederate service, and a courier on the staff of the commanding general himself: P.G.T. Beauregard. Now, there is a real soldier for you, not some dusty cracker from the hills of western Virginia."

Jackson's chest rose as if to engage the boy. He stopped himself, though, and muttered a silent, closed-eyed prayer. When he opened his eyes, he saw Lucas grinning victoriously.

"You keep praying, General. You're going to need all the prayers you can get with the way this army regards you." He laughed out loud.

Unaffected, Jackson ignored the boy and slogged away, another murmured prayer on his lips.

A second boy, this one in a cadet uniform, rushed up to Lucas and shook his hand enthusiastically. "Holy hell, fellow," he said, grinning. "How do you get away with treating a general like that? What's your secret for not getting court martialed?"

Lucas said, "It's no secret. It just depends on the general. That one there isn't worth a damn."

"Well, no matter. I'd still like to introduce myself. I'm Archie Bagwell. Lieutenant Archie Bagwell from the Citadel, South Carolina. I'm a courier for General Beauregard."

"Lieutenant Lucas Ashcroft, Virginia Military Institute. The same."

"I suppose we're going to be seeing some of each other then."

"Yeah," Lucas said. And he walked off with the energetic boy in tow.

CHAPTER TWENTY-THREEE

---●---

General McDowell's Headquarters
Centreville, Virginia
July 20, 1861
10:00 p.m.

GENERAL MCDOWELL HAD NOT EXERCISED HIS PREROGATIVE AS A FIELD commander to displace a local family and take over their home for head-quarters use. With an eye toward appeasing a populace already hostile due to the plundering and pillaging of Fairfax Court House, he had issued decrees forbidding such depredations and set himself up in a tent. It was an unpretentious tent with a dirt floor and few appointments. It contained a cot, a desk, a few camp stools, and, of course, a dinner table. The canvas shelter could barely accommodate the officers and the one prominent Washingtonian who had gathered inside for a council of war.

Some of the officers insisted upon rushing headlong into the fight, a position staunchly supported by the chest-thumping Senator Henry Wilson. Others wanted to wait for more supplies and training, but all of them could agree on one thing: just how much they would enjoy two or three drinks and a rich, soothing cigar to complement them. But they knew the prudish commander would not allow that, especially when he had not yet finished his second apple pie for dessert. Thus, tense and agitated, they argued their points, crowded onto the stools and into the standing room available to them.

"I'm telling you, General McDowell," Colonel Richardson said. "We've lost two good days here. Why are you waiting to attack?"

His mouth full, McDowell mumbled, "Partly, Richardson, because you and Tyler exceeded my orders at Blackburn's Ford, and your repulse there shook the confidence of this entire army."

"That is not true," General Tyler said. "You would have taken these two days regardless of what happened at the ford. You said yourself that you needed the time to bring up rations and to scout the rebel left."

A portly, bald colonel with huge muttonchops spoke up. "But are you all too blind to see it? It doesn't matter if we attack now or two weeks from now. Our men are not ready."

"Oh, not that again, Burnside," Hunter said. "General McDowell has thoroughly considered and dismissed those reservations."

"But you know they are true," Colonel Burnside said. "Our men don't know the rudiments of maneuver. They can barely load their weapons, and they have no idea as to the real nature of war."

Ambrose Burnside, a friendly Indianan and an 1847 graduate of West Point, had little more experience with warfare than the rest of the men. His greatest military feat had come after he resigned from the Army and designed and manufactured the Burnside breeching-loading carbine, a marvel in its day.

Colonel William T. Sherman wiped the nervous sweat from his hands and said, "Burnside, you know I agree with you in principle, but we must be realistic here. Do you really think Lincoln or the Cabinet or the Northern people would allow us to come out all this way and not engage the enemy?"

"Never! Never!" the Honorable Senator Wilson said.

"That is right, Colonel Burnside," McDowell said, wiping pie from his mouth. "Not fighting is no longer an option."

Indian killer Samuel Heintzelman said, "General McDowell. I think you know me as one of your supporters, but I believe that the Rebels are growing stronger daily, by way of the railroad."

"They are coming down from the Shenandoah," General Tyler said. "And because of your delays here, we will have to fight Joe Johnston's army as well as Beauregard's whenever we do move."

"You have no way of knowing that," Catfish Hunter said. "Every dispatch from Washington assures us that Patterson is still holding the Rebels in place up there in the Valley."

"Yes," Colonel Sherman said, "but who is informing Washington of that fact?"

"Why, Patterson, of course," Hunter said. The tent went quiet.

McDowell rolled his eyes, saying, "Well, that is neither here nor there for I have made my plans, and that is why I called you all here."

"To discuss them?" Richardson asked.

"No, to order them. There is no time for anymore debate or counsel. We move out at 2:00 a.m. and will be engaging the enemy by daybreak. Here, General Hunter, spread this map out on the floor so I can show them."

CHAPTER TWENTY-FOUR

◆—•—◆

The Union Encampment
Centreville, Virginia
July 20, 1861
11:00 p.m.

Voices were hushed around a wood-scented campfire not far from General McClellan's tent. Sparks from its embers crackled up into the air in searching fingers of orange. A lonely rendition of *Shall We Gather at the River* lilted upward from a mouth organ played by a blue-clad boy absent from his hometown church for the first time. A few dusty young men in their early twenties sat around the cheek-reddening flames, speaking tautly about their girlfriends and families. Those who had letters, read and re-read them, carefully folding the tattered stationery back into their envelopes as if they were holy writ.

A couple of campfires over, a gruff man who looked like Blackbeard the Pirate pierced the quiet with callous laugher. Most, however, gathered in their circles with serious faces, smoking pipes, gnawing at tasteless hardtack, and whittling sticks down to shavings. A few spoke tentatively of sweeping strategies as if merely talking about victory would make it come to pass. Others read Bibles, nervously fumbling through the thin paper's chapter and verse. Crickets, bats, and owls interrupted the quiet as did a few muffled sobs. Every man and boy here had heard the rumors that they would be marching into gunfire in the morning, something almost none of them had ever done before, and even Blackbeard's laughter eventually ceased in apparent recognition of his own inexperience.

No one was sleeping much this haunted night out under the stars. These uninitiated warriors were sweating in spite of the late night chill and shivering in spite of their fires. Dew was dampening their blue woolen uniforms, but it was thoughts of the Rebels that were chilling them most: tortured images of those slave-whipping savages, those soul-less bloodthirsty beasts. They worried and wished that the long drum roll would hurry up and rattle, to start the battle and get it over with. But it had not rattled yet and hearsay that it might at 2:00 a.m. was no more believable to these men and boys than any of the other hundreds of unfounded rumors that had been circulating through camp for the past two days.

Private Billy Anderson, the chubby boy Ol' Mex had taken under his wing at the barricade in Washington, tossed his playing cards and French nude carte-de-visites into the pulsing campfire, where they curled into blackened wisps of smoke and ash. Dressed in an over-sized but shining new blue uniform, he pushed back his drooping sleeves and said, "I ain't takin' no chances on angering the Lord tonight. I'll admit I've been runnin' a mite crazy these past few weeks, what with them being the first that I was ever away from the orphanage an' all. But I'm turnin' back to the Lord right now, and I don't give a good goddamn what nobody says about it."

"That ain't a bad idea," Ol'Mex said, still wearing his powder-blue Mexican War uniform rather than the modern dark blue style like the one hanging so loosely on his young friend. "I was gettin' more than a bit concerned about your eternal soul the way you was sinnin' in whole cloth. Here, take a read on this a while. It'll do you good." He handed the boy a weathered Bible.

Billy leaned to accept the book, tears glistening in his eyes. "I reckon I h'ain't never been scared the way I am right now. There don't seem to be nothin' I can do to make it stop neither."

"That's the way it is, son," Ol' Mex said. "And it's gonna get worse before it gets better. That's the way I found it to be anyways, down in Mexico. And believe me, I'm just as scared as you are right now. It don't no never mind how many times you've seen the elephant, it just don't never get easier."

Billy hid his tears in his hands. "I reckon you're right. I just hope I ain't the only scared one here tonight. I mean to tell you, I'm down right ashamed of how scared I am."

"Don't worry none about it, boy," Ol'Mex said. "I guarantee you, you ain't the only one that's scared."

"But you don't understand," Billy whispered, hanging his head. "You don't know how scared I am."

"Oh, I reckon I do."

"But you h'ain't never done what I've gone and did," Billy said, a tear running down and streaking his dirty face.

Ol' Mex reached over and clasped the boy's shoulder. "What in the hell are you talkin' about Billy, you ain't no worse off than me or any of the rest of these fellers here."

Another tear broke free and ran. "Oh, yes I am. Yes I am."

"What are you goin' on about, boy. What are you cryin' for?"

The boy looked both ways and whispered, "Because I done pissed my britches clean through. Clean through, I tell you. I know there ain't nobody else around here that's gone and did that." He turned away from the fire and began to sob.

Ol' Mex took a closer look and saw the evidence. The stain in the boy's trousers was dark and spreading. "Don't you worry now, son. You'll dry out and ante up when the time comes. You mark my word you will. I've seen better men than both of us do worse than that in their drawers before a battle." He patted Billy's shoulder until the crying stopped and the boy had steadied himself with a few recovering breaths. Then he cocked his nose away from the stench of urine and listened as the long roll sounded at last.

"It's time, boy," he said grimly, "wet trousers or not. It's time."

CHAPTER TWENTY-FIVE

General Beauregard's Headquarters
The McLean House
July 21, 1861
4:00 a.m.

COLONEL THOMAS JORDAN SAT ALONE IN THE DARKENED PARLOR AND fretted over the papers strewn before him. He had just spent hours transcribing copies of orders for all the brigade commanders so he looked frazzled and tired but, worse, distressed. He bore none of the spymaster élan that had won him the heart of Rose O'Neal Greenhow in Washington. His face was drawn and gray despite the flickering gold of a single oil lamp.

He had been reading the various orders over and over again, hoping to prove himself wrong, but he could not escape the conclusion that Beauregard's orders were terribly written, confusing and contradictory. They were bound to paralyze his grand offensive sweep around the Federal left flank.

Joseph Johnston had reached Manassas the day before and taken overall command from Beauregard, but he had allowed Beauregard to remain in tactical control due to his greater familiarity with the ground and disposition of troops. Thus it had fallen to Beauregard to choose the strategy and issue the orders required to execute it. And as far as Colonel Jordan was concerned, therein lay disaster.

"My God," Jordan muttered. "What in the hell am I supposed to do? Wake the man up and tell him to re-write a score of orders on my say-so alone?"

He knew no one in the Army would have done that but he clearly saw what the problems were. Beauregard broke down battle groups in one order into brigades and in another into two-brigade divisions without specifying who was to command these combined units. In another, he referred to dividing the entire army into what could only be construed as two 18,000-man corps without specifying the chain of command. Jordan's brow furrowed deeply with the question of what he should do.

He looked up and saw two boys, one dressed up like a cadet in a triple-buttoned jacket and white trousers, the other in Confederate gray with knee-high cavalry boots. "Who are you?" he said. "Couriers?"

"Yes, sir. I am Lieutenant Archibald Bagwell," said the first. "I came up with General Beauregard from Charleston, the Citadel actually. I have been with him since Fort Sumter."

The other said, "And I am Lucas Ashcroft, Lieutenant Lucas Ashcroft. From the Virginia Military Institute. I got my assignment with the General in Richmond."

Jordan said, "You mean your daddy got you your assignment in Richmond, don't you?"

Lucas did not reply, knowing that the assertion was true.

"What do you want?" Jordan snapped. "Neither of you should be in here. I don't care how well you think you are connected to the General."

"I know, sir, and I apologize," Archie said, "but Lieutenant Ashcroft and I and the other couriers outside want to know if we can get a bit of sleep, sir. Before the orders are ready. Don't get me wrong, sir. We are up and rearing to go right now if the orders are ready. There is not a man among us who can't ride all night long if that's what it takes."

"That's right," Lucas added.

Jordan looked down at the floor and did not speak for a long moment. At last, he said to the boys, "The orders are ready. Follow me. I will assign them to you all outside."

Lucas nodded with a silent salute.

Archie grinned irrepressibly and nearly shouted, "Yes, sir!"

Colonel Jordan snipped, "Silence, boy, or you'll wake up the General. And we couldn't have that now could we?"

"No, sir," Archie said.

The boys trailed Colonel Jordan out of the house, Archie playfully poking Lucas with his elbow. Lucas tried to look annoyed but he could not fully mask his excitement. He had come for war and now he was about to have it.

CHAPTER TWENTY-SIX

The Road to Sudley Ford
5:30 a.m.

COLONEL AMBROSE BURNSIDE CHECKED HIS POCKET WATCH AND SNAPPED it tightly shut. Dawn was already lightening the horizon behind him and his regiment still had three miles to go before reaching Sudley Ford. He had been directed onto this flanking road just past Cub Run by Generals McDowell and Hunter, but he had no idea how impassable the overgrown lane was. He had tried to move his force faster by dividing it into three parallel columns, one on the lane and one on either side. But the time lost hacking and chopping their way through the undergrowth and low trees had cost them any advantage they might have otherwise gained.

As much as Colonel Burnside had always tried to get along with everyone and support the plans of his commanding officers, he knew that General McDowell had mishandled practically everything on this march so far. The commander had ordered Daniel Tyler's vanguard division to move out at 2:00 a.m., but it left an hour late. The fact that McDowell had even chosen General Tyler to go first had been an amateur's mistake. Since Hunter's and Heintzelman's divisions had the farthest to go to complete their flanking march, they should have left first. As it was, Tyler's anguished pace and the behemoth of a heavy artillery piece he was lugging along seriously delayed the entire right wing of the army.

After Tyler's division had finally been ordered off the Warrenton turnpike to let the divisions of Hunter and Heintzelman pass to the front, Burnside had crossed his men, Rhode Islanders of the 2nd Regiment mostly, over Cub Run and veered right onto the flanking lane. He watched General Tyler, still slowed by the mammoth thirty-pounder rifle, head straight ahead for the feint at the Stone Bridge over Bull Run.

Blinded by the darkness under the low canopy, he had seen his men strike their heads on hanging branches, bruising, cutting, and even knocking themselves out. His Pioneers did their best to hack their way through the thicket but his men continued to run into trees, stumps, and each other. Four of his men had already been shot dead by accidentally discharged muskets.

Southern citizens living in hovels along the way, some of the dirtiest people Burnside had ever witnessed, taunted his men with threats of a massive Rebel force awaiting them. Adding to his frustrations, the guide who was leading them took a wrong turn that cost the column another two hours wrapped up in this stunted wilderness. He knew it would only be a matter of time before General McDowell's Napoleonic plan would come undone, and he feared that he would be the scapegoat.

The signal to begin his attack was to be a blast from Tyler's thirty-pounder in front of the Stone Bridge, planned for 6:00 a.m. He dreaded the starry dawn now, expecting to hear that explosion, already shamed that he would not reach Sudley Ford in time to respond to it. He raised his hat and cheered on the trotting recruits, but he doubted that anything in his background, not West Point, not his affable manner, not his love for his men, made him qualified for command.

"Quickly, men, quickly," he shouted. "Double-quick, double-quick, for Union, for Liberty. Please. We must pick up our pace. We must, we must. Harder, men, harder, you must run harder, faster, forward, forward, forward to victory." Ducking low branches, he spurred his horse along the lane.

"Well, I reckon that's all easy enough for him," Billy Anderson said, struggling to keep his trouser-legs pulled up, "what with him bein' on top of that there horse and all an' having a pair of britches that fits him proper."

"Well, you'd best get used to it, son," Ol' Mex said, keeping up, "because that's the way it is in the Army. The officers do the ridin' and the fighters do the walkin', or runnin' as the case may be. An' they always gets the tailor-made uniforms."

"Well, that Burnside oughta at least give us a rest once in a while," Billy said between breaths. "Hell, we'll be all played out before we ever git to the damned Rebs."

"Duck down, boy," Ol' Mex said. "Jesus Christ, one of them branches is gonna take your head off if you don't pay better attention."

"Aw, let it," Billy said. "I'm gettin' too tired to keep up as it is."

"You're gonna make it, son. Just keep puttin' one foot in front of the other and keep lookin' ahead. You wouldn't want to have to tell your youngun's someday how you missed the great battle to end the rebellion 'cause you fell out, would you?"

"I reckon not," Billy said. "But we've got to at least stop for some water. If'n we don't... "

"Watch out, Billy!" But the warning came too late. Billy slammed his head into a large, low branch and fell to the ground, moaning. Men stumbled over him, shouting and cursing.

Colonel Burnside rode up and ordered, "Get that soldier out of the way, off the road. Keep the column moving. Keep it moving."

Ol' Mex dragged Billy out from under the pile-up and shook him but he got no response. "Wake up, son. Wake up. Your gonna miss the whole she-bang if you don't wake up."

"Fall in, soldier," Burnside said, nearly pleading. "I can tell by that Mexican War uniform of yours that you know something about discipline and you need to get back in the column."

"But, sir... "

"Fall in, private. Your friend will be all right. When he comes to, he will join whatever regiment is passing by at the time. Now get moving."

Ol' Mex stood up. He looked down at Billy, then up at his strangely apologetic colonel. "Yes, sir," was all he could muster and he got back into the column. Over his shoulder, he heard the boom of an unusually loud cannon followed by a series of lesser blasts. "The battle's on," he murmured to himself. "My God, it's really on." And his soul filled with fear.

CHAPTER TWENTY-SEVEN

General Jackson's Headquarters
July 21, 1861
6:00 a.m. Sunday

GENERAL JACKSON STOOD ALONE IN FRONT OF HIS MAP TABLE, FACING THE sound of the booming guns. He seemed mesmerized by them. His eyes were closed and his lips were moving, but he blinked each time one of the distant cannons reported. Even motionless, he was clearly tense and preoccupied with the battle developing on the left flank, at the Stone Bridge. He knelt and began to pray.

He stayed that way, head bowed and hands clasped, until he heard someone enter the tent and clear his throat. "They told me outside to come on in so that's what I did. I'm here with the latest orders from General Beauregard."

Jackson raised his head but he did not stand. Eyes veiled, he looked at the straw-blond lieutenant and said softly, "Cadet Ashcroft."

"It's *Lieutenant* Ashcroft, and I was sent here by your commanding general."

Jackson studied him but said nothing more and went back to his prayers.

After a silence, Lucas said, "Now listen here, I have orders from General Beauregard himself and you have to get up and receive them. You are obligated under the courtesies of war to receive me, as an officer and a gentleman."

General Jackson creaked to his feet and walked slowly over to the courier.

"Lieutenant," he said, "you know nothing of war or its supposed courtesies. And you mind your tone with me. At the Institute, I was your professor. On this field, I am your senior officer. Now give me those orders."

Rankled, Lucas did as he was told.

The General stepped to the entrance and held the paper up to the dawning light. He read it once, then twice, and a third time before saying, "These are highly confusing. But one thing is certain. General Beauregard is still going to attempt his move around the enemy's left."

The guns echoed their deadened thumps. He gazed in their direction and envisioned the enemy getting behind the Southern forces at Manassas Junction before General Beauregard could take Centreville? "We will be surrounded and destroyed," he muttered.

"We're not going to be destroyed, General. If General Beauregard devised the plan, it is a good one. For Christ's sake, he is the greatest general this country has."

"Rein in your tongue, Lieutenant. The Lord will not favor those who take his name in vain."

Smirking, Lucas shook his head but curbed his instinct to speak.

General Jackson went over to his map table and wrote something on a piece of paper. Folding it three times, he gave it to young Ashcroft and said, "Take this to General Beauregard. Tell him of the enemy's guns on our left. Tell him to look north. Now go. Quickly. You have responsibility now. Prove yourself worthy of it."

Unmoved, Lucas offered a sloppy salute and left. General Jackson, his solemn face fixed toward the sound of the big guns, knelt once more to pray.

CHAPTER TWENTY-EIGHT

Cub Run Bridge
6:30 a.m.

"DAMN IT, TYLER," GENERAL MCDOWELL SHOUTED FROM HIS HORSE. "You were supposed to have your division at the Stone Bridge two hours ago. You are holding up this entire operation." Hundreds of blue-uniformed men were still rattling across the rickety, wooden Cub Run bridge. They were too exhausted to care about their commanding general's tirade.

"But, sir," Tyler said, "the men are green on the march. They haven't been able to see one foot in front of their faces all night. And dragging along that thirty-pounder you wanted has cost me two hours and then some." It and several other cannons boomed up ahead.

"I don't have time for your excuses, General Taylor," McDowell said, rubbing the ache in his stomach.

"Tyler, sir."

McDowell growled, "Just get your men in position. And remember, you will only demonstrate with the artillery until you hear further from me. Are you capable of following your orders today, General?"

Tyler flashed hot but said only, "Yes, sir. I am, sir."

"Good. Now get to it."

General Tyler saluted with an angry snap and spurred his horse back toward the sound of the artillery.

Colonel Sherman approached. Reining in, he saluted and said, "General McDowell, I have just personally reconnoitered the ground up ahead and found a proper ford where my brigade can cross. It is just north of the bridge, and a hill on the other side will screen my crossing from the Rebels' view."

Shaking his head, McDowell said, "Now just hold on a minute, Sherman. A brigade commander has no business going anywhere near that creek yet. There are bound to be Rebels all over that area."

"Yes, sir," Sherman said with a nervous laugh. "It was some of them, in fact, who revealed the ford by crossing it in pursuit of me."

"Damn it, man, that is just what I am talking about. Did they fire on you?"

"Yes, sir, but my escort and myself easily turned them back."

Reddening, McDowell said, "Colonel, I hereby order you to cease and desist from personally doing your own reconnaissance. And I don't want to bring on a general engagement there."

"Yes, sir, but my boys are heady for fight. And I must admit, I am, too."

"You have your orders, Colonel. You will cross the creek and attack the Rebels only when Hunter and Heintzelman have flanked them. Is that clear?"

"Yes, sir. It's just that… "

"Goddamn it, Berman, stop that incessant banter of yours and get back to your brigade. Are you incapable of doing what I say?"

Sherman's nerves percolated at the rebuke, but he wheeled his horse and left before his anger could boil over.

CHAPTER TWENTY-NINE

Lookout Hill
Overlooking Mitchell's Ford
7:00 a.m.

GENERAL BEAUREGARD PACED NERVOUSLY ON TOP OF THE TREELESS HILL, pausing every few seconds to pour over the map table in front of him. He had an unobstructed view of the center of his line and the Unionist artillery on the opposite heights, but he still seemed confused about the Federals' intentions. The battle seemed to be developing in two separate places, here at Mitchell's Ford where he had already identified "Fighting Dick" Richardson's brigade massing for an apparent frontal attack and somewhere upstream where he could hear the booming of cannon.

Waving his arms, the General barked an angry monologue at his staff. "What in the hell is McDowell up to? Sweet Mother of God, is he truly attacking in two places at once or is one of them merely a feint? And which one is which? Can none of your scouts find that out for me?"

General Joseph Johnston, standing nearby, said, "General, does your lack of certainty mean a change in your plans to hold here in the middle and attack them from our right?"

"No, sir," Beauregard said emphatically, "not at all. My orders stand as issued at 4:30 this morning. Why, do you see a problem with that?"

Johnston, ever the Virginia gentleman, said, "No, General. I told you when I took command that I would defer to your tactical judgment, you being more familiar with the situation here than I."

"But I sense that you do not support my judgment, that you do not think I should go ahead with the attack." Officers and couriers were exchanging worried glances at their commander's agitation.

"I think, sir," Johnston said, "that you know what is best. And I will support you until and unless circumstances clearly mitigate otherwise. And they do not at this point."

The cannon to the north thundered again. One was particularly loud. "That sounds like a thirty-pounder," General Johnston said. "I don't have to tell you the damage one of those guns can do."

Beauregard's eyes were fixed to the north. "I am fully aware of their range and power, General, but I am also aware that the Unionists could have never transported such a monster on these roads. It is probably just an atmospheric amplifying of the report of a twelve-pounder."

"Perhaps, but we should keep an ear cocked in its direction."

"I have already sent Bee's brigade along with Bartow's two regiments up there."

"That makes for a total of how many men?" Johnston said.

"About 3,000."

"When will they be deployed?"

"Within two hours, no more."

Johnston looked down and toed the dirt with his knee-high boot. His polite silence brought more looks of consternation from the cluster of men around them. Beauregard masked his thoughts by mulching it over into irritability at the loosely jointed lines of Southern infantry slouching in reserve behind him.

He turned back to Johnston and asserted, "3,000 men arriving in two hours is all that will be needed up there, General. And pressure will be relieved from them once I attack the enemy on his left."

"Of course, General," Johnston said, bowing slightly. "You know best. Please, carry on."

Beauregard turned and called, "Colonel Jordan. Get your couriers up here and dispatch them with orders to begin the attack. Have them read them and recite them back before sending them off."

Jordan called for the youths and several appeared. One was Archie Bagwell.

When his turn came, the eager boy stepped forward, read, and recited.

When finished, he said to Colonel Jordan, "Sir, I am certain it is due to my own dullness of wit, but I must confess that I have some measure of difficulty understanding what it is that General Beauregard wants the various brigade commanders to do."

"Is that a fact?" Jordan said, not sounding at all surprised.

Carefully and uncomfortably, Archie said, "Well, sir, it seems unclear to me as to whether Ewell is to actually attack Centreville or merely demonstrate or even wait for some further order. But they order Holmes and Jones to support Ewell as if he were definitely attacking without further word. And it almost sounds as if Ewell and Jones are to cross paths somehow, and I know the General couldn't mean that."

Overhearing, Beauregard's face heated. "Are you quite through, Lieutenant? Boy? I will have you know that my orders are clear and will be understood by the professional officers for whom they are intended. And you will never again question me. Is that clear?"

Archie dropped his eyes and said, "Yes, sir, forgive me, sir. I will deliver the orders."

"See to it, Lieutenant. Immediately."

Colonel Jordan walked away, hiding his own concerns.

The Federal guns on the opposite heights let out distant puffs of smoke and their concussive booms followed closely behind, scattering men and horses for cover on the Southern side as the solid shot came screaming through. Voices yelled.

"They're beginning their attack!"

"They're going to hit us in the middle!"

"Good Christ Almighty, here they come right at us!"

"Silence, you fools!" Beauregard shouted. "That is just one brigade of infantry. I have twice that facing them right here alone."

All eyes watched the methodically evil descent. Halfway down the slope, the soulless bluecoats halted, realigned, and unloosed a crackling volley. The Southerners in the foliage below shot back but few fell on either side. The Federal artillery opened up again, sending balls into the bushy treeline. Screams of the Rebels could be heard.

"Where is our artillery?" Beauregard cried. "I want those Yankee guns silenced!" Several staffers flew into action, flagging down artillery teams as they rumbled by.

"There is no need for that," General Johnson said darkly. "They are using rifled guns. You can tell by the flat trajectory. Our smoothbores will never reach them from here."

"Then by god I want my attack launched, while the Federals are committing here. Colonel Jordan! Get those couriers riding." More Union cannons puffed and boomed, scrambling Confederates on the hill like roaches in a sudden light.

Lucas Ashcroft rode in low and saluted Generals Beauregard and Johnston. "Sir, begging to report, sir."

"Yes, what is it?" Beauregard snapped.

"Coming back here from General Jackson's, Captain Alexander stopped me. You know, Porter Alexander, at the middle wig-wag tower."

"Of course I know who he is. Report." A shell burst overhead. Everyone ducked.

"Yes, sir. Well, anyway, sir, Captain Alexander wants to know if you see that dust cloud rising up beyond the Stone Bridge. Up there. Over those farthest woods."

Both Beauregard and Johnston studied the yellowish cloud through their field glasses.

"It could be Patterson coming down from the Valley," Johnston said. "Or McDowell on a wide flanking maneuver."

"Patterson is too cautious to have executed such a maneuver," Beauregard countered. "And McDowell could not have marched that many raw troops that far in the middle of the night."

"But the cloud is there, General Beauregard," Johnston said. "How else would you account for it?" More Federal cannonballs plowed the hillside around them, burrowing in and exploding with muffled thumps. The staff men tried not to flinch but failed.

Beauregard said, "It could be the last of your men, General Johnston. Kirby Smith and Elzey. Perhaps the train broke down and they had to finish their march on foot."

General Johnston approached the map table and took another look. "You might consider sending Jackson in that direction. I believe he would now be the closest reserve brigade to our left flank." Rifle and artillery fire from across the creek made him glance up.

"But General, if I do that, I will weaken my striking force. I would have to abandon any offensive action and the swift, decisive victory that it might bring. No, I am not prepared to do that. The brigades up at the Stone Bridge will simply have to hold the Unionists off until I can make my strike down here and relieve the pressure on them. Down here is where the issue will be decided." He poked at a spot on the map.

"And what of this advance before us?"

"The men we have here can stop it. The Unionists haven't moved in several minutes. They are no doubt just demonstrating, trying to keep me here, and I am not going to succumb to that ruse."

Johnston carefully eyed the dust cloud again and said, "Whatever you think best, General Beauregard. But should you not inform Colonel Evans of the threat to him?"

"Yes, yes, I will do that." Scribbling a note, he handed it to the closest courier, Lucas Ashcroft, and said, "Ride to the Stone Bridge and tell Evans to be ready to face a possible flanking maneuver. Tell him he must defend our left to the last extremity, until my attack on the right is underway. Repeat that."

Lucas did and galloped off.

General Beauregard raised his field glass toward the hills and wood lots two miles to the south where his own men's dust should have been rising. General Johnston, looking north, studied the dust that was already there.

CHAPTER THIRTY

The Stone Bridge
7:30 a.m.

COLONEL NATHAN "SHANKS" EVANS PACED BENEATH THE SMOTHERING sun. His gray tunic was black with sweat and reeked of whiskey. He dipped into his tent for shade but found the humidity there just as suffocating. He needed a drink and headed back outside to find his orderly with the barrelita of whiskey strapped to his back. Evans figured that General Beauregard had placed him this far from the expected Federal attack due to his legendary drinking, but he did not much care what that primping general thought. He was a tooth-and-nail Indian fighter, always agitating for a fight, and the whiskey fueled his rage.

Evans was finishing a draw from the back-borne barrelita, wiping off his scruffy chin, when Lucas Ashcroft rode up. He did not appear to notice the young lieutenant storming back-and-forth on his bowed legs, bruising the air with rank banality.

"Goddamn it, goddamn it to hell! I don't like it. Virgin Mary mother of God, I don't like it a bit. Shit, piss and goddamned fornicatin' hell!"

The profane colonel pushed through his staff men, roaring epithets and filth. "Sweet Jesus, what are the goddamn Yankees up to anyways? Are they going to attack or just sit over there on the other side of this fucking hill and do nothing but hurl shells at us? I want them to attack. Please God, let them attack!"

He stopped in front of Lucas and stared fiercely into his wide eyes, causing the youth to lean back in the saddle as if blown by a hot wind. "And just who in the goddamned hell are you, boy? And what in the goddamned shit are you lookin' at me that way for?"

Stunned, Lucas did not answer.

"Well, talk to me, you little asshole!"

"Colonel Evans," he blurted. "General Beauregard sends his compliments and his latest orders."

"Fuck his compliments! And I'm surprised that little gamecock even bothered to send me any orders. Hell, he was so convinced that the sons of bitchin' Yankees were going to hit the middle of the line that he didn't allocate me a shit's worth of men or cannon. Let me see those." He snatched the paper and read it for himself, his lips slowly moving.

"Goddamn it! An ape could've written better orders than these. But I can tell he still isn't going to reinforce me the way I need. I'm facing what looks to be half the goddamned Unionist army with my two under-strength regiments and all the fart-sucker can tell me is to 'hold out to the last extremity'. Shit. Piss. And goddamned fornicatin' hell!"

A huge Federal shell exploded overhead, driving everyone to ground except for the drunken general. "There goes that sister-rapin' thirty-pounder again. They can probably hear that son of a bitch down in Richmond but no, it's not loud enough to shake any sense into that bastard Beauregard five miles away!" He barely noticed a series of lesser blasts, his lips already attached as they were to the spigot of his barrelita.

"Colonel Evans," Lucas shouted over the din, "General Beauregard wants me to inform you that there is a dust cloud forming to the north, up in the trees around Sudley Ford. He doesn't know who is causing it yet, but he wants you to be apprised."

Before Evans could respond, another dispatch rider thundered up and jumped down from his mount. Handing over a message, he said, "Colonel, this just come in from the wig-wag tower. It's the Yankees, sir. They've done turned our left. Thousands of them. They're crossing up at Sudley Ford. This must just be a feint here at the bridge. And there ain't nobody up there at the ford to stop the main force."

"Goddamn it! I knew it. I knew those sons of bitches were up to something. Jesus Christ on crutches. Come on! We've got to get these men over in front of those bluebellies before they roll up the entire army like an old carpet."

"But sir," the second rider protested, "you can't stop them with the few hundred you've got here. I took that the wig-wag captain was meanin' for you to retire, and fast."

Evans thundered up to him, eyes ablaze, and said, "Well, by god, I don't know what kind of pettycoats are up in that fucking tower, but I for one can indeed try to stop them, now can't I? Who in the Hell has reconnoitered that area up there? Who knows the lay of the land between here and Sudley's Ford? Well, speak up, goddamn it!"

When no one answered, Evans roared, "Hells-bells! Do you mean to tell me that not one of you so-called staff officers bothered to have our exposed flank scouted? The Yankees are bearing down on us and I need to know where we can best make a stand. Somebody speak up before those bastard nigger-lovers sweep us away!"

Slowly, haltingly, Lucas cleared his throat and said, "Uh, sir, I am familiar with that area, somewhat. I surveyed it once with some of General Beauregard's staff."

Evans whirled around. "You, boy? You can lead me to a good defensive position up there?"

Lucas hesitated, "Uh, I guess so… but you see… I'm supposed to get back to General Beauregard to report. He's going to want to know what's going on up here."

"Forget him, goddamn it! I'll send this other fellow back to him. I need you here. Now! Unless you're afraid of a real fight." He grinned at Lucas like a pirate.

"No, no, it's not that, sir, not that at all."

"Then lead the way, you little sissy-boy. We've got us a mess of Yankees to kill!" And shrilling a warrior's shriek, he took charge of his troops with a grasp and a clarity that no common drunkard ever could have.

CHAPTER THIRTY-ONE

Sudley Ford
9:00 a.m.

GENERAL DAVID HUNTER RODE UP TO COLONEL BURNSIDE AND SHOUTed over the tramping soldiers. "Colonel Burnside. Deploy the first two regiments of your brigade into line of battle on the far side of those woods up ahead. Your men will have the honor of spearheading the attack that will crush the rebellion, and I will personally lead them."

The mutton-chopped Burnside looked a little miffed at Hunter's glory-grab but a little relieved at not having to lead from the front himself. He listened carefully as his senior officer further ordered him to align the succeeding brigades on his right and splash them across the rippling run.

Hunter surveyed the noisy, odorous sea of blue clamoring forward and said, "Isn't it grand, Colonel, my boys rising to the task. The day is mine. I am... I mean, we are about to become the stuff of legend."

Appearing embarrassed at the thought, Burnside nodded unconvincingly.

Hunter scraped his saber out of its scabbard and rode ahead, calling, "Cold steel, men! We shall give them cold steel!" The General thrilled at the rousing cheer he received in response, a cheer in which at least one man, a Mexican War veteran in faded powder blue, did not take part.

Fifteen minutes later, Ol' Mex stood at the edge of the woods where Colonel Burnside had led his first two regiments. He surveyed the double lines stretching out along the leafy green murk and assessed the number of men to be about two thousand. Wiping the sweat from his face, he scanned the cleared yellow slope before him leading up to a thin line of woods on the crest. Even a lesser experienced soldier than him, he figured, had to know that they would be advancing up that open hillside.

He could not see any Southerners on top, but he knew that the position would be a perfect place for them to be hiding. In Mexico, he had learned to identify a likely spot for an ambush, and he had tormented himself for two years down there fearing sudden death around each bend and in every clump of trees. This low ridge dripped with danger, and he knew that they would be walking into a trap unless they had truly stolen a march on the Confederates.

That was their only chance, he thought, their only hope. Perhaps the grand flanking plan had somehow worked in spite of all the miscues. Perhaps there would be no Rebels on this hill at all, and they would completely dust away those to the south by surprise. Perhaps by noon they would really have the rebellion crushed and be on their way home as heroes.

General Hunter rode boldly before them swirling his saber. "Men of the Union!" he cried. "You are the vanguard of the United States Army! You shall be the first to drive the traitors from the field! You shall be remembered in the annals of history as the men who first drew blood from those who would destroy our beloved country! Christian soldiers, at the route step, march!"

The undressed lines of blue lurched forward out of the cover of the forest and onto the naked slope. Their weapons at shoulder arms, they shuffled their brogans though a small wheat field and into the tall, golden pasture grass beyond, creating a whisking sound like that of a giant broom.

"Dress it up!" Hunter yelled. "Dress it up!" His orders devolved down the chain of command to the ranks, and the men were soon pressing their shoulders one against the next, until a solid wall of brass-buttoned chests presented itself.

"That's the time, boys!" Hunter yelled. "That's the time! Now, you're looking like soldiers!"

But Ol' Mex did not feel like a soldier. He waited for the youthful flush of exhilaration to overwhelm him the way it had at Cerro Gordo and Chapultepec, but it did not come. He swallowed hard, licked his parched lips, and wiped his palms on his hot, woolen pants. His legs felt heavy. They ached with a weakness that gave him an ungainly, dragging gait in the uneven soil.

He sensed a vague light-headedness. Was it the sun pummeling down, the heat waving up, or had thirteen years of peace turned him into a coward?

"Dress it up, men!" General Hunter cried, waving his saber. "Dress it up and advance. Advance to glory!"

But where was the glory, the veteran wondered, the thrill that turned fear into anticipation, fright into overcoming action? It had been there in Mexico when he was eighteen. Where was it now?

"Regiment!" Hunter called. "At the quick step! March!"

Ol' Mex doubled the pace of his walk. His head felt lighter; a shudder of nausea waved through him. Darkness began to crowd his peripheral vision. Did he see movement in the trees up ahead? Were those glints of sunlight reflecting from the bushes? Perspiration burned his eyes. He rubbed at them and the blur worsened.

"Forward, men, forward," Hunter shouted again. "Dress it up! Dress it…" Suddenly, the tree line ahead ruptured with smoke and flash. Singing bullets sucked air overhead, driving the Federals to ground as one.

Ol' Mex dug his fingers into the dusty-dry earth and clawed for cover that was not there. More bullets whined nearby. These were closer. He heard a few hit flesh with that sickening thud that flashed him back to Mexico like a wildfire scorching his memory. Screams of pain and panic rent the air.

"Get up!" General Hunter shouted. "Get up, you sons of bitches, and advance! Advance! Advance!"

But no one got up. The men in the two confused lines hid in the yellow grass and behind each other. Ol' Mex heard prayers and curses, pleas and whimpering moans. But not a man stood up to face the zipping lead.

"Goddamn it, you bastards!" Hunter cried. "Get up and advance like men! Get up and fight, you… " A bullet smashed into the General's face mid-sentence and somersaulted him backwards to the ground near Ol' Mex.

It appeared that the wound was fatal. Bright red, Halloween blood was pouring from the man's cheek and neck. But then the General moved. He was still alive, somehow, and he began gagging and thrashing about like a hooked fish on a muddy bank. Colonel Burnside braved the fire and rode to his aid.

"General Hunter," Ol' Mex heard Burnside cry, "my god, your face!" He dismounted and called for help. A few brave men crouched up the slope to drag the general off. The Rebel fusillade pinned the rest down.

Hunter rose up for a moment, revealing the white of his jawbone and the shattered teeth embedded in his sausaged cheek. Choking on blood, he sputtered, "Get them… on their feet… Burnside. Don't… let them… be stopped here."

"I will do that, sir," Burnside shouted above the racket. "I will personally rally them."

"Do that... Colonel, please... please... "

"I will, sir, I will."

"I leave... the matter... in your hands," General Hunter said, and he collapsed for the agonizing jostle to the rear.

Shaking violently, Ol' Mex saw Burnside remount and begin riding up and down the line exhorting the huddled men to stand and fight. But no one seemed able to force himself up into the lead-storm, and he was not about to be the first.

Burnside kept trying to rally the skulking men but with no success. Galloping up and back two more times had no effect. But then the Colonel's horse reeled from a splattering of bullets. It's legs crumpled and it crashed to the ground tumbling the Colonel out of his saddle and nearly crushing him. Ol' Mex cautiously raised his head to see if Burnside was dead, if the regiments were truly leaderless on the field. Burnside did not move. Interminable moments passed. Finally, Ol' Mex saw an arm flinch and a leg. Burnside shook sense into his head and struggled to his feet. Unstable yet defiant, the bald, portly officer grabbed his saber and thrust it mightily into the sky. He stormed about on foot amid a scatter of bulletry, shouting, "Rally, men! Rally! For General Hunter! For the Union!"

Feeling suddenly roused and utterly foolish, Ol' Mex arose and came to attention at shoulder arms. Others around him followed, raising the Colonel's pitch to heroic tones. The new commander ran to get behind the lines and gave the command. "Regiment! Ready! Aim! Fire!" And the United States Army entered the fray with a ripping roar that sounded like the tearing of a thousand sheets.

"Reload!" Burnside called. "Fire at will! Fire at will!"

An erratic pounding of Union musketry ensued. Men, young men, and boys began loading and firing, firing and reloading their weapons, blast after ear-stunning blast. It was impossible to tell if their bullets were striking the Rebels, but they blasted away into the smoke where they had last seen the vicious enemy sparks. The fight dissolved into a gut-grinding misery of incoming and outgoing lead. Unionist soldiers dropped in anguish at the feet of others who were trying to out-scream their own terror.

Confusion jumbled over into a mayhem of shouting officers, riderless horses, and crumpling Federals. Ramrods jammed barrels, bullets ripped air, and sinew and flesh burst apart with butchering blows. Amid the vomiting and cursing, the pleas, and clouds of reeking sulfur, the two thousand animalized Unionists packed into their line, trying to discharge their skillet-hot weapons before the next Rebel bullet struck them down.

Those whose rifles did not foul with powder residue and whose hands were not shaking too badly fired about three rounds a minute. Most could only manage two. Yet even at that rate, the two regiments were unleashing thousands of deadly missiles. The Rebels managed to keep up a daunting fire of their own, and Ol' Mex did not see any signs of it lessening.

The Federals were out in the open, suffering grievous casualties. The only hope of survival were the fresh Federal regiments pouring onto the field to the right, extending their lines across Sudley Road. Perhaps soon, Mex thought, a flanking action might drive the traitors off the hill. But for another twenty mired minutes, the gun battle raged on, neither side able to budge the other. The stand-up duel ended when a line of gaudily dressed Rebels showed themselves and launched a wild assault down the hill with a barrel-chested buccaneer leading the way.

"Dear God Almighty!" Ol'Mex shouted. "Here they come! Here they come!"

CHAPTER THIRTY-TWO

Matthews Hill
9:30 a.m.

FROM THE CREST, SHANKS EVANS WATCHED ROBERDEAU WHEAT'S FIVE hundred New Orleans dock ruffians pour down the slope waving Bowie knives over their heads. *"Look at 'em go, the sons of bitches! Look at the magnificent bastards go!"*

His jaw dropped as the Zouave hoodlums rushed headlong toward the Union line, baying like wolves and brandishing their razored blades. He saw some toss their rifles away altogether as if they were mere encumbrances to the expression of their rage.

They ran, leapt, and screamed, surging down the hill. The Yankees fired. Some Tigers went down but the rest kept going. Forty yards, thirty yards, twenty and closing, the butternut Zouaves roared on, until they crashed into the Yankees like a hurricane wave, slashing and stabbing and clubbing with rifle butts.

Through his field glass, Colonel Evans could see steel slice faces, chests gush blood, and fingers getting lopped off to spurting stubs. Victims yowled hideous screams as cold blades were plunged into warm bodies. Men crumpled, vomiting blood from gashes to stomachs, lungs, and throats. Fists slammed noses, rocks crushed skulls, and soldiers yelped like scalded dogs. Even the most hardened of soldiers might have recoiled from the sight, but Evans licked his lips hungrily and said, "Yes, Wheat! Yes!"

He watched the Zouaves grapple hand-to-hand and boot-to-boot with the enemy for fifteen demonic minutes, but the Yankees would not yield and the wharf toughs would not relent. The slain bodies underfoot began tripping those left standing. They kicked up from the ground and wailed. Then, amid the roar of cannon and musketry, Evans saw a flanking Federal regiment enter the fray and the Louisianian survivors begin to recede. He marveled at their heroics, how they dragged their bleeding friends back up the hill with dangling limbs of their own.

A stunned calm settled over the smoking battlefield. The rifles stopped. The silence chilled Evans like a night without whiskey. Then the cries of the wounded arose with the haze, filling the air with a tastable misery. The air went humid with anguish, permeating men and boys like their sweat and urine had not.

Evans could not shut out the moaning, the crying, the praying of the wounded, the thrashing about, and the pleas for help: help to crawl, help to drink, help to plug their draining wounds. The most pathetic of them moaned for their mothers or begged to be mercifully shot.

Suddenly angered, he jumped up on a tree stump, shook his white-knuckled fist down the hill and shouted, "Goddamn your Yankee eyes! Goddamned your sons-of-bitchin' Yankee eyes! Come up here. I'm beggin' you. Please come at us!" He would have yelled that way for the rest of the morning had Lucas Ashcroft not rushed up to him and tugged on his trousers.

"Colonel Evans! Have you seen the others? Across Sudley Road? There must be ten thousand of them lining up by now. They're outflanking us by a quarter of a mile."

Evans wobbled down from the stump and said, "What in the hell are you going on about, boy?"

"Over there on our left, sir, where the smoke is thinning. Use your glass. You'll see them. They'll have our rear as soon as they move forward. We don't have anybody over there to stop them."

Evans studied the left and said, "Damnation. Damnation to hell."

"They're going to turn our flanks," Lucas said, "and swallow us whole if we don't get out of here, sir. And it won't be a battle. It'll be a massacre. Don't you think we ought to fall back while we still can, sir?"

Colonel Evans whipped his field glass down and snapped, "Hell no, I don't think we ought to fall back, you damned little coward. I'm here to buy time for the rest of this bastard army of ours and, if that means sacrificing every man I've got including you, that's exactly what I'll do!"

"But sir, shouldn't somebody at least ride back and try to find Bee or Bartow. They were supposed to be heading this way."

Evans smirked. "And let me guess, Lieutenant, you'd like to volunteer for that duty. You'd no doubt like to turn tail and run about now, now wouldn't you?"

"No, sir, it's just that…"

"Don't make excuses, boy. Just mount up and get me some reinforcements."

"Yes, sir." Lucas looked decidedly cowardly in spite of his denials. This was the closest he had ever come to real battle and his trembling lips belied it

"And hurry, goddamn it! Those damned black abolitionists are deploying another regiment in front of us as we speak."

"Yes, sir," Lucas said, and he saluted properly.

"Get the hell going, you damned little school-boy. Those Yankees aren't going to wait for your toy-soldierin' salute."

"No, sir." And he remounted for the ride back, glad beyond expression to be leaving.

Evans strode over to the returning remnants of Wheat's Tigers and slapped a few of them on their bloody backs.

"Well done, men," he said. "That's the way to give those Yankee bastards cold steel."

A demoralized Zouave with something blackish oozing from his ear said, "But we didn't break through, Colonel. They didn't turn and run like they was supposed to."

Another added, "No, sir, they didn't turn tail a lick."

"No matter, men," Evans said. "You threw them into a confusion. You disrupted them. You bought time for Beauregard and that's all anyone can expect of you this morning."

He glimpsed Major Wheat being borne to the rear on his regimental flag. "Wheat. Wheat. Good God, man, what in the hell happened to you?"

The four bearers lowered the huge, bleeding man to the ground. He grimaced and said, "I appear to have been pretty well ventilated, sir. Some son of a bitchin' Yankee got lucky and sent a bullet clean through me from armpit to armpit."

"I'm sorry to hear it, Major. This army is going to miss a man with your kind of style."

Struggling, Wheat said, "You talk about me like I was already dead, Colonel."

Evans had seen scores of Indians and white men die on the frontier. He had personally stabbed two Indian chiefs to death with his bloody hands and held his own troopers in his arms as their life drained out. He knew what death looked like and he knew he was looking at it now. "Well, Wheat, I've seen plenty of mortal wounds in my time and yours surely does appear to be one of them. I don't believe anyone as torn up as you has ever recovered."

"Well, then, sir, I will put my case on record, 'cause I don't feel like dying just yet."

Evans smiled and nodded. "You're a good man, Wheat. If I get out of this one, I'll see to it that you and your boys get all the laurels you got comin'."

"Thank you, sir," he said, groaning.

"Don't mention it. Can I get you any comfort before your bearers take you on back. A little whiskey maybe."

"That would be right Christian of you, sir," Wheat managed to say, "right Christian indeed."

Evans bellowed, "Orderly! Bring me my goddamned barrelita for this hero here!" When the frightened boy arrived, the Colonel gave Wheat an ample dose.

Evans was sucking on the spigot himself watching Wheat's men carry him from the field when he saw Lucas ride back up. He downed another swig and said, "What in the hell are you doing back here so soon? Where are my goddamned reinforcements?"

"They're coming, sir," Lucas said. "I ran into them right over there on that hill behind us, the one with the white house. The Henry House hill, I heard somebody call it."

Evans peered across into the morning sunlight. "Who is it? How many of 'em are there?"

"It's Bee's brigade, sir, and Bartow's is right behind him. Close to two thousand of them I'd say. They're hot and tired and thirsty as sand, but they appear to be spoiling for a fight nonetheless."

"Any guns?"

"Yes, sir, Imboden's battery. Six twelve-pounders, not like these two puny six-pounders you've got here."

"Good. Good. Now, you ride back and guide Bee's infantry onto my right flank and Bartow's onto his right flank. And have Imbodden set up his battery on the Henry Hill or whatever the hell you called it. Have him break up those Yankee formations on the left, across the Sudley Road. Do you understand me, boy?"

"Yes, sir," Lucas said and he whipped his horse to a frothing gallop, knowing better than to waste time saluting.

Evans found his stump again and jumped up on it, announcing to his men, "We're gettin' reinforcements, boys! This fight ain't over yet!" The worn and weathered Southerners let out a shrill cheer that could be heard in Sunday morning churches for miles around.

CHAPTER THIRTY-THREE

———————◆•◄———————

Matthews' Hill
10:30 a.m.

Ol' Mex sat on the ground and fingered his throbbing head. He turned over his palm and winced at the blood. He had obviously been clubbed by someone but he did not remember who did it or when. For all he knew, one of his comrades had accidentally bashed him in the swinging, beating, out of control melee with those crazed Rebel Zouaves. The thought crossed his mind that the wound might have saved his life. He had probably fallen unconscious to the ground and looked dead. How else, he wondered, could he have escaped any worse a wound than this one that matted the hair on his scalp.

He heard the Rebels cheering from the top of the hill and could tell that the amount of musket fire pouring down on him had increased. More cannon shells were exploding around him, too. The Rebels had definitely been reinforced and he saw no end of the battle in sight.

He rose to a kneeling position, unsure how long he had been knocked out of the fight. Head swirling, he hid behind standing men as much as he could until he was able to load and shoot his weapon. The brave and stupid boys in blue offered him considerable cover, and they were paying for it with exploding wounds to every part of their bodies. The firefight might have lasted an hour or it might have lasted two. He could not tell.

The fear of death, death in the next instant, searing painful death distorted time and reason. The only solace he found was in the mechanical loading and firing of his musket. Only by hiding behind the dead and losing himself in the shooting could he deaden the horror of being shot.

He bit off cartridges, poured powder down the barrel, and jammed bullets in after it. He fumbled percussion caps onto nipples, cocked the hammer back, and shot over and over again until he heard it or felt it, the electrocution of his nerves. It was a cry, a whelp, an awful, fearsome jolt. "What the hell is that?" someone shouted. "It's the Rebs screaming," another said. Ol' Mex listened. It felt like a corkscrew was going up his spine. He would have run away but his legs would not move him. He did manage to stand up, fix his bayonet, and face what could only be another Rebel charge.

He fired his rifle, adding to a sheet of flames that demons could have danced on. Smoke thickened the woolen air. Only shouts and bullets could penetrate it. He loaded and shot, shot and loaded, though he could barely make out his targets. He prayed and cursed and sweat and feared, waiting for Southern steel to burst upon him from the fog. He readied himself for a hand-to-hand scrap, but the Rebels did not emerge and their yells withered. Please God, he beseeched at some deep, voiceless level, let me kill everyone trying to kill me. Please O Holy Father, let me kill so that I might live.

But lead balls kept thudding into men all around him, revolting him with their moans. He did not look down at the red-black gore puddling beneath his feet. He had learned that in Mexico: don't look at the wounded, look away, always look away. He kept loading and firing, praying for deliverance from this evil.

Finally, the noise began to diminish. Or was it that his stoved ears could hear no more. No, the Southerners really were slackening their fire. The clamor and smoke were thinning. He waved a pungent mist from his face, peered toward the enemy, and saw what warriors throughout time have always longed to see, the backs of their enemies retreating with that unmistakable abandon that signifies defeat.

The Yankees let out a waving whoop from one end of the line to the other and started after them at a run. It was all that the officers could do to push them back into reasonably ordered rows and try to keep them together. Ol' Mex trotted up the hill with the rest, bayonet at the fore though his head was on the verge of exploding like a shell and his vision was growing dark.

He leapt over the flotsam of battle, bodies and hats and blood. The Rebel survivors were streaming away from their tree-lined defenses. He saw some of them turn and fire. He ducked and crab-crawled. He heard bullets pounding into men to his right and left. And then he reached the trees.

"Hell's fire, looky over there!" he heard an old man shout. "To the left! It's more Goddamned secesh comin' in from the side! "

Ol' Mex peered in the direction of the Stone Bridge, but he could not shake his sight clear.

"They's dressed in gray, all right, the sons of bitches," a younger voice said. "And look, the Rebs down there is wavin' them in."

"It's secesh reinforcements, all right!"

"Goddamn, let's open fire on 'em!"

Ol' Mex strained again to see. Something did not make sense. Could he trust what his eyes were telling him? "Don't shoot at 'em yet!" he yelled through the blur. "They might be our boys after all."

He watched the Southerners below him wave their flags for some identification from the approaching gray-coats and saw them get it in the form of an unfurling United States flag and a two hundred gun volley.

The bullets minced the secessionists. The few still on their feet ran all the harder down the hill, past a stone house, across a narrow run, and back up the next hill. Ol' Mex tried to squint away the darkness to better watch them flee. They could never turn and rally now, he knew. The battle was truly over. He had done his duty, lived through the maelstrom, and now he fell to his knees in the heat and dropped his head into his hands.

"Victory! Victory!" he heard someone cry. He looked up. It was General McDowell. "The day is ours! The day is ours!" And that was the last thing he heard before sliding into a tingling blackness.

CHAPTER THIRTY-FOUR

COLONEL WILLIAM T. SHERMAN LED HIS GRAY-CLAD WISCONSIN MILITIA-
men onto the grassy slope along with another nine hundred behind them in
blue. As they chased after the Confederates, he rode to the top of Matthews
Hill where the Rebels had made their stand. There he joined Colonels
Burnside and Porter whose men had undertaken the brunt of the fighting.
They had a sweeping view of the Warrenton Turnpike, a two-story stone
house, and the Henry House on the next hill over.

"Glad you could make it, Sherman," Colonel Burnside said, beaming a
smile. "I was about to think that Porter and I were going to garner all the
glory for ourselves."

Porter tried to grunt a laugh in spite of the pain rising around them.

Sherman's fritzing nerves and the writhing wounded would not allow him
any mirth. He clenched his teeth and clipped his words. "If McDowell would
have ordered me over sooner, we would have caught all the secessionists and
there would have been glory enough for everybody. Look at him down there,
riding up and down the line like a damned giddy lieutenant. He ought to be
back up here with his maps and his couriers overseeing the entire operation

instead of putting on a show for one regiment here and one there."

Porter nodded glumly. Burnside grinned and said, "Oh, don't be so hard on the man, Sherman. Hell, he has reason to be happy. After an admittedly rough march, the battle is unfolding just the way he wanted it to. Porter and I are pretty well used up, that much is true, but you are fresh, and Tyler will be crossing the Stone Bridge soon and Heintzelman is already across at Sudley Ford. That means that half the army is now on this side of the creek and bearing down on the Rebel flank. There is no way they can stop us now."

Sherman scratched at his short, red beard with shaking fingers. "Perhaps. But if we don't keep the pressure on and keep driving them without let up, they will still be able to form a line over there somewhere and contest the issue. The worst thing we can do right now is to stop to reform, and what do you wager that that is exactly what McDowell will order us to do."

Burnside laughed like Santa Claus. "You worry too much, Sherman. If you are not careful, your pessimism is going to land you in a sick-bed."

"I agree, Sherman," Porter said, trying to sound like he was not just as worried.

"Speaking of sick-bed," Burnside said. "That house back there looks like it might serve the purpose." He pointed east along the ridge. "Porter's and my men are fought out for the day. I'll have some of them gather up the dead. I must say I was not expecting to be inundated with this number of them."

Sherman looked down at the ground beside him. "They are not all dead. Some are still moving. Like this one with the old Mexican War uniform. Where the hell do we get these men that one war does not satisfy them?"

"I don't know," Burnside said, smiling, "but I'm glad we won't be needing any more like him today."

Porter made a repulsed face at the blood and nodded.

"We'll see about that," Sherman said grimly. "In the meantime, I'm going down there and see if I can get McDowell moving again before we see some real casualties start to mount."

CHAPTER THIRTY-FIVE

One Mile South of Henry Hill
11:00 a.m.

SLIM COCHRAN, THE GANGLY REBEL FROM HARPER'S FERRY, WAS SCARED AND confused the way he had been since hearing the muffled battle sounds starting up around the Stone Bridge at dawn. But now, he was also hot and tired, struggling to keep pace with General Jackson's brigade as it rushed in column, four abreast, toward the towering cloud of dust and smoke rising into the sky up ahead.

He had fretted away the night and misty morning with fears of failure and cowardice scratching his mind like briars. He was mired in the twilight bog between exhaustion and sleep when the long roll had shocked him to frazzled alertness. He had strapped on his gear along with his comrades and been swept along with them, as much from inertia as any willful push of his own. He felt sick with shame and dread and heat. His head went light before they had been on the road long. His stomach churned with the morning's rancid bacon and bitter coffee.

He trudged on, alone amid a thousand stinking men, through the dust and torridity and the fright of what lay over the next yellow hill. His blue, woolen uniform was sweat-soaked. His wet hair was plastered to his head. He was parched with thirst but had long since emptied his canteen and knew better than to ask another man for his. Panting and huffing, straining and struggling, he felt nothing like the hero he had always longed to be when trapped on his widowed mother's tiny farm, and everything like the lost, stumbling child that these recent days had made him.

And then the wounded began to stream back from the fighting, some walking, some limping, and others groaning in bouncing wagons, but all were smeared with dirt and leaves and blood and most were warning of the disaster ahead.

"We's whipped!" came the shouts. "Don't go no farther!"

"They's right on our heels, comin' by the thousands!"

"Go back! Go back while you still can!"

"We've done lost! It's over!"

But the officers kept driving the brigade on in spite of the warnings, and the warnings became worse because they became more plentiful, more tortured, and closer to the pursuing Yankees. Where there had been cheering and laughter earlier, at least among the boastful, faces now soured, eyes hardened, and voices fell silent. The wails of the wounded and the taunts of the stragglers were wiping away any hungry smiles that had been on men's faces and that at least made Slim feel a little better about his own fearful face.

"Quickly, men, quickly," a rider pulled up beside him and droned. "Press on. Forward. Forward." The boy glanced to his right and saw General Jackson jostling gracelessly atop his graceless horse. He shriveled from the General at first. He thought the laconic man might recognize him as the drunkard from Harper's Ferry and single him out. Maybe he could even tell what a coward he had become on top of everything else. The boy sneaked a peek at his ungainly leader and was struck by how big he was for his unimpressive little mount. His huge feet nearly dragged the ground as if he were riding donkey and he exhibited no rhythm in his ride whatsoever.

"Pick up the pace, men," he heard Jackson say without a trace of command presence in his voice. Slim was at least glad to see that the General was not addressing him in particular. It barely sounded like he was addressing anyone but himself. "Press on. Press on."

A rider crested up over the rise ahead and galloped like a centaur down the four-breasted column. Slim watched the courier rein in right beside General Jackson and pace the commander's horse in a walk. The young rider had straw-blond hair and a bright red face. Slim crooked his ear toward the two of them and listened.

"General, General," he heard the straw-blond say. "There must be fifteen thousand Unionists up ahead. Our boys fought hard, you know, Evans and

Bee and Bartow, and they held the Yankees off for nearly three hours but the blue-bellies finally flanked us and now they're reforming to take the Henry Hill, the one you can see right up ahead."

General Jackson said, "Are any of our forces on that hill still able to fight?"

"I don't know," the blond said. "Hampton's Legion, the South Carolinians, were coming onto line as I was leaving, but they only looked to have five or six hundred men. I think they went down over to the north side of the hill. Over there on the right. There's a sunken lane leading down to a little white shack. I think Colonel Hampton is going to make a stand there." He pointed in the direction of a hazy pine grove.

"What about artillery," the General said. "How many guns can we bring to bear?"

"I think Captain Imboden has wrangled up a dozen or so. But they aren't in action now. I don't know what happened to them. Maybe he limbered them up and got them the hell out of there. I sure would've. And I think you ought to turn around and do the same damn thing. While you still can. At least until more reinforcements arrive. You can't do a Goddamn thing by yourself except get slaughtered like all the rest."

"First, Lieutenant Ashcroft," Jackson said, "you will refrain from swearing. God will not tolerate the profane nor will I. Second, our Heavenly Father has placed me at the head of this brigade, this instrument of His will, not you. And I will put my trust in Him."

"Well then, sir, if you read your Bible right, you know that the Israelites lost damn near as many battles as they won, and it was usually because of some jackass commander who was out of step with God and who wouldn't read the obvious signs that God gave him. And you are about to do the same thing here."

Jackson simmered. "I will deal with you and your insolence after I deal with the enemy. For now, leave my sight and that of these brave men before your cowardice infects their hearts any more than the wounded already have. Go back to General Beauregard and tell him that I intend to hold that hill. Tell him to send more reinforcements up here as quickly as possible."

"But I'm warning you, General..."

"Go, Lieutenant, before I have you arrested."

Slim Cochran watched the courier shake his head and whip his horse to a thundering departure without bothering to salute. Returning his gaze to the General, he chilled. The solemn man was staring into his soul, it seemed, with blazing-blue eyes. He appeared to recognize him. Jackson said nothing, though. Instead, he put him out of his mind and trotted off to the front of the column, jostling in the saddle with his right arm raised.

CHAPTER THIRTY-SIX

Near the McLean House
Noon

LIEUTENANT LUCAS ASHCROFT RODE HARD FOR FIVE MILES BACK TO Lookout Hill. Once there, he dismounted and was starting for the crowd around General Beauregard's table when Archie Bagwell caught up to him.

"Where have you been?" he said. "Do you have any news?"

"Hell, yes, I've got news," Lucas said, pointing to the plume of smoke to the north. "Everything is falling apart up there. The Yankees are breaking through by the thousands. Why isn't General Beauregard sending more men up there?"

"I don't know," Archie said, "Maybe he's afraid that the Yankees will attack us here. Or that he can still pull off that plan of his to attack the Federal left and cut them off at Centreville. I just don't know."

Lucas shook his head and said, "But can't he see that the Yankees are coming at us from the north, in force? They are flanking our left. And why in the hell haven't our men down on our right crossed the creek, if that's his plan? I don't see any smoke or hear any fighting from that direction. What's he thinking?"

"I don't know," Archie said. "I've been delivering dispatches down there and back all morning, and I can't make any sense of it. He has ordered

Longstreet's brigade and Jones' and Ewell's back and forth across Bull Run three or four times already and in the confusion none of them has done much of anything. It's like he's paralyzed by the action to the north and he can't make up his mind what to do."

"Well, I sure as hell know what to do. I see General Johnston up there. If Beauregard won't do anything, maybe he will. Hell, he ranks Beauregard anyway. Let me pass."

"General. General Johnston," Lucas said, boldly approaching the highest ranking Confederate on the field. "Begging to report, sir. I've just come from our left flank, where the real fight is."

"Yes, yes, what do you have?"

"Sir, you must send reserves to the left immediately. Those sent already are too few and have been driven back. General Jackson has the only intact brigade up there now, along with Hampton's Legion, but their men will be chewed up in the same mincer as all the rest if you do not immediately reinforce them."

General Johnston studied the left and then the right, his gray eyes darting back and forth like a shuttlecock.

"Sir, I know what you're thinking. You're thinking that the Federal threat is here and that we should hit them from the south, but that's not the way that things are shaping up. The battle is not down here. It is up there. To the north, our left. I have seen it. And begging the General's pardon, but I think anyone with the sense God gave a goose could look at the smoke and listen to the guns and see the wounded men coming back and know that that is where the battle is. And that is where you and I and everyone else ought to be going. Sir."

General Johnston stroked his beard and glanced over at Beauregard who was still pacing indecisively. "Thank you for your report, Lieutenant. You are confirming what I have already been deciding for myself. Now, get back to General Jackson and tell him that substantive reinforcements will be forthcoming."

"Do you need me to guide you up there or anything?" Lucas asked.

"No, Lieutenant. That will not be necessary. Just tell General Jackson to hold on. That help is on the way."

"Yes, sir," Lucas said, breathing a satisfied sigh.

General Johnston called over to General Beauregard with more authority than Lucas had heard him do so all morning. "General, remain down here if you wish, but I believe that the battle is up there." He pointed emphatically toward the smoke. "Yes, the battle is definitely there. And I am going."

CHAPTER THIRTY-SEVEN

The Matthews House
12:30 p.m.

Ol' Mex's eyes sprung open like roller blinds and he vaulted up among a slop of bloody bodies. He had already seen enough of that this morning so he powered his way out of the tangle. As far as he could tell, no one was even attempting to offer these moaning men any relief though he doubted that it would do them much good. If they were piled here in this stench-ridden bedlam, they were already too far gone to benefit by even the most modern of medical efforts.

The Matthews house was filled with criers and wailers, and the yard outside was overflowing as well. It did not seem possible to him that a single battle could have produced so many pitiable casualties but he saw them and more keep streaming in.

There were many Southerners mixed in with the Northerners, the grisly by-product of the morning fight, but it did not matter to him whether the victims whose blood he smelled wore blue or gray. To him, they were all just legless, armless, faceless boys, now, whose stumps and dreams of glory had been rendered a crusty black by the Sunday heat and the swarming flies. His head swirled. He bent over and vomited.

Ol' Mex pulled himself up and began stumbling away. He had no reason, no direction. He just started walking until he broke through the haze on top of Matthews Hill and saw thousands of blue-uniformed soldiers in varying stages of readiness. Some were aligned in long double rows with bayonets fixed and gleaming. Others were rushing to form up their lines under the coarse, verbal flailings of officers while still more advanced four abreast through fields and on the two dirt roads that intersected near a stone house in the valley below.

A rancid taste in his mouth, he shuffled down the hill to where the two roads crossed. Sweat glistened his face, dust grimed it, and his peripheral vision began to darken again. He heard a low rumbling, a vibration beneath his feet. There was a voice but he could not place it. He knew the tone, but not the person, the words but not the meaning. The vibration got louder and closer with its banging wheels and pounding hooves. He heard the voice again, closer this time. "Get out of the road! Get out of the road!" The clattering rumbled, the rumbling kept tumbling, but it was not yet to him. It was somewhere else.

"Get out of the road! Now!" He heard but did not move. The crashing rolled nearer, shaking and shuddering until a blast of pain and force drove him down to the ground.

He opened his eyes and saw Billy Anderson on top of him, panting, sweating, and scared. Behind him a dozen or more artillery pieces and caissons pulled by six horses each were rampaging by without a thought of stopping for anyone. An eternity passed, an interminable earthquake of man, beast, and machine until the battery turned left and charged up Henry Hill.

"What the hell is wrong with you, Mex?" Billy said. "Didn't you see those damned guns a'comin'? Damn man, if I hadn't have tackled you out of they way when I did, you'd have been squashed flat. An' by your own damn men no less."

"What...who..."

"Jesus Christ, Mex, you're head's covered in blood. An' your touched by the sun. Looky at your face all splotchedy. Here lemme give you some water." The boy uncorked his canteen and splashed Ol' Mex' face clean. He propped him up in front of the stone house and helped him to a long, grateful chug.

Eyes beginning to focus, the veteran said, "What's going on? What happened to you? Where have you been?"

"Hell, I figured you'd know better 'an me. I must've hit my head on somethin' on the march out here. All I know is that I woke up with a lump an' some damned officer was herdin' me in with them pretty-colored Zouave boys from way up to Brooklyn, New York, you know, that dead Colonel Ellsworth's boys. And I just stayed with 'em. That's them lined up all neat and clean over there, waitin' for the chance to go in an use them long, curved bayonets of theirs. An' they say it's gonna come right quick, the advance. Come on, get up and get in it with us, if'n you're up to it, I mean."

Ol' Mex tried to squint his headache away. "No...no...don't go over there, boy. Stay right here with me. Don't go up the hill."

Billy grinned and said, "What are you talkin' about. We're about to win this here battle, I hear tell, an' I aim to get in on at least the tail end of it. I don't know what I was so all-fired worried about last night. There's nothin' to this warrin'."

"No, Billy, no. You don't know what's up that hill and if it's anything at all like what I seen this morning, you don't want to know. Stay back here with me. It's safe here."

"I can see why you don't wanna go. Hell, you already done got your red badge and your glory. But I h'ain't. You just wait here for me. I'll be right back for you. This charge won't take long but, if'n I don't hurry on over there, I'm a'gonna miss it altogether."

Ol Mex clutched the boy's arm. "No, Billy...no. I ain't never had no family to speak of, no brother or nephew or son and you've come nigh on to bein' all those things to me. I can't let you go, I just can't." His eyes moistened.

"Ah, don't you worry none about me," Billy said, pulling free, "I'll do fine. I'm over bein' scared. But, damnation, it sounds like them Zouaves is gettin' ready to advance now. I gotta go. You wait for me here. I'll come back for you after we finish whippin' the secesh." Smiling, he turned and trotted off toward the gaily-dressed New Yorkers, pulling up his trousers as he went.

CHAPTER THIRTY-EIGHT

—————————◆———◆—————————

Henry Hill
1:00 p.m.

BRIGADIER GENERAL THOMAS J. JACKSON RODE OUT ONTO THE PLATEAU of Henry Hill in time to see what appeared to be the final dissolution of the Confederate army. The only troops showing any semblance of cohesion were his own whom he had ordered to lie belly-down at the edge of a pine grove along the northern end of this quarter-mile-by-quarter-mile meadow. The descending ground through the trees behind him was choked with wounded and exhausted men who had fled the earlier fighting, and the grassy, rolling plain to the front was being overrun by retreating Rebels.

Jackson knew that Colonel Wade Hampton, the South Carolina planter who had paid for his own "legion" of infantry, cavalry, and artillery, was holding the ground down the slope to the right and, from the sound of it, they were putting up a wolverine's fight, but the General's own left was wide open and inviting disaster.

But he had faith in God and faith in Captain John Imboden's battery of eleven field pieces spread out before him. He did have his doubts, however, as to whether or not Generals Johnston and Beauregard would arrive with reinforcements before the Federals launched their second attack and, when the last wave of fleeing Southerners surged onto the far end of the field, his doubts grew all the more grave.

"They're comin'!" came the shouts of the beaten Rebels.

"The Yanks are comin'!"

"Millions of 'em!"

"Run! Run!"

Jackson watched General Bernard Bee gallop up and rein in. The gentleman Indian fighter from South Carolina pleaded, "My boys are getting beaten back, General. They fought hard all morning and don't deserve the dishonor of this rout. We must do something. What shall we do?"

Eccentric, absent-minded Ol' Tom Fool Jackson said simply, "Sir, we shall give them the bayonet."

Bee leaned forward in his saddle and asked, "The bayonet, sir?"

"The bayonet," Jackson confirmed.

General Bee's face slowly lit and he said, "Yes, sir. Yes, sir!" He wheeled his horse and rode back into the plain. "Rally, men, rally!" he began calling. "There stands Jackson like a stone wall! Rally behind the Virginians!" He galloped around the smoking field until, at last, the retreat did slow.

A battery of Union artillery that had been unlimbering at the other end of the plateau, opened up with canister. Thousands of small leaden balls furrowed the field and chafed the air. They struck Bee and most of the men he had just inspired.

Behind the holocaust, General Jackson droned, "Steady, men, steady. Do not rise up until I give the command." A group of sergeants, file-closers, fanned out behind the brigade line to enforce the order. Jackson ordered Imboden to commence his barrage and the earth shook like a wet dog.

Lucas Ashcroft galloped up.

"Report, Lieutenant," Jackson said. "Are reinforcements coming?"

"Yes. General Johnston is seeing to it. But I don't know how many brigades he is going to send. General Beauregard still seems fixed on the right flank, wanting to attack from there."

Jackson flexed his jaw. "Could you not make them see that the battle is here, on the left, on this hill, or will be as soon as the Federals reform?"

The Unionist guns blasted a salvo across the smoky hilltop that exploded in the trees, terrifying the men on the ground. Jackson did not flinch.

Lucas did. "I think General Johnston may be coming himself, but I don't know how many men he's going to bring with him."

"Well, you should have found that out, Lieutenant," Jackson said. "Do you have *anything* useful to report?"

"Only that the Yankees will be up here shortly and if reinforcements don't arrive in time to meet them, then I think you ought to high-tail it to the rear and wait for help."

"Avoiding the action. Stay with me, in the front. I am going to need every courier I can get."

"But, sir…"

Jackson waved him quiet and raised his field glass toward the Henry House across the plateau. He could see Confederate sharpshooters firing at the Union artillerists. The shooters were apparently remnants of Rebel infantry who had fought earlier on Matthews Hill. Scanning the rest of the field, he lowered his glass and said, "We may have an opportunity here."

"An opportunity? Here?"

Jackson chided, "Tone, Lieutenant, tone."

Lucas shook his head and muttered something that a cannon blast concealed.

"Get over to the 33rd Virginia, on the left." Jackson pointed.

"You mean those boys in blue?"

"Yes. Tell Colonel Cummings to attack the Federal battery. He already has their right flank and Hampton is providing a diversion on their left. All he needs to do is move out of the woods he is in and advance."

"Advance? Five hundred men against a battery and however many Yankees are coming up the back side of that hill?"

"You heard me, Lieutenant. Go to the 33rd." He pointed again and his hand flew back, his left ring finger struck by a bullet.

"Damnation! You are hit!" Lucas said, looking aghast at the splattered blood.

The General held his left hand in his right, trapping a crimson pool in his palm. "Go, Lieutenant. Get my orders to the 33rd."

Lucas pulled away, glad to do it. "Yes, sir, right away, sir."

Jackson bandaged his finger with a handkerchief and put the wound out of his mind.

He heard a commotion of breaking twigs and rustled leaves crackling up through the wooded hillside behind him and saw General Beauregard leading troops up through the trees. Beauregard had obviously abandoned his grand offensive scheme, Jackson thought. God be praised for that. When the Creole's officers brought the reinforcements into line, General Jackson ceased the fire of his artillery and listened as the Napoleon in Gray made a clarion address, prancing on his charger in front of the brigade.

"I seek," Beauregard called, "to infuse into the hearts of you officers and men the confidence and determined spirit of resistance to this wicked invasion of the homes of a free people which I truly feel. Be of stout heart, men, for reinforcements are rapidly coming to your support, and we must at all hazards hold our posts until they arrive. Remember always, we fight for our homes, our firesides, and for the independence of our country. I urge you to the resolution that we achieve either victory or death on this field!"

Jackson's men erupted into cheers, throwing their caps into the air. General Beauregard doffed his own ornate kepi and galloped on down the line to give the same speech until every gray soldier had thrilled to it along the distance of the crescent-shaped front.

Beauregard snatched up the flag of one regiment and bore it back up the line, the banner fluttering and flapping in the hot breeze. The souls of men stirred and the flesh of boys pimpled. General Johnston appeared on the scene with his own patriotic banner and rallied his end of the field.

Both men wanted to lead the forces firsthand but since, Beauregard argued, Johnston ranked him and was technically in overall command of the army and the battle, Johnston should retire to a safer distance and direct the battle from there. Johnston reluctantly accepted Beauregard's logic and rode off with his staff to set up his headquarters. Far behind him, long lines of colorful Unionist soldiers crested onto the field, looking like the Duke of York's own 10,000 men.

CHAPTER THIRTY-NINE

Henry Hill
1:30 p.m.

BILLY ANDERSON STRUGGLED TO KEEP UP WITH THE NEW YORK FIRE Zouaves as they shouted their way up the slope, but the best he could do was to stumble along several steps behind and avoid the sword-slaps of the file-closers. They had already driven him over the Warrenton Turnpike, across Young's Branch, up a cornfield, and now onto the plateau of the hill when he looked over at a white house to the left and saw secessionist sharpshooters firing from it. Following the Zouaves into their supporting lines to the right of the Unionist battery, Billy saw an artillery officer training two of his guns on the house.

He watched them set sights, crank elevations, feed their iron beasts. He heard the order, "Guns one and two! Prepare to fire! Ready! Fire!" The gunners yanked the lanyards, sending sparks down into ten-pounds of black powder and unleashing volcanic explosions from the monsters. The wheels spun backward, recoiling wildly, and the shoulders of sweating men rolled them back into place for the next feeding.

"Reload!" he heard the officer cry. He saw barrels sponged, powder and shells rammed down, lanyards fit with primers and pulled. The earth shook again beneath the flaming muzzles, driving him to the ground with his hands pressed against his ears.

When he raised his head, smoke and sulfur choked him and stung his eyes. Straining, he could make out the second floor of the house blasted open with flames lapping out. He saw what he thought was an old woman dangling half way out, thrashing about in agony. Billy jumped up in horror. "Lordy, Lordy! Stop! Don't shoot them guns no more." He broke through the Zouave lines and bolted for the artillery officer. "Hold your fire! Hold your fire!" He grabbed the captain. "There's an old woman in that house. I seen her. Don't shoot no more."

The officer pulled his arm away. "Unhand me, boy, I am a captain in the Regular Army. I have had men court-martialed for less."

"I don't care. Somebody has got to go over there and help that old woman. She appears to be hurt somethin' awful." Billy took off running low to the ground amid a furious escalation of the duel between the Union and Confederate cannon. He rounded the house and balked at what he saw.

A middle-aged woman was wandering about aimlessly, shocked, devoid of her senses. A man was on his hands and knees sobbing, "They've killed Mother…they've killed Mother…" A black woman was crawling off toward a cluster of scrubby trees, crying from a foot-long shard of wood stuck in her back.

"Lordy, Lordy!" Billy said. "What have we done? What have we done?" A salvo from the Unionist guns jarred him to motion. He weaved his way into the house and up what was left of the staircase, back-peddling to a stop at the second floor as if it were a crumbling cliff. Most of the roof was blown off, exposing the blue sky, and a portion of the wall was gone. He soon saw the old woman moaning deliriously, blood draining from a splintered leg.

"Lordy, Lordy! What can I do? What can I do?" Billy said. He froze until blood pooled beneath his feet. Hopping to a dry spot, he pulled down a curtain and ripped a long strip off to use as a bandage. He tied it around her bony shard as much to hide the gore from his eyes as to offer aid. The old woman was nearly unconscious but not free of pain. She uttered low, groggy moans. Billy prayed over her, knowing that she would be dead soon, hoping that she would be dead soon. But she did not die. Not right away. So he kept on praying with tightly closed eyes. But then he heard something else, something worse, a clatter, a rustling, a rattling, leathery rumble. He looked out through a crushed wall and howled at his comrades below.

"It's secesh riflemen! Off to the left, behind their guns! They's risin' up to fire! Get down!" But no one responded. Billy waved his arms and shouted, but no one saw or heard.

The ground opened, the sky tumbled down as 2,000 Confederate muskets roared out their lead as one. Minie balls sucked the air like a siren, whining and whistling, before splattering into jerking bodies. A scream went up, a common, mashed scream, a scream from pain-purpled lips. It started with one voice and swelled into hundreds until the cacophonous misery devoured itself like passing thunder.

Most of the Federal survivors broke and ran back down toward the Stone House. Only the stunned and reckless remained at their posts, and they were digging into the earth with their fingers when the second Rebel volley tore across the hilltop. Zouave officers quickly began sword-whipping the recalcitrant in an effort to stem the fleeing tide. It took several minutes but the semblance of an artillery support line took shape again, and those Zouaves returned the musketry, driving the Rebels across the plateau back to ground and enabling the Unionist gunners to extend two of their field pieces farther across the field. From there, they could blast shells and canister into the Southern left flank.

Suddenly, beyond the right flank of the Zouave line, Southern cavalry came pounding down the hill. They were charging from a stand of trees on the next ridge over, to the rear of the guns, with a hell-bent, saber-flashing fury. They crashed into the Federal musketmen with screams and shouting, bugles and neighing, hooves plowing soil and flesh. Shots rang out. Swords clanged against bayonets. Men crashed to the ground. Blades slashed fingers, bayonets ripped stomachs, bullets churned faces to bloody stew.

Billy's eyes teared. Lead set up in his legs. He tried to look away but couldn't. He watch, transfixed, until the merciless slaying finished. It took only a matter of minutes. A bugle sounded and the Rebel horsemen galloped back to the woods from which they had come, leaving the dazed Zouaves frenzied and bleeding but still in possession of those mighty guns that could determine the outcome of the fight.

Billy rocked back and forth, his arms wrapped around himself. He tried to see his mother and he did: her full waist, the apron, the smell of cinnamon, and her robust Norwegian laugh. No one had ever called him lard ass or butter butt when she was around, and any tears he had ever shed had always been dried by her cookies and hugs.

A stink brought him around like smelling salts.

Billy opened his eyes and looked outside, across the width of the plateau. Even with this dead woman's blood boiling and the sickening smell wafting up his nostrils, nothing could have scared him more.

CHAPTER FORTY

SLIM COCHRAN ADVANCED OUT OF THE WOODS AGAINST THE CLOSEST PAIR of Unionist guns. He was in a double line of blue-clad Virginians and they were methodically stepping toward the enemy battery. He kept ducking behind the big man in front of him, but he was still terrified that the cannon ahead would shift to the right and send a shell through him in the next angry instant.

His hands shook and his heart pounded. It seemed he could not breathe. Sweat ran into his eyes and his mouth. It drained down his back in cold rivulets. Every awkward step was one closer to lacerating death or worse. He could not shake the fear of being rendered meat and bone and then suffering for days in the dirt.

He leaned into the inevitable, the certain incoming of shot and shell. He bent down lower behind the large man and waited for the bullets and bombs to cut him down. All the Yankees had to do was wheel their guns a quarter-turn and discharge one volley to turn the entire company into bloody mist and gurgling muck.

Slim kept walking, tripping over thick roots and sticks. He pressed himself closer to his cover. He felt like he was in a quagmire of boot-sucking steps and more steps, nightmarish steps, moving ever closer to pain. But the Union guns did not wheel, they did not fire their canister, they did not lash out with their fiery shards of iron. They were prolonging the unavoidable torture, he thought. They were not opening up. It had to be some kind of trap, a heartless pleasure of waiting until they saw the whites of his eyes. But then he looked at his jacket and it suddenly became clear. "They think we're Yankees!" he shouted out loud. "We're wearing blue and they think we're Yankees!"

"Quiet in the ranks," a sergeant with a pistol snapped.

"But we've gotta fire on 'em before they find us out. We gotta lay 'em down."

"I said quiet in the ranks, you bastard."

And the blue Rebel lines kept marching on through the wisping haze. Now, Slim could make out Federal Zouaves lying on the ground, the ones supporting the guns, and tell that they were still unaware of what was happening. They had to fire. Fire now!

Finally, fifty yards out, the commands came down: "Regiment! Halt! Fire by regiment! Ready! Aim! Fire!" In the next moment, all other sound, sight, smell, and taste was lost, swallowed by the smoke and fury of three hundred blasting rifles.

The Federal Zouaves, the artillerists, and dozens of horses collapsed like rag-dolls with Saint Vitas' Dance. Slim Cochran heard a cheer rise up from within the billowing smoke. It was a rebellious cheer, a victorious cheer, a distinctly Southern cheer. The blue-coated Confederates burst through the cloud they had created and charged wildly toward the rest of the shambled guns.

It was over in moments. The battle had ended. There were no unbloodied Unionists contesting the hill and any still able were running to the rear, taunted by the Rebel jubilation behind them. The Southerners had won. Thank God, Slim thought, thank God. And he grinned like his face might split.

But the celebration was short-lived.

"They's comin' back!" a Rebel yelled.

"More damn Yankees is comin' up the hill!"

"They ain't beat yet!"

"Skedaddle! Skedaddle!"

Slim joined the other blue Rebels as they tore back toward the woods they had just left, Yankee bullets nipping at their heels like dogs. Diving among the trees, he buried his face into the green-smelling mulch and waited for the gunplay to end. He sensed more than saw, he felt more than heard the fresh wave of Unionists gushing up onto the crest of the hill in their savage hundreds, surging to re-take the Federal guns and keep the fight alive. They stopped there but did not attempt to man the field pieces. Perhaps, Slim thought, all their artillerists were dead.

"Hell's crackers," Slim said to the man lying next to him, the big one he had hidden behind before. "This battle ain't over a 'tall."

But when he saw the man's soupy gray brains oozing out of a shattered hole in his head, he pressed his body into the humid earth and prayed, "Dear God, dear God, if you get me outta this, I swear I'll go to church every Sunday and I'll never leave my poor mama and my little brother to do the farmin' all by themselves again and I'll be a good boy and I won't never harm another creature." But before he could utter an amen, a Union volley drove his face even deeper into the brain-strewn ground.

CHAPTER FORTY-ONE

Chinn Ridge
2:00 p.m.

LIEUTENANT COLONEL J.E.B. STUART RODE ALONG THE REFORMING LINE of his 1st Virginia Cavalry grinning robustly through his bushy auburn beard. "That's the way, men," he said. "That's what cold steel is all about!" His ostrich plume waved in the hot breeze that blew along this wooded hilltop west of Henry Hill. His redlined cape flapped like the Stars and Bars itself. "Now you are in school, troopers, the school of real war. Dress up your line. With any luck, you'll be going in for another lesson against those Yankee guns soon!" His knee-high boots and his triple-buttoned jacket resembled many of the three hundred he commanded, but none could match Stuart's zest for battle. "Praise the Lord, you patriots! Death to the invaders! May God render our sabers instruments of his righteousness!" And a cheer mushroomed from the gray riders.

"The man is amazing," John Mosby said. "The way he revels in the killing of Yankees. I saw him. He was laughing. Laughing! I swear to you that I am going to mold myself in his image before this war is over."

Wild-eyed and rattled, Jacob Sebastian panted, "To hell with his image. His image is going to get us killed."

John chiseled his face. "This is war, school marm. Men die in war."

"So you're not afraid to die then, is that what you are saying?"

"I took care of myself down there just now, didn't I? And a few Yankees, too."

"And you think I didn't?" Jacob said, pushing his spectacles up.

Bloodied troopers rode up and filed into battle line.

"Do those red badges make you want to turn back, marm, head home with so small a wreath of glory?

"What sane man wouldn't want to be home right now?"

"And therein lies the difference between you and me. I know that Colonel Stuart will order us back in again, and I welcome another opportunity to face death saber-to-saber. For I am determined to become one of the great cavalry commanders of this war, should we be blessed with enough of a war to allow it. I have what is required. You, sir, do not."

Jacob tried to hold his stare, but his nerves would not support it. He glanced away with the look of a guilty man discovered. Lieutenant Colonel Stuart passed them in line again and cried, "Dress it up, men, dress it up. We're not out of this fight yet. I guarantee you a heap more fun shortly. Be ready to attack on my command. Dress it up! Dress it up!"

As the line of men and horses tightened, the lawyer's lips curled into a tight grin. The schoolmaster, wiping beads from his spectacles, could only muster a sigh.

CHAPTER FORTY-TWO

———◆●◆———

Henry Hill
2:05 p.m.

GENERAL JACKSON LOOKED OUT OVER THE DIPS AND SWELLS OF THE SMOK-
ing field and assessed the situation. The Confederate line was stretched in a
thin crescent around the edge of the cleared hilltop with his own brigade of
Virginians and Imboden's battery lashing out their bluster from the middle.
The rifle-cracking line was bending around to face the Unionist guns whose
current infantry support was trading them body part for bloody body part, a
butcher's contest which he knew that the Federals with their greater numbers
would eventually win.

As formidable as the Rebel position might have appeared to amateurs,
Jackson knew that it was a shaky, hodgepodge of thrown-together regiments,
batteries, and squadrons that could never hold up against a concerted frontal
assault or flank attack. And the Rebels were still being blown to chunks by
the many Unionist guns posted on Henry Hill and beyond, making a wait-
and-see strategy that much less sensible. Attack was the only answer, as
Jackson saw it, and he would be the one to lead it.

He knew that the charge of the 33rd Virginia had stirred the passions of
his boys and that he could not hold them back if General Beauregard did not

harness their vigor and push them forward in a managed advance. Wade Hampton on his right had already lost control of his six hundred hellhounds. As Jackson watched, the wealthy planter had been shot out of the saddle by a Yankee bullet, his Legion foundering in the Yankee smoke.

General Beauregard soon rode up, soot-faced and streaked, and said, "It is your turn, General Jackson. We must send more men across in unison. We will be defeated in damned driblet's if only one regiment goes in at a time."

"Yes, sir," Jackson said over the din. "I agree." He licked his lips hungrily.

"Good. Then I am sending you across with the center and what is left of the right. I do not dare risk the left yet."

"Yes, sir," Jackson said eagerly.

He did not waste a second. Wheeling his dancing sorrel, he commanded, "Brigade! Attention! Forward! March!" His officers were there to pass the commands down through the ranks and spread them to neighboring regiments until 2,500 men lurched out onto the hazy plain.

Beauregard, waving the Stars and Bars, rode to the fore, crying, "The day is ours! The day is ours!" The men cheered madly even as he passed back through them on his way rearward. He had to flag down Jackson, nearly grabbing his reins, to make him follow. "Do not be foolhardy, General," Beauregard said. "I cannot afford to lose my brigade commanders." Frustrated but obedient, Jackson stopped and watched his men march forward to a fate he could not share with them.

Lucas Ashcroft approached and drew rein. Saluting, he said, "General Beauregard, sir. I come from the left. I mean, I went over there to get the 33rd moving, but they took off before I ever found Colonel Cummings and..."

"Yes, yes," General Beauregard said. "I know about all that. Wait. Wait. I must see what happens here."

Beauregard raised his glass and tried to pierce the fog. Bullets and artillery shells scorched the air around him. "I can't see. I can't see. I think our men have retaken those guns and driven the enemy back down the hill, but I can't tell with a certainty."

Jackson listened and smelled and tasted the brimstone field, his eyes fixed on the Yankee battery. He did not have to wait long to discover whether or not his men had taken them. After appearing to capture the eleven guns, he watched another force of blue infantry swarm up from the other side of the hill and retake the pieces, sending his remaining Southerners clamoring for their lives to get back.

"Goddamn it!" Beauregard said. "We had them. Goddamnit to hell, we had those sons of a bitching guns."

"Sir," Jackson monotoned, "may I remind you of our Heavenly Father's admonition against the use of such language."

"General, this is neither the time nor the place for such..."

"General Beauregard," Lucas said, "I must report on the situation I observed on our left. The enemy is..."

"Silence, boy! Here come the damned Yankees at us this time. It had to happen. I knew they wouldn't just stand over there by their guns all day. General Jackson, rally your brigade and prepare to receive the attack."

"Yes, sir," he said, still more concerned over his commander's vile tongue than the approaching blue line. With Beauregard and Lucas' help, he hastily drove his returning men back into line and had them unleash a decimating volley of musketry and canister. The whining balls raked the field, dropping dozens of Federals and putting the rest to flight. Jackson narrowed his eyes at the lumps of writhing meat and smiled perceptibly. "God's will be done," he thought.

"Well done, lads, well done!" General Beauregard cried. "You have pushed the invaders back!"

"But only a regiment," Jackson said, "and they still hold the guns. We will need to attack again."

"Yes, but not now. I must let these boys here rest. I will send in the left next."

Lucas shook his head and said, "Not the left, sir. You can't send in the left."

"What?" Beauregard snapped. "Who in the hell do you think you are, boy, to question my command decisions?"

"May I just make my report, sir? Then you'll know what I'm talking about."

"Report then," he said grudgingly.

"It's our left, sir, the enemy's right. We are stretched awfully thin over there, as far as we can go, down to the Sudley Road with infantry and a very little bit of cavalry on Chinn Ridge beyond. And no guns to speak of."

"I know that, boy. Do you think I got to be a major general by failing to be aware of my troop dispositions?"

"No, sir, of course not, sir, it's just that, maybe because of all the smoke and confusion and the lay of the land and all, you can't see what the Yankees are doing over there."

"And just what do you think they are doing, Lieutenant, I mean in your experienced, professional opinion?"

"Sir, they are lengthening their lines steadily with reinforcements, and they are getting a passel of them. It won't be long before they'll have our flank and rear. I'm even wondering if all this here on this hilltop is just a ruse to keep us busy while they pull off their main attack around our left."

General Beauregard immediately lifted his field glass and looked in that direction. Jackson did the same. Mist and topography prevented the generals from getting a complete look beyond their left, but they could see enough United States flags out there to decide that this boy lieutenant might be onto something.

Whipping the glass down, Beauregard said, "Listen carefully, Lieutenant. This is going to be the most important dispatch you will ever carry and you had damned well better get it right."

"Y-yes, sir," he said with a gulp. "I'll get it right."

"Go back to General Johnston and tell him that I need all the reserves he can muster. Tell him to lengthen our left flank with them. Do you understand me, boy?"

"Yes, sir."

"Tell him that I have ascertained that the enemy is attempting to flank us over there and that I need every available man sent to that end of the line. Immediately. And tell him to still be on the lookout for Pattersons' Yankees coming down from the Valley, perhaps by the same cars that brought him. If they managed that, then they would be hitting our rear and left."

"Yes, sir, I'll tell him all that, sir."

"Now, repeat everything back to me. I have never seen such a worthless set of couriers as I have during this campaign, and I will not trust any who cannot spit my orders back to me exactly as I gave them."

Lucas repeated them verbatim in spite of the increasing incoming and outgoing fire.

"Go then, damn it! Go!" Beauregard said. "Time is blood and not to be wasted."

"Y-Yes, sir," Lucas said saluting, and he cowered his way through the clutter of men to the rear, a shell bursting in the trees behind them.

Jackson studied Lucas' timid departure, pulling out a half-eaten peach from his pocket and sucking on it nonchalantly. He watched him, quietly, intently, and rolled his tongue over his fruit as if its flavor might sweeten his own unforgiving thoughts.

Beauregard turned and said, "General, I must send your men in again, tired or not. I dare not weaken our left. Now is the time, reorganize your brigade and the regiments to your right for another advance. Attack, sir, when you are ready. Sweep the field and regain those Yankee guns."

With a calm nod and fired eyes, General Jackson did as he was told and within minutes, the right and center of the Confederate line were once again in motion across Henry Hill. Unionist riflery across the plateau banged and crackled to life. A bald man clutched his exploding chest and dropped beside him; a suspendered boy screamed and grabbed his spurting face. Smoke cloyed around Jackson and he heard bullets suck air past his ears. Glowing artillery shells roared in like locomotives and burst in mid-air, ripping a leg off a mustached man and a hand from a bearded one. But most stumbled over back-packs and bodies, the flotsam of previous killings, and slipped and slid forward on red-glistened slicks, their shoes sucking and popping from older, stickier blood.

Waving his flag, Beauregard caught up to Jackson halfway across the plateau and cheered the charging men on, "Give them the bayonet, boys! Give them cold steel! Give it to them freely!" Then he reined in and reached for Jackson's arm. "Stop, General. This is as far as we go. I told you before that this is not our place. Our place is back here." He pointed his gauntleted thumb over his shoulder.

"I cannot inspire from the rear," Jackson said over the blare. "These men are giving their all and I must do the same. It is imperative that I lead by example."

"No, General Jackson, I am finding you to be one of my most capable brigade commanders, j187
and I cannot afford to lose you. Stay back. That is an order."

Oblivious to the compliment and the command, Jackson looked to the front and watched his men being tossed into death like rag-dolls. He said sadly, "At least their souls are saved…and their cause is God's cause. Their reward will be in Heaven."

Like all of the other exchanges in this see-sawing battle, the Federals sent up still more men who, in turn, drove the Rebels away with their own debilitating volleys. The surviving Southerners, hot, tired, thirsty, and scared witless, crawled, leapt, and ran back to safety. Beauregard and Jackson, for all their flag-waving and rallying calls, could do nothing to stop them. The Southern troops had taken flight like flushed grouse, and they could only hope that they would again be predators before this hellish day wound down. But for now, the generals knew, it was the sanctuary of the trees, the protective swales, and Imboden's cannons that the retreating gray soldiers most sought.

CHAPTER FORTY-THREE

Warrenton Turnpike
2:30 p.m.

OL' MEX WAS WANDERING AMONG THE HORDES OF MILLING FEDERALS WHO had already been up Henry Hill and been driven back down. There were still plenty of formed and fresh regiments and brigades aligned and ready for their first attempt, but the number of dazed, saucer-eyed men idling about was growing.

He saw General McDowell bouncing his girth in his saddle, furiously shouting orders to groups of men numbering less than fifty. It was clear to Ol' Mex that the General had lost sight of the overall situation. Closer to the Stone Bridge, he stumbled upon Colonel William T. Sherman looking nervous. But at least he was trying to attend to his entire brigade, struggling to keep them lined up and ready to advance as one. Ol' Mex watched McDowell ride up to Sherman and begin shouting at him.

"Good," the veteran said to himself, though he could barely hear his own voice over the musketry, artillery, and yelling. "A full brigade now should end this madness."

But he shook his head when he saw just one regiment, less than a thousand Wisconsin boys, the ones clad in gray, separate from the other two regiments in Sherman's brigade and start up the slope alone. The Wisconsins might still have a chance, though, he thought. They would be marching up the northwest side of Henry Hill against the right flank of Hampton's Legion, which had been heavily engaged since early morning. Ol' Mex groped up the opposite slope to a shade tree overlooking the action and picked up a discarded field glass for a better view.

From beneath the foliage, he could make out the remnants of Hampton's men. They were faced to the front, toward the contested Unionist guns at the other end of the Henry Hill plateau. It looked like Sherman's single regiment just might make it if it could hit the South Carolinians' flank before they could wheel right to face Sherman's threat.

"Come on, come on," he muttered from beneath the glass. "You're almost to the top and they still don't see you yet. Just a bit farther, just a bit..."

Suddenly, scores of Rebel rifles volleyed out from behind trees, rocks, and out buildings. Their fire snapped the Unionist line like a bullwhip. The gray Yankees convulsed and fell, they twitched and jerked, a few got off a single round and then fled. As quickly as their advance had started, the Wisconsins overwhelmed their file-closers and tumbled back to where they had begun. Ol' Mex pounded the ground angrily. A few minutes passed and then the next piecemeal offering started up: the New York Highlanders, whose colonel was the brother of Secretary of War Cameron and whose captain had chased a pig in his bare-assed kilt on the march out from Washington.

Wiping a cold drop of blood from his face, Ol' Mex watched the Scots start up the slope, striding over the remains of their comrades. Rifles touched off on both sides this time and the Highlanders inched closer to the top. Colonel Cameron was aligning his New Yorkers for a second volley when Ol' Mex saw him lurch backwards clawing at his chest.

Wiping off another blood droplet, he spotted an officer in blue running up and down in front of the line, evidently ordering the New Yorkers to ceasefire. The men did stop firing and simply stood there taking the Rebel bullets like mule kicks without returning the blasts. The loss of momentum seized them in their tracks and forced them back down the slope. Ol'Mex listened as cheers and jeering rang out from the Confederate side. But those voices were consumed by the Unionist artillery pieces pounding into action from the ridge behind him.

"Good God Almighty," he said, clasping his ears. "Don't they see it? Hell, it's as clear as day. They have to send in at least a full brigade all at once, maybe two, or three...like Chapultepec...Chapultepec..."

He saw Colonel Sherman order in the last of his three regiments, but they could barely swim against the tide of the retreating Highlanders. By the time they were halfway up the hill, he could tell by the volume of fire that the Rebels had been reinforced. He could not make out the difference between United States and Confederate States flags on this windless day, and he doubted those poor dumb bastards trying to climb the opposite hillside could either. A gun battle flared in the close-quartered confusion and the Federals gave as good as they got, but they eventually withered under the fire and went staggering back down like all the rest, adding their dead and writhing wounded to the hillside morass.

"Damn, damn, damn," Ol'Mex said. "Who in the hell is running this mess?"

He looked down at the jammed turnpike and saw General McDowell still circling on his horse like a commander in search of a command, barking orders for squads to form, companies to advance, and regiments to take the hill, but the general showed no sign whatsoever of pulling together a full-scale, simultaneous assault.

Ol' Mex shifted his field glass to the left, across Bull Run, and noticed an unused brigade standing idle, poised to move across the Stone Bridge. Behind that stood at least two other uncommitted brigades seemingly waiting for McDowell to order them in. To his far right in the little valley beyond the intersection at the Stone House, he watched a brigade extending the Federal right flank. Maybe, he thought, McDowell might yet end this battle decisively over there. Certainly, he had the men positioned for it.

More blood hit his face and ran down his cheek. He touched it and looked at his hand. He shot a glance straight above him just as another dollop splattered into his mouth. "No...no..." He gagged. Cringing, he looked up again. A naked boy was impaled on a branch overhead, or at least, half of him was, his head and limbless torso. Bluish intestines were hanging out from what had been his waist, dripping a reddish-black slime. "No...no..." was all he could get out before he plunged into dry heaves.

It took an artillery blast from the battery above him to jar him to his senses. He jumped up and scrambled off into a nearby wood. All thoughts of generals and colonels and unused brigades evaporated, as did the shouts and explosions and gunfire. He was stunned on his feet, bumping into and off of trees, horrified by the smell of feces and the sight of scattered meat. Not even the piteous cries of the wounded could slow him down, tripping over bodies and ragged parts of bodies.

He stumbled around in circles until he could not stumble anymore. Slouching against a tree, he slid down to the ground and scrubbed at the muck on his face. He tried to spit it out of his mouth but his mouth was too parched to do it. Tears flooded his eyes. He wept softly, at first, but then harder and harder until, soon, he was gasping in hoarse spasms. His shoulders rocked and his nose ran freely. He tried to squeeze the maelstrom from his ears, the images from his mind, the stench from his nose, and the tastes from his tongue, but he could not do it. The battle, with all of its revulsions, had finally done its work and left him a collapsing wreck.

CHAPTER FORTY-FOUR

---◆•◆---

West of Henry Hill
3:00 p.m.

A QUARTER MILE AWAY, THE YANKEES WERE FLEEING AGAIN FROM THE CON-
tested Union artillery pieces, fanning out westward along the turnpike to
Warrenton after being decimated by the muskets of Jackson's men. Billy
Anderson, struggling to keep his trousers up, was tripping over bodies,
weapons, knapsacks, and cartridge boxes: the refuse of fought-out units. Prior
to this latest retreat, Billy had been corralled into a rag-tag company of survivors by General Heintzelman's file-closers before bullets had shred the
white-bearded, Indian fighter's arm. The closers under Colonel Franklin then
pushed them across the Henry House plateau but had been unable to keep
them there under the galling gunfire.

Billy veered down the hill, across Sudley Road and the Warrenton
Turnpike until he was past the most distant battery of Unionist guns in the
westward pasture on the way back to Sudley Ford. Surely, he thought, he
would be safe there from both the Rebels and any other officers bent on
rustling up stragglers. He jumped into a dip in the high yellow grass to catch
his breath, drawing his knees tightly to his chest. He was through with fighting now. Ol Mex had been right. It was time to go home, home to his stout,

laughing mother with her embracing arms and the smell of fresh-baked bread in her hair. The way to get there, back to Washington, looked clear enough but he was so exhausted, more exhausted than even eight hours of drill or all night picket duty had made him. He had gotten no sleep the night before and, responding to the long roll at 2:00 a.m., he had strapped everything he owned on his body and been force-marched through the dark until dawn.

He had hit his head on the branch and been knocked out for an hour or so, but that had not given him any rest, just a sickening headache. The heat of the day had sweated him dry. The sun had left him splotchy. His thirst had not been quenched for an instant, even when he had found enough water to fill his belly to bursting. His legs felt leaden. His vision was blurred. He was on the verge of throwing up. If ever he had needed rest, it was now and it was here, and he determined to get some before making his final push to safety.

He burrowed himself into the warm grass and pulled his cap down over his face. Unbuttoning his sack coat, he fanned himself for a moment and waited for sleep to descend, to come down and calm the shattered mirror of his mind, to envelope him with its muffling wings. And though the artillery bursts kept jolting him awake, he did fall into a fractious slumber, and he stayed that way until a square-toed boot kicked him hard in the ass.

"Get up, fat boy, and fall in line. I don't see no red badges on you."

The voice sounded gruff and older, like a tough professional. It had to be a file-closer. Glancing up, the boy could see a grizzled, acne-pocked sergeant with the fire of an Indian killer in his eyes.

"I said, get up, fatty, right now or by God I'll sword whip you where you lie."

"Whose troops are these," Billy pitifully asked, looking at a fresh line of blue men marching past him.

"Colonel Oliver Howard's. Maine men mostly, not that I need to explain nothing to you, boy. All you need to know is that if you don't get up right now and get in this second line comin', I will personally take this here saber to you. Now get the hell up!"

Billy arose reluctantly and squeezed into a second line. When he thought the closer had moved on, he slipped out of that line, working his way to the rear. He was beginning to feel clever about his escape when he felt a sharp, stinging pain slap the backs of his legs.

"Get back in line, skulker," the closer ordered, his breath tallowed, "or so help me I'll turn the sharp edge of this blade on you. I guarantee you I will."

"But I already..."

"Get in line!"

Billy knew he was trapped now. There was no way out. The closer had him identified as a coward, and he knew that the belligerent man would be keeping a particular eye on him, falling in right behind him, shouting into his ears. It looked like he would have to fall in for his third attempt to take the hill, at least until the closer moved on down the line. The only thing that gave him any comfort at all was that he was not out in front.

After crossing back over the Warrenton Turnpike, a spray of Confederate bullets zipped down the hill into the first line, scattering dead and wounded men in all directions. Billy tried to duck out again but the file-closer slapped his legs even harder.

"Ouch! Damn it! Why in the hell are you picking on me?"

"Because you're the only one I see tryin' to yellow out. Now keep movin' and you had best know that I am takin' a personal interest in you."

Billy rubbed his legs and wiped away a tear before it could fall. A second Rebel volley hit the line in front. He saw blood spritz into the air and stricken men drop. He heard anguished screams. Artillery shells burst among them, cleaving bodies into butcher-shop scraps. The surviving Federals broke and burst through to the rear. He started to join them but stopped when the grizzled closer drew his saber again. Colonel Howard rode back to guide in the second line, Billy's line.

He reeled ahead, pushed along by the closer. The gunplay heated up, crackling like frying grease. Billy heard bones snap and flesh thock. He saw solid shot smash through faces and limbs. The balls spewed whirling blood into the air and splattered it wildly as if done by a child's pinwheel. Billy returned a few musket rounds on the move but he did not know where to shoot. The Rebels on the high ground had melted away and he could not see them.

Fearing that every instant was his last, Billy held his own but, when Unionists began to retreat and the closer became overwhelmed, he, too, broke for the rear. It was a wild, disjointed flight and, pulling up his trousers, he could do no more than bring up the rear.

"Regroup, men," Colonel Howard was shouting. His officers and closers began wrangling the men to a stop in the little valley. "Regroup and form up. We are not out of this fight yet. We can still take that hill and carry the day. For Maine! For Vermont! Rally! Rally!" He began to get some response from the bloodied New Englanders though less from Billy.

"I'll be damned if I'm goin' back up there," he shouted up at the Colonel. "I've done all the attackin' I'm gonna do for my whole entire lifetime. If them damned Rebels want me, they're gonna have to come down here after me. I ain't attackin' them no damned more, and I don't give a lick about no damned file-closers and their swords neither!"

"Is that right, fat boy?" the Sergeant said, suddenly appearing and clutching him by the neck. "Now, we'll just see about that, won't we? From here on out, you're going to be my special project and you're gonna do your duty." And he laughed as more and more of the retreaters were herded back into their ranks.

CHAPTER FORTY-FIVE

Portici
3:45 p.m.

LUCAS REINED IN HIS HORSE IN FRONT OF THE ESTATE HOUSE. HE JUMPED down and handed the bridle to an orderly who looked even younger than himself. He could hear the battle raging a mile or so to the northwest and see the smoke cloud looming ever larger but, worst of all, he saw the steady stream of bloody men passing by on their way to the rear.

He was starting toward the crowd around General Johnston when he heard an old man's voice bellow, "Turn around, you damn worthless skulkers. There's nothing wrong with you except that you're cowards. Get back to the fighting!"

He glanced behind him and saw an upright old man in uniform, his long, angel-white hair flowing past his shoulders. The man was brandishing an iron pike and looked madder than a rabid dog.

One wounded Rebel supporting another said, "Aw, go to hell, you old geezer. Who are you to think that you know the first damn thing about fightin'?"

"Why you little whip," the old man said, shaking his fist. "I am Edmund Ruffin. The dean of the *Secessionist Press* and the man who fired the first shot at Fort Sumter, that's who the hell I am."

Another passing straggler added, "Well, hooray for you, you old coot. If you're such a damned good soldier, why don't you go on up there and throw in a musket. Them boys could use another about now."

Ruffin pounded his pike down and said, "Sonny-boy, that is exactly what I intend to do. I'll show you shirkers what Southern manliness is all about. Get the hell out of my way." And he stormed off with a determined thrust in his step.

Lucas shrugged the old man off and approached General Johnston to report, but another courier stepped in ahead of him.

"Sir, I come from our left." He bent over, panting.

"Go on, Sergeant," Johnston said. "Report. Report."

"Sir, we held off two flank attacks over there. Kershaw and Cash did anyways. Then Coke and Bonham and Kemper showed up. And none too soon neither."

"Where exactly did the enemy strike?"

"Up the hill along the Sudley Road. That's where we beat 'em back. Just barely. But the Yanks are reforming again and they're getting' reinforced. You've got to send more men over there, General."

A spotless staff colonel puffed up his chest and decried, "But we have committed all we have to commit. We don't have any more men."

"I heard that Colonel Early is supposed to be on his way," the sergeant said. "Up from the run."

General Johnston gazed worriedly in the direction of Mitchell's Ford and said, "But his brigade cannot turn the tide alone. We would still need Kirby Smith and the last of my men from the Shenandoah to arrive by train in time." He aimed his field glass toward Manassas Junction. "There does appear to be some dust rising down around the rail station."

"But sir," Lucas spoke up. "General Beauregard told me to tell you to be on your guard against anybody coming up from that way. He said it might just as likely be Patterson if he figured out that we gave him the slip."

"Jesus Christ," the sergeant said. "If that's Patterson..."

"But if it is Smith and Early," General Johnston said, "then, by Heaven, we have a chance."

The subordinates exchanged doubtful looks. Then Johnston announced, "I want a rider. You." He pointed to Lucas. "Get down to the junction and find out who those new arrivals are. If they are Confederate, guide them to our left flank. If they are not...then...well...get to General Beauregard and tell him to disengage and retreat posthaste. Repeat that."

Lucas did so and mounted up. He galloped off toward the thickening yellow cloud, frightened, and drenched with sweat. He murmured a prayer, his first in a long time, and, oddly, thought of General Jackson.

CHAPTER FORTY-SIX

Henry House Hill
3:50 p.m.

A MILE AWAY, GENERAL JACKSON WAS MUTTERING HIS THIRD PRAYER THAT minute. He was mounted in front of his black-mouthed, haggard men, holding his bandaged hand in the air. These were the survivors behind him, ramroding and banging away with their muskets at the latest batch of Yankees to attempt a crossing of the plateau. Rebel cannon to their front pealed away at uneven intervals, fraying nerves and senses. Jackson, however, maintained his aloofness through it all and calmly studied every corner of the body-clogged meadow through his field glass.

A cowering captain approached on foot, shouting up at the General, "Sir, there are several Unionist regiments reforming and getting ready to move up the hill on our right. It's the same ones as before, Sherman's, a prisoner said, plus some fresh ones, I think. We can't hold them off this time. We were just plain lucky last time that they didn't hit us all at once."

General Jackson did not even lower his glass amid the wind of incoming bullets and cannonballs. "It was not luck, sir. It was Providence. The divine will of our Heavenly Father."

"Well, maybe, General, but that prisoner told me that similar flags and uniforms kept confusing them or some such thing. I don't know."

Jackson lowered his glass and looked down on the captain. "It was the hand of God and anyone who cannot see that, sir, is blind, definitely blind."

"Well whatever it was, we'd best get it again because our right flank cannot withstand another assault." He flinched at a shell that burst the intestines out of a screaming horse.

Jackson remained passive in the saddle, holding his mount in check. "Then my advice to you, Captain, is to go back to the right and prayerfully prepare a defense that will withstand such an assault."

"But, sir..."

"Leave me, Captain," Jackson said, dismissing him with a wave, "and trust in the Lord."

Slim Cochran ran up and saluted wildly. He looked overwhelmed by his new assignment as a courier and thoroughly intimidated by Jackson. "S-sir, I don't know why Colonel Cummings picked me of all people, m-maybe because all the runners are dead, I don't know, but he told me to come over here to you with a message."

Jackson paused, a glint of recognition in his eyes. "Well, what is it, boy? What does Colonel Cummings have to tell me?"

Slim tried to swallow back his fear, but it lumped in his throat and nearly gagged him.

"I said report, son. Are you drunk again?"

Slim tried again, as much shaken by Jackson's courage as his disapproval. "No, sir. Not at all, sir."

"Then report, boy, before the Lord sets his sun on this, his Sabbath day."

"Sir, Colonel Cummings told me to tell you that the Yanks are reforming to flank our left. They're bringin' on a brigade at least. He says they're going to break us over there this time for sure if you don't help, sir. He said him and Colonel Kershaw and Colonel Cash want you to order another frontal assault to take the pressure off us over there, sir."

Jackson looked at him coolly, "You are talking to the wrong man, private. Only General Beauregard can give that order."

"But, General Jackson, you have the only brigade that's even close to being able to make such a charge. And you've got to order it now before the entire left falls apart."

"Go to General Beauregard. He is up ahead, on the right. One hundred yards this side of that burning house."

"Sir, I wish you'd hear me out. Time's short and I..."

General Jackson stared hotly into Slim's eyes. "I said go, son, go! To

General Beauregard. And come back to me with his orders immediately. I want nothing more than another chance to sweep these godless invaders from our soil, but I will not, I cannot, do so without orders from my commanding officer."

When Slim took too long, the General fired, "Go, boy, go! Get me those orders while there is still time for me to execute them!"

CHAPTER FORTY-SEVEN

Henry Hill
4:00 p.m.

GENERAL BEAUREGARD PACED WITHIN SMELLING RANGE OF THE HENRY House, the aroma of burning wood in definite contrast to the niter of gun smoke. Wild-eyed Colonel Evans paced alongside him, pausing only long enough to take long draws from the spigot of the keg of whiskey still being borne on the sagging back of his orderly.

"Colonel Evans," Beauregard said, "When you have finished inebriating yourself, I need a professional opinion."

Evans grinned and gave a sloppy salute.

"Both our flanks are endangered," Beauregard said. "Would you advise staying here and fighting it out or withdrawing?"

Evans swayed on his bandy legs and belched over the artillery fire. "I don't know, General, I ain't the commanding officer here. But Jesus Christ on crutches, you'd best do something and do it right quick. We can't go on like we have been for the last hour, each side just trading bullets and bombshells. Hell's bells, we can't match 'em one for one. They got more men on the field than we do. Jesus, Mary, and Joseph, any son of a bitchin' bastard can see that."

"Curb your tongue, Colonel Evans. That *barrelita* is beginning to do your talking for you."

"Sorry, sir," Evans said, but he did not look sorry at all.

Beauregard let it go. His confidence was shredding and he had to talk to somebody. "If I order a general assault with the last of our troops and it should fail, what would prevent the enemy from waltzing into Manassas today and Richmond by week's end?"

Evans took another swig and shrugged his shoulders. "I don't know, General, maybe we ought to pull back and dig in for a last stand. The sun's headin' west and maybe McDowell will call off his dogs before gettin' a clean sweep on us today. I hear tell he's cautious like that."

Slim Cochran ran up, panting, and saluted General Beauregard. "Sir, I am reporting from Colonel Cummings and Colonel Kershaw and Colonel Cash over yonder on the left. And General Jackson, too."

"Yes, what is going on over there? On the left?"

Slim stood at attention, trying once again to stress the danger there and ended with, "...so you've got to order a general assault, sir. Everybody thinks so."

Beauregard ground his teeth and hissed "You, boy, will not tell me what I must and must not do! I know what to do and I will do it!"

Slim stepped back, stinging, and hung his head.

"Goddamn and sweet Jesus!" Evans said. "Looky over there, General. It's somebody's pissin' brigade or maybe two. I don't know who or how many, but somebody's comin' for certain. Looky there at that dust cloud risin' up behind our left."

Beauregard raised his field glass and looked. He saw the cloud beginning to ascend from beyond Chinn's Ridge a half mile away. "I cannot tell who it is either. There are no flags cresting the rise yet."

"It's our boys!" Evan shouted exultantly. "It's gotta be!"

"Or Patterson's Yankees," Beauregard said.

Evans had his field glass up now. "There! There is the first flag."

"But I can't read it," Beauregard said. "There is no wind. It could be either the Stars and Stripes or the Stars and Bars. Damn it. Our banners look too much alike."

"Then this is it," Slim said. "If they's Confederate, it means we win and if they's Yanks then..."

"I know what it means, boy," Beauregard snapped. "If they are Federals, then they will strike the very rear of our left flank and roll up our entire army. Colonel Evans, get back to General Johnston and tell him that I am withdrawing. I can wait no longer to act."

"Yes, sir. I'll do whatever you tell me to do, General, but don't you think that..."

"I have made my decision, Colonel. Go."

But Evans did not leave right away. He and everyone else on the hill were stilled by the prickly silence that had suddenly fallen over the battlefield. No one spoke. The gunfire wound down and the heavy, humid air seemed to press the men of both armies into their places. All eyes were on the approaching column and on the limp, furled banners, which would signify defeat or victory in this titanic struggle.

"Who are those men?" Beauregard said to himself. "Who?"

CHAPTER FORTY-EIGHT

The Stone House
4:05 p.m.

OL'MEX STUMBLED OUT OF THE WOODS AND INTO THE SLOPED CLEARING, shielding his eyes from the sun. He would have stayed in the trees for the remainder of the day had it not been for a single, gnawing thought: Billy Anderson. He ambled in the direction of the Stone House, the last place where he remembered seeing his young friend. Still touched, he had the entirely unreasonable thought that he could somehow find him in the chaos.

Descending into the disorder of the Federal ranks, he recoiled from a horse stepping on its own dragging guts without so much as a whimpering neigh. There was an armless, shoulderless man, equally silent, whose heart he could see beating and whose lungs he could see expanding and contracting deep within his cracked open thorax. Ol' Mex turned away, his mouth parched to cracking, and collapsed on the bank of little Young's Branch. He scooped up a handful of water but immediately spit it out when his tongue registered the coppery taste.

"Blood. Damn it." He shrunk back and saw several bodies, blue and gray, with their life juices leaking into the muddy, red rivulet. He crawled to a tiny mud hole made by a horse's hoof and sucked up the thick liquid. Struggling to his feet, he teetered into the heat waves.

Caissons were overturned and artillery pieces shattered, cartridge boxes and leather straps were strewn in disarray. The ground undulated with the wriggling wounded; marbled meat lay about in clumps. Smoking shell holes were blown out of the ground and clods continued to fly as more cannonballs augured in. Men ran from stinging wasps whose hives had been disturbed. Boys wept. Youths screamed. Men wandered about like zombies.

Ol' Mex made it over to General Howard's soldiers, the ones that had been hitting the Rebel left. What had been one thousand ordered men was now little more than a mob of a few hundred confused men. He could see Howard riding among the men hurling insults and provocations in an attempt to rally them, but many were slipping through his grasp toward Sudley Ford or the Stone Bridge in search of a way out.

Suddenly, a gust of hot wind unfurled the mysterious flags and a scythe of gunfire sliced through the Unionists.

"They're Rebs!" someone yelled.

"Run! Run!"

Most of them did run, knocking Ol'Mex down in their maddened rush to the rear. General Howard tried to stop them but with no more success than a flea-catching expedition. What might have been called falling back to regroup before was now nothing less than full, unbridled retreat. Honor was nowhere to be seen, nor pride, nor glory. It was a matter of survival now. Survival, capture, or death.

Panicked bluecoats cried and hollered as they blew past the dazed veteran. "Turn back! Turn back! We've lost! We've lost!" Those who started the run, spooked those behind them until clots tumbled over into a herd and a thundering stampede ensued. The turnpike jammed. The rutted roads congealed with the masses. Men pushed men who pushed other men down to be trampled by wagons, boots, and horses' hooves. Mex was jounced, kicked and blocked until he, too, yielded to the raging current.

Nearly lifted off of his feet, he bobbed with the white-water of humanity. It spit him out and beached him near the Stone House. He was trying to heave himself up for one more attempt against the current when he heard a cacophonous collage of torment.

"Help me...help me..."

"Dear God in Heaven...help me..."

"Somebody...kill me...please...kill me..."

"Put me out of my misery..."

He tried to crawl out of the mire but plunged his hand into a disembow-eled gut until he felt the man's spine. The victim yowled. Screaming himself,

Ol'Mex ripped away and ran for the rear, at least he thought it must be the rear. It was the direction in which the rest of the army was fleeing. His head went lighter. He stumbled further into the swamp of casualties before toppling into an even louder chorus of moans. The butchered bodies of the half-dead electrocuted his nerves, the sulfur, the copper, the crusty-black gashes sucked on by thirsty flies.

He heard a terrifying, high-pitched wail descend from the sky as if from the voice of a vengeful God or the devil or both. He turned toward Chinn Ridge and saw a tidal wave of Confederates pouring down onto their right flank screaming the angry scream of victory. He collapsed back into the bloody morass, too exhausted, too defeated, and too confused to get up and run any more.

CHAPTER FORTY-NINE

Chinn Ridge
4:10 p.m.

"Yip-yip-yip-yip-high!" came the ghostly chorus from the sky. Red O'Riley led the avalanche of 3,000 hellhounds in their snarling tumble down Chinn Ridge toward Young's Branch and the Warrenton Turnpike beyond. He was rolling up his part of the slope as if it were an old carpet. Colonel Elzey was the only Rebel ahead of him and he was on a horse.

Rifles fired, bayonets gleamed, sabers whirled devilishly. Friendly artillery boomed behind them rocketing iron balls overhead and into the mob of fleeing Unionists. It was a stampede, a rushing torrent, a giant reaper gone mad. Kirby Smith's Confederates, the last to leave the Shenandoah by rail, were turning the tide. They were winning the battle. They were the heroes of the day. Their cries, their yelps, their shouts mulched over into one triumphant, vanquishing shriek. "Yee-yip-yip-yip-yip-high! Yip-yip-high!"

Red O'Riley was panting, almost tasting the blood of his enemies, his eyes were stinging with sweat. But he pressed on through the heat, musket in hand, straining for a Yankee to kill. He bounded over the crawling wounded. He ignored those trying to surrender. He could not kill a man who was down, a man who had thrown his weapon away. He needed to catch one who still had fight left in him, one with a rifle pointed his way.

He saw a few of the blue bastards turning to fire, standing their ground. He felt their bullets rend the air by his head. But most of the cowards were running away. "Come back here, you damned Yankees," he shouted. "Come back here and fight like men!"

Red spotted one promising tangle of resisters still offering to duel, but a cannon shell blew them to butchers' scraps not thirty yards to his front. Another group of nearby bluecoats, stunned by the blast, joined in the panic to the rear. But two of those Yankees stayed behind: a man with a saber and one fat boy in a baggy uniform. Red took aim at the saber-wielding man and pulled the trigger. He missed, he was sure, but a moment later, the swordsman crumpled over anyway, apparently the victim of another Rebel's bullet. The Yankee in the baggy trousers released as if freed. Red saw him try to break for the rear.

He bore down on this personal enemy, his goal, his quarry, his dream and he leveled his bayonet. The Yankee turned and Red slammed into him with a sharp, crack of rifle wood. He butted and thrust and jabbed, but the Yank managed to parry and counter back.

The great swarm of Confederates passed by Red but he did not notice. He was consumed by his rage for this one monster. His bayonet locked with the beast's in a banging clangor. He pushed and grunted, deflected and forced. Veins swelled to rivers in his head. He clenched his teeth. He lunged and snarled and grappled.

Then it came, the chance, the opportunity, the opening. He kicked the Yankee hard between the legs, reared back, and plunged his blade through the boy. The steel went in hard and deep, tearing more than slicing, ripping more than cutting. He heard the sound or felt the feeling of pulling jerky apart. The Yankee hissed like steam.

Red had to leverage the brute off of his bayonet with his foot before he collapsed into a doubled heap. He stood over his trophy as if it were the carcass of a panther and cried out a victorious Rebel yell. He was about to catch up to his comrades sweeping across Young's Branch when his enemy let out a whimper. He kicked him over and looked into his face and saw it for the first time.

The Yankee looked no older than himself. He was a peach-fuzzed, chubby-cheeked boy. Red drew up his rifle butt to bash out the youth's brains, to finish the job, but something stopped him, an impulse, a blip, the twitch of his own sweaty face. He suddenly had a troubling urge to speak to the agonizing boy.

"Hey, Yank, Yank," he said. "Hey, Yank." He shook the Yankee's shoulder, but all he got out of him was a moan.

"Yankee. Hey, Yankee." He uncorked his canteen and poured water over the boy's blood-frothed lips. They would not part, though, and the water ran into the thirsty dust. "Hey, Yank, take a drink. Take a drink. It ain't poison." But he got no response.

Red pulled the Yankee's hands away from the wound. Blood pulsed out of the over-sized jacket. He tried to wipe the warm red from his hands, but not even a dousing of water could do that.

His face scrunched in repugnance, Red said, "Here, I'll get you help. I reckon I can do that much for you." He began to lift the boy up but blood and anguish gushed out of his mouth, so he quickly lowered him back down.

"My god, Yank! What do you want me to do? I can't get you any damned help if I can't move you." But the bleeding boy offered only a low, rattling sound.

"Do you want me to kill you? Put you out of your misery? Is that what the hell you want?" The balled-up boy said nothing. He just twisted and whimpered, lost in some distant torment.

"Damn it, Yankee," Red said. "This never would have happened in the first place if you hadn't come down here, if you hadn't invaded us. It's your own damned fault. You had it comin'. And I ain't takin' no blame for it neither. You asked for what you got and you got it. Pure and simple."

The gutted boy did not answer.

"Goddamn you, Yankee, why don't you just die then? Or by god, I will kill you. You're the same as dead anyways."

There were sobs now but still no words.

"That's what I'm gonna do, by god. I'm gonna kill you and put you out of your damned misery. I'd do the same for a buck deer, wouldn't I?" Red stood up and hurriedly reloaded his musket. He put the muzzle to the Northern boy's head but his hands began to tremble.

"Goddamn you, you bastard. I'm gonna do it. I'm gonna pull this trigger and put you behind me. I swear I am." He squinted his eyes to slits and squeezed but he could not squeeze it all the way.

"Damn you, Yankee," Red said, snapping his rifle down. "Just go ahead and die slow then. See if I care. That's what you deserve." He dropped to the ground and forced his tremoring hand through his hair, nearly ripping out a shock of red. He fell silent, rubbing the fatigue from his face. He was plugging his fingers into his ears to jam out the sounds, when he felt the hooves of a horse pound up behind him.

"Did you kill that Yankee, son?" a slovenly Rebel colonel asked.

"Who's askin'?" Red said.

"Damn you, boy, don't you back talk me. I am Colonel Early. Colonel Jubal Early and I am in command here."

"What happened to General Smith?"

"He's lying back up on the ridge with a bullet in his chest. Colonel Elzey took his place and I rank him. Who in the hell do you think is responsible for leading this flanking charge anyway?"

"Why, General Kirby Smith's brigade, of course."

"And mine, too, you little whip. I rank everybody on this end of the field now."

Red turned back to the Yankee, appearing to care little about any of that.

"That Yank there," Early said, "did you kill him?" He produced a flask and drank deeply while awaiting an answer.

"No, no," Red said tiredly, "he ain't dead. But I reckon I did do him the damage."

Burping, the colonel said, "Oh, he's dead all right. I saw enough corpses in Mexico to know the sight."

Red looked closer. "Really? He's dead? I really killed him?"

"You're damn right you did, boy, and that's commendable, commendable. But you can't rest on your laurels now. Catch up to your regiment and chase the rest of these sons of bitchin' invaders back to Hell."

Red stared blankly at the Yankee boy's graying face.

"I said, move along, boy. This battle isn't over yet. There's a passel of killing left to be done."

"Killing?"

"That's right, now get up and get back into the fight before you end up on my bad side. And believe me, you don't want that."

Red slowly stood but he kept staring down at the dead Yankee, one of dozens on this slope but the only one he showed any interest in.

"That's it, boy. There are plenty more where he came from. If you're lucky, maybe you'll be able to bag yourself another one before they all surrender. Now get moving. I'll bet you assholes to apples that that little priss Beauregard is going to be sending the whole kit-and-caboodle in once he sees that I won this damn battle for him."

Red shook his head at this nasty little man but kept his mouth shut. He was studying the lifeless form at his feet when another shrilling yell descended from the sky.

"What'd I tell you," Early said. "There's Beauregard now and that holy-roller Jackson up on the hill. By god, I'm not going to let them or any other damn glory-hound steal my thunder. I'm going to be waiting down there for them." He spurred his horse into action, his bottle bouncing at his lips.

Red finally started after his comrades but without the spring in his stride that he had begun this charge with. He heard the battle sounds raging around him again and wondered if they had stopped and restarted or if he had somehow blotted them out for the past several minutes. He turned to glance back one last time at his kill, the maelstrom in his ears going silent again. It took an explosion of Unionist artillery from far out on the Sudley Road to jar him back to his senses and send him on his way.

CHAPTER FIFTY

Henry Hill

SLIM COCHRAN WAS CHARGING THROUGH THE HIGH GRASS AS FAST AS HIS legs would carry him. He was screaming and yelling, rejoicing in every way known to rejoice on a battlefield where artillery shells were still exploding. He tripped and fell many times, the dips in the pasture and the lumpy meadow preventing him from displaying the grace he felt in his soaring heart, but he bounded up each time and kept pressing gloriously onward.

His senses rushed and his joy effervesced. He saw Southern banners fluttering and heard Southern voices cheering. He joined in, shouting wildly, "We won! We won! Praise God Almighty, we won!"

He dropped his musket and almost left it. He wouldn't need it again, he thought, and he feared he would miss the great celebration ahead. He retrieved the weapon, though, at a sergeant's insistence, and caught up with the surge of unwashed humanity, the racing mob advancing beyond anyone's ability to control it.

Stray Federal shells detonated here and there but to no great effect that Slim could see. Nothing could stop the unbridled momentum, the overwhelming wave of Confederates chasing the tails of their prey. Slim yowled and yipped and grinned like a jack O'lantern, leaping over rocks and logs and dead bodies. "Come back here you damn Yankees!" he bellowed. "Come back here you damn cowards!" A shell went off to the left and then to the right of him. But he felt invincible, protected by the hand of God. He ran on and on. He was nearly to the edge of the hill, past the burning white house and the abandoned Union guns they had been fighting over all afternoon. He reached the edge of the hilltop and saw the Unionist army panicking in the valley below him. He shrieked to the heavens, "Hot damn! We's truly won! We's truly won! We got you now, you bluebellies! We got you...!" But suddenly the earth convulsed with fire and fury, hurling him into the air like a rag doll. He crashed to the ground and all went black.

CHAPTER FIFTY-ONE

Chinn Ridge
4:20 p.m.

"YEE-HIGH!" COLONEL JEB STUART CRIED AS HE LED HIS CHARGING HORSE-men down the slope. "Yee-high! Yeeeee-high!" His beard flew up in his face but could not mask his grin. He waved his saber furiously at all enemies, real and imagined. "Come on, boys, this is where the fun begins. Get to 'em before they all surrender!"

There were still some foolish Yankees holding their ground and thrusting their bayonets upward, but they were few and growing fewer with every pistol shot and slash of razored steel. Most of the Unionists were dropping their weapons and running or throwing up their hands in terror.

"Come on, boys!" Stuart shouted. "We've got to cut 'em off before they can get back across Bull Run. Quickly now, quickly!" He led his troopers across Young's Branch, then the Warrenton Turnpike, and up the Sudley Road, routing the last of the Federal artillerists along the way.

John Mosby pounded up beside him, his tight-boned face grinning like a skull. For a moment it looked like they were racing. Colonel Stuart was flashing his most playful, competitive smile. John looked mean as death. "Watch out for these stragglers, Private!" Stuart called as dozens of the surrendering

Yankees dove out of the way. At least one could not make it and the angry lawyer trampled him.

"That's enough, Private, that's enough." Stuart said. He leaned over and grabbed John's arm. "Whoa! Whoa!" The rest of the horsemen slowed to a canter behind them.

"Let me go, Colonel, let me go," John said. "There are hundreds of them up ahead, and they are going to get away if we don't stop them."

"We can't catch them all, Private. We've got our hands full right here just rounding up these men." The horses slowed to a trot and then stopped.

"'Men' my ass," John said, "these blue-bellied cowards were trying to kill us not five minutes ago."

Colonel Stuart smiled big and said, "Alas, Private...what is your name again?"

"Mosby, sir. John S. Mosby."

"Alas, my good Private Mosby, such is the nature of war. And civilized warfare has no place for the murder of unarmed prisoners. I commend your spirit, though, and look forward to times and places where it can be better employed." He slapped John on the back. "You're a good trooper, a good killer. I will remember you. But for now I want you to help gather up as many prisoners as possible and take them back to that stone house. We can guard them better there."

By then, scores of Federals were pressing close to the horsemen trying to give themselves up. They were all in search of the safety of a captor and many had chosen the snarling lawyer. He circled his nervous horse and swore at them with an upraised pistol. "These damned cowards? I didn't come all this way to capture them. I came to kill them!"

The grimy Unionists tried to back up and find refuge with someone else, but the crush was too great for them to move anywhere. They took heart when Colonel Stuart firmed his voice and said, "Private Mosby, there will be no more killing here. Round up these prisoners and march them back."

"But, sir, we've got their whole army on the run. We can cut them off before they get back to Washington."

"And set these men free to fight us again. No, you have your orders, Private. Now carry them out."

John shook his head. "If it were anyone but you giving me that order, sir, I would not obey it. And I still don't agree with it."

Stuart laughed, his eyes dancing. "I can appreciate that, Private, and I can appreciate your zeal, but do as I tell you. See to these prisoners." He waded his mount through the swamp of beaten men and cantered on up the dirt road with the remainder of his riders.

"Goddamn you sons of bitches!" John shouted at the pleading faces around him. "Move to the rear!" He began herding the Yankees back to the Stone House. "Come on, you bastards. Somebody make a run for it. Please." But he got no takers.

Back at the Stone House, John found Jacob Sebastian already standing mounted guard over a morass of wounded Unionists. He noticed that the bespectacled man looked a little queasy. "What's the matter, school marm, not what you expected of war?"

"No...no." The teacher tried to look away from the casualties, but everywhere around him laid the foul fruits of victory.

The lawyer husked a bitter laugh and said, "Hell, boy, this is nothing. And with any luck, it's not even over yet. Look down toward the Stone Bridge. Some fresh Yankees are forming up in front of it to cover the retreat."

Those Yankees suddenly unleashed a volley that felled several celebrating Southerners. The Rebel infantrymen fell back and regrouped, returning the fire. For a time a standoff ensued, allowing a flood of potential Yankee prisoners to escape over the bridge. Many of those who had already surrendered saw their opportunity to make their break and bolted away in the confusion. One of them wore the light blue of the Mexican War.

"Come on, marm!" the lawyer said. "This is just the chance I was hoping for. These bastards are fair game now. Let's get them!" And they rode up the slope behind the house after the scurrying bluecoats.

"Hurry, marm, hurry! If they reach those woods up there, we've lost them." He fired his revolver at the man in light blue, but he did not go down.

"Damn it! I'm going to kill that bastard if it's the last thing I do. If it's the last..." A spray of Federal bullets plowed up the hillside in front of his horse. He emptied his revolver into the Federal line below him while Jacob turned his terrified mount and galloped back to safety.

"Goddamn you, you black devils!" John cried, his pistol empty. "You haven't seen the last of me. If you ever come down to Virginia again, I'll haunt you like the avenging angel of death!" Tall in the saddle, he wheeled his horse and proudly trotted it back to the Stone House.

Once among the moaning, he looked back toward the bridge. The Yankee line was still holding, but it was clear that it would not hold long. A torrent of Rebels was moving down Henry Hill against their flank. John Mosby should have been pleased but he was not. His hawkish eyes were penetrating the smoky woods where the Yankee with the Mexican War uniform had disappeared.

"You coward," he shouted. "You bluebellies are all cowards, by God, and bastards, too." Then he ripped into Jacob, "And you're no damn better, school marm, leaving me out there by myself, not that your prissy ass could have done me any good!"

Tired, hot, and too disillusioned to care, Jacob slouched in the saddle and hung his head.

CHAPTER FIFTY-TWO

The Stone Bridge
4:30 p.m.

COLONEL SHERMAN AND GENERAL MCDOWELL STRETCHED IN THEIR STIR-rups and peered up over the Federal firing line. The bombast was incessant and they were glad to hear it. It afforded them the cover to push their way down to the Stone Bridge and force themselves across with the horde of shoving, screaming men. They turned and, between volleys and cannon fire, shouted to make themselves heard.

"Sherman," McDowell said, "do you have your brigade across the bridge yet?"

Sherman replied that it was and that it probably would have been trapped on the other side had Sykes and his battalion of Regulars not covered the retreat so efficiently. Sykes and his Regulars had been bragging all along about how they would save the day for the volunteers and, indeed, they had. A shell exploded to the front, spooking their horses. Their hooves pranced nervously, kicking up dirt clods

"Yes, they are a bright light," McDowell said, "but what went wrong, Sherman, with the rest of the battle? Tell me what went wrong."

Sherman said that it had been close, much closer than anyone would ever know. General Tyler had commanded a fresh brigade ready to storm Henry Hill from the undefended Rebel rear. The secessionists never would have known what hit them. Tyler was minutes from ordering the assault when the Northern right flank gave way. A few minutes more, the fidgety Colonel said, was all that the Unionist forces needed.

The Yankee Regulars delivered and then received a ripple of smoke and lead. Stray bullets whined above them. "But we did not get those minutes, Colonel Sherman. The Rebels did and I will be the goat because of it."

"General, do you think that you should order Sykes back? He is taking some serious casualties up there, and his left flank appears to be threatened."

General McDowell agreed and said that he would order Colonel Sykes to fall back fighting, hopefully fending off the Rebels until the Federals got back to Centreville. Miles' and Richardson's brigades were still fresh back there, McDowell said and perhaps they could stabilize the Unionist line there. He shouted the necessary orders to an aide, who pushed his way against the current on the bridge to recall Sykes' rearguard.

"General," Sherman said. "Look up there, on the high ground to the left."

"What now? What further misfortune could befall us this day?"

It was Rebel cavalry and they both knew that where there was cavalry, infantry could not be far behind. The fleeing blue soldiers would soon be fish in a shallow barrel. A spate of bullets raked through the leaves above them to prove it.

McDowell exclaimed that they had to get their men over the Cub Run Bridge, a mile to the rear, or all was lost. It was just a little wooden suspension bridge, he knew, and pretty much wrecked by the Federal advance, but it was the army's only hope of survival. The banks of Cub Run were too steep to get wagons and horses or even men across, and there was no time in which to build another bridge. He ordered Sherman to see to it.

"Yes, sir," the redheaded Colonel said. "I will do my best."

And as Colonel Sykes' eight hundred Regulars came trotting over the Stone Bridge in orderly fashion, Sherman took off riding as fast as his exhaustion, and that of his horse, would allow.

CHAPTER FIFTY-THREE

Portici
5:00 p.m.

LUCAS ASHCROFT RODE UP IN FRONT OF THE HOUSE AND NUDGED HIS mount through the celebrating crowd toward the last place he had seen General Johnston. General Beauregard had joined Johnston there, and staff officers and the curious of all ranks surrounded both men. It was clear from the blaring musicians, the celebratory gunshots, and the wild whooping that the Confederates had achieved a major victory, but the blond could tell that the two commanders were still actively planning the exploitation of the rout. Dismounting, he squeezed close enough to the inner circle to be able to report.

"Do we have any word yet?" he heard General Johnston say. "Is the enemy truly advancing on our right at Union Mills Ford?"

"Only more of the same rumors," General Beauregard said over the partying. "We are waiting to hear from Longstreet and Bonham. They are all we have down there since Ewell and Holmes started up here. But they are ready to advance on Centreville as soon as we can ascertain the intentions of the Unionists."

"I cannot let Longstreet and Bonham go chasing after the Federals," General Johnston said, "until I know that the right flank is secure. Where are those couriers we sent down there? Surely one of them must have returned by now."

The crowd bustled and then parted. Archie Bagwell broke through and said, "Sir, I just got back from General Longstreet and General Bonham."

"It is about time, Lieutenant," General Beauregard said. "Your dallying could have cost us any opportunity to block the enemy's retreat."

"Let him report, General," Johnston said. "Go ahead, son. Tell me what is going on down there."

The triple-buttoned boy snapped to attention, saluted, and rattled off grandly, "Sir. Begging to report, sir."

Beauregard rolled his eyes.

Johnston returned the salute and said, "Yes, yes, Lieutenant. Your report. Your report."

"Yes, sir. General Longstreet and General Bonham send their regards and say that the Yankees do not appear to be making any offensive moves toward Mitchell's or Union Mills Fords. They ask permission to move against the Federals at Centreville in order to cut off their retreat to Washington. Sir."

Johnston considered the report and said, "General Beauregard, I am still doubtful that there is enough daylight left to launch such a potentially risky move. I prefer to focus our efforts on the Warrenton Turnpike and push against Centreville from the west. We do not leave ourselves vulnerable that way, and we can still overwhelm the enemy with our momentum."

"But our men over there are tired," Beauregard said. "Longstreet and Bonham are fresh."

"True," Johnston said, "but they would be going up against fresh Unionists as well. I prefer to hold on our right and pursue on our left."

"Whatever you say, General Johnston. I am, of course, merely your humble servant and will defer to your judgment in this matter." His eyes simmered with sarcasm.

"Very well then. I want you to remain in tactical command on the left and press the enemy up the Warrenton Turnpike, at least until nightfall. I will stay here and try to get the stragglers reorganized. I will send them to you as soon as possible. And have General Jackson report to me. That man has shown mettle this day and I want to use him more. His men are already calling him 'Stonewall,' I hear, the 'Hero of Manassas.' Let's see what else our new hero can do for us."

"Yes, sir," Beauregard said, visibly peeved that someone seemed to be eclipsing him.

"And what about General Longstreet, sir, and General Bonham," Archie said. "Do you want me to ride back to them?"

"Yes," General Johnston said, scribbling on a piece of paper. "Go to them with these orders. Tell them not to advance against Centreville, that we are losing daylight and do not have enough time to exploit the situation there. Tell them to continue to be on guard against a flanking attack on Union Mills, that we are still receiving reports of enemy activity there and cannot afford to jeopardize the day's gains."

Archie repeated the orders, took the paper, and set off.

"And you there," Johnston said, pointing to Lucas. "You, the one who led General Smith and Colonel Early into place on our left. That was fine work, son, fine work indeed."

The straw-blond beamed.

"Now I want you to find Colonel Kemper and his battery and tell him to rustle up every gun that can fire. Captain Imboden must surely be low on ammunition by now, but Kemper should still have enough for one more good fight. Tell him to find high ground and open fire on the enemy before they can reach the Cub Run Bridge. And find Colonel Kershaw and Colonel Cash, if you can, and have them send their infantry along as support. Now go, go before this opportunity slips away. We have the chance to win this war today if we hurry." The filthy, cheering men slapped backs and threw hats in the air.

Lucas worked his way through the mob to his horse. Mounting up, he felt an exhilaration, a rush. He was on the scent of stricken prey, the blood of a wounded buck. He rode hard and fast, horseflesh rippling, scared but happy, exhausted but wide awake. Then an uneasiness streaked across his mind, a burr, a blemish, a comet trailing dirty ice. Were people really calling Ol' Tom Fool *Stonewall?*

CHAPTER FIFTY-FOUR

The Warrenton Turnpike
5:30 p.m.

TWO ROADS, EACH THRONGED WITH HUNDREDS OF TERRIFIED MEN, WERE trying to merge onto the one-lane bridge over Cub Run. Ol' Mex recognized the smaller of the two roads, the one on the left, as the one he and his young friend, Billy Anderson, and thousands of other blue-coats had taken to flank the Confederates in the pre-dawn darkness so very, very long ago. The men had been in a neat column of fours then, most expecting an easy victory. Now they were kicking, clawing, and fistfighting each other in the crush to flee to safety.

Every man was the only man. They were cannibals eating each other's chances for survival. And Ol' Mex devoured all the chances he could. He would not be left behind even if it meant that others would be. Hell had erupted in the Earthly realm, reducing men to seething, selfish beasts, and the only antidote he had ever known for Hell was prayer, though he had rarely used it. On this Sunday evening, however, it poured from him in torrents.

"Dear God, help me." The pandemonium swelled. "Dear God, dear God, save me." The chaos kept spreading, growing more ghoulish. "Dear God, sweet Jesus, I'll be good, I'll pray more, I'll go to church, please, just let me live." But the panic, the surge, the ripples of alarm continued waving throughout the grappling masses.

When it appeared that it could get no worse, it did. He heard the cries of men and boys shrieking behind him.

"Rebel infantry!"

"On that rise back there!"

Ol' Mex turned his head to look.

"They're gonna shoot us down like dogs," a bearded man shouted into his face. "We ain't got a chance! Run! Run!"

A long, gray line of riflemen began firing at will, filling the air with whizzing bullets and that nail-scraping Rebel yell. The angry lead punched into flesh, collapsing bodies to the ground like feed sacks.

Ol' Mex prayed harder and louder. "Dear God, help me." But if God was listening, he did not show it. "I'll do anything, anything!" He saw Rebel artillery wheeling into line. "Dear God. Let me live!" The hysteria of voices peaked around him.

"Guns!"

"They're bringin' up their guns!"

"Move! Move! Move out of my way!"

"God Almighty Jesus, let me through!"

The pushing and shoving grew ugly and fiercer. If these men had ever been comrades, they had forgotten it now. "Out of my way, you sons of bitches! Out of my Goddamned way!"

Ol' Mex felt a mighty ramming against his back. His legs buckled and he went down. Hundreds of feet started kicking and trampling him. He could not get up. He was being crushed. Curling into a ball, he waited for the fatal blow. He was kicked once in the head, then twice, and three times. Others tripped and fell on top of him. He could not breathe.

"Get up..." he tried to scream but he did not have the strength to make himself heard. "Get off me..." The most he could do was whimper...and pray. "Please...God...help me...help me please..." But that was all he could get out before he tumbled into a painful delirium. The last thing he heard was the thundering of horses.

CHAPTER FIFTY-FIVE

Overlooking Cub Run Bridge
6:00 p.m.

LUCAS REACHED THE RISE OVERLOOKING CUB RUN IN TIME TO HEAR THE hooves of some two hundred Confederate cavalrymen pounding down on the Yankees. The riders were Radford's Virginians, someone told him, but he did not much care who they were. It was enough for him to know that they were on his side and that he was not one of their victims.

The charge was over in a few swells of agonized cries, animalized shouts, saber sliced meat. Enough Unionists still had rifles to fend the attackers off and unhorse a few of the emboldened Rebel boys, but the escalation of panic the riders caused made their wounding seem worth the cost.

The riflemen on the rise had lessened their fire to let the cavalry have their turn at the Yankees but, now that the horsemen had withdrawn, they resumed their rabid loading and reloading. Gun smoke once again burned the blond's nostrils. Musketry hammered his ears. It sounded like God was tearing the sky in two.

Lucas watched the Yankees down below being shot and trampled as they clawed their way across the spindly bridge. He wanted it to be over soon, for the sake of the wounded if no one else's. He could see them crawling and limping, clutching arms, bellies, and faces. Wagon wheels were crushing those who could not get out of the way. Their cries echoed through the leafy trees.

He heard a familiar voice shout over the bombast, "Boys, let me do the honors!" It was Edmund Ruffin, the white-haired old man he had seen earlier at Portici.

The artillerists quickly sponged, loaded, and hooked the primer to the lanyard. A colonel ceremoniously handed the lanyard over to the robust senior, proclaiming like a politician, "It is my pleasure and my honor, sir, to let you fire the first shot here, as you so admirably did at Fort Sumter." A cheer went up as Ruffin bowed and accepted the cord.

"I have always been called a fire-eater," Ruffin announced, "and I have borne that appellation proudly. Now, however, it gives me even greater satisfaction to cause the Northern infidels to eat a little of my fire. Stand back! Let me have at them!" The men cheered and Ruffin yanked the lanyard with the force of a young man, touching off the gun and sending a gush of noise, flame, and iron down the slope.

Lucas watched the shell explode directly in the center of the bridge, hurling horsemeat and men into the water and wagons onto their sides. The bridge was suddenly clogged by the broken wagons, impassable, and on fire. He saw Federals dive into the run, discarding everything of value to a fighting man, some down to their underwear. They were beating the water like crazed side-wheelers to get to the other side. The frenzied Yankees pushed each other beneath the murky stream and dug mud out of the steep, glistening banks trying to escape, but hairy heads ruptured and backs blew apart and lifeless bodies slid down to become rungs for those still thrashing.

"Look at them run!" Edmund Ruffin cried. "They are skedaddling now. They are whipped for sure. I have driven them from our sacred soil. They are repelled! Praise God, they are conquered!" The Rebels hollered and threw their kepis up like the hats were so many flushed quail.

Lucas should have been happy, too. He attempted a couple of shouts but, strangely, he could not muster much enthusiasm. But why? The battle was unfolding just the way everybody said it would. The Southerners were winning. They were gloriously driving the Northerners from the field. But the killing, the maiming, the flesh hanging from trees like Spanish moss, had become too much. And when the Confederate infantrymen began forming up for a bayonet charge sure to generate more of the same, he mounted and rode off in the opposite direction.

CHAPTER FIFTY-SIX

Henry Hill
6:30 p.m.

LUCAS GINGERLY STEPPED HIS DROOPING HORSE THROUGH THE FIELDS, hills, and wood lots that had been forever transformed by this day, unaware of how much he himself had changed. Aching deeply, physically and mentally, he found himself both drawn to and repulsed by the gore. It seemed he had to look at it in spite of the sickening effect it was having on him.

Blood doused the cornfields and puddled up in high grass. It ran in muddy streamlets, soaking to black spots in the dust. It caked on faces and dripped from bushes, miring every acre of the hilltop plain. He did not know if it was Northern blood or Southern blood and it did not much matter to him. It was just blood, red blood, thick blood, blood so bright or so black that it reeked of something evil, and its smell was curdling his stomach.

Rancid vomit rose up in his throat, but he forced it down as a small party of riders approached. They were all wearing gray except for one man in a black civilian frock coat. Lucas absently patted his trembling horse until the riders drew rein in front of him.

"Lieutenant, Lieutenant," a well-tailored colonel said. "Look alive, boy. Are you wounded or something?"

"What?"

"Are you all right?" the officer said gruffly.

"Oh, yes, sir. I'm all right, I guess." He shielded his eyes from the setting sun to get a better look at the party.

"Well, then come to attention, soldier," the colonel ordered. "Don't you know who this man is?" He motioned to a tall, gaunt-faced civilian with a pointed spear of beard on his chin.

Lucas squinted at the man and said sluggishly, "Why, no, sir, I can't say that I do."

The officer started to upbraid the youth but the civilian stopped him. "That is all right, Colonel. Allow me." He gazed warmly at Lucas and said, "Why, son, I am the President."

"The President?" Lucas managed. "You're Abraham Lincoln?"

A tense murmur ran through the party. The Colonel was visibly angered but the civilian stepped in again. "No, son, I am the other President. President Jefferson Davis."

"Jefferson Davis? The Jefferson Davis?" Lucas straightened and saluted. "I'm sorry, sir. I don't know what I was thinking. I…"

"That is all right, Lieutenant, quite all right. From the looks of your uniform, I would say that you have served your country well today and your confusion is, no doubt, understandable. I was a soldier once, too, you know, and I remember how I felt at the end of a battle." He nodded and smiled like a wise uncle.

"Yes, sir. I'm sure you do, sir."

Davis leaned forward in his saddle and said, "Tell me, son. What unit are you with? What part did you play in the victory?"

"I am a courier for General Beauregard. I delivered orders most of the day."

"Well, Lieutenant, a grateful nation congratulates and thanks you for your contribution. Please accept my personal commendation on a job well done."

"Yes sir…" Lucas' head began to swirl. He tasted the vomit in his mouth again and smelled the blood. Glancing down at a severed hand, he said, "Thank you, sir." He felt hot all over. His mouth began pumping saliva. Queasiness overtook him. "Yes sir…yes…sir…" And before another word could come out, he puked a vile, soured stew that splattered on the ground in front of the President's horse.

"Damn it, boy," the Colonel barked. "Watch what you're doing. What kind of damned soldier are you anyway?"

"No shame, son, no shame," President Davis said. "I've seen plenty of good men do the same or worse."

Trying to spit the bitterness out of his mouth, Lucas said, "Sorry, sir, sorry. I'm just not feeling myself right now. I'll be fine in a second."

"Understandable, Lieutenant, understandable. All you need is a little rest. It looks like you have done enough for one day. But perhaps you could do one more thing. My escorts and I just arrived on the battlefield from Manassas Junction. Can you take us to Generals Beauregard and Johnston."

Wiping his mouth on his cuff, Lucas said, "Yes, sir, I know exactly where they are. It's no more than a mile from here."

"Please lead the way then, Lieutenant," Davis said. "I wish to confer with my generals."

And Lucas rode off at the head of the Presidential party, less impressed with the grand men behind him than the dead ones on the ground.

CHAPTER FIFTY-SEVEN

Warrenton Turnpike
7:00 p.m.

AN ARTILLERY SHELL EXPLODED CLOSE TO OL' MEX, JOLTING HIM BACK TO consciousness and throwing a dead body off him. He stumbled up and slid down the muddy bank into the water. Stampeding legions were thrashing their way across, splashing and gagging. The mash of sounds, the screams, the curses, the spatter of the muddy water filled his ears as did the yipping yell of the Confederate infantry bearing down from behind.

He dug his way up and over the solid mass of arms and backs and shoulders, scrambling onto the far side. He tried to run but could not. The stampede instantly bogged him down to a mad stumble. He packed his way onto the Warrenton Turnpike for the flight back to Centreville and eventually Washington. He thought that the Rebels were breaking off their pursuit but, even if they were, he knew there was still the retreat to survive.

Order had completely broken down. No one was safe. It was every man for himself. Chaos swirled through the mob. Riderless mounts galloped headlong over youths. Six-horsed caissons banged by without drivers. Soldiers who had not done so already threw down their rifles, chucked their cartridge boxes, and shrugged off every other accouterment except for their canteens to strip down to running weight. They tore off jackets and coats, shirts and hats, some ended up half naked.

The gowned ladies and top-hatted gentlemen who had come out from Washington City to picnic and enjoy the battle were caught up in the maelstrom, too. Their buggies were rocked and buffeted by maddened men who would have killed them as quickly as a Rebel. Some of the civilians were Congressmen, Ol' Mex knew, men who had blustered for a quick march to war and glory. But now that the soldiers they had sent out here were running them off the jammed road, all the politicos could do was lash out with their whips and curse the volunteers as traitors.

After a five mile run, Ol' Mex collapsed, prostrate, on the wooden porch of the church in Centreville. He heard that the last reserves were forming somewhere to the south in an effort to cover the retreat, but nothing in the prevailing disorder suggested that there was any truth to the rumor. Spanking white tents and all the necessities of camp life stood abandoned in fields. Even one pound of extra equipment was too much for the retreaters to carry on their way back to Washington. Rowdies were breaking windows and trashing homes, but no one looted for fear that the added weight would encumber his escape.

Ol' Mex glanced up and saw General McDowell ride by. He watched the commander nudge his horse into the middle of the rout and begin brandishing his revolver at the swarm of Yankees.

"Turn back, men!" he shouted. "Form up on me!" But the soldiers shoving to get past him roundly ignored the general. It was as if he were a rock of no consequence in the middle of a swollen stream.

"Stop! I command you!" he said. But they paid him no heed. It would take the Potomac River to slow down this crush, Mex thought, and then only if someone burned the bridges before they got to it.

He got up and was trying to make his legs move again when he saw a civilian in a carriage lashing the backs and shoulders of every man who got in his way.

"Get out of my way you worthless shirker!" the civilian was shouting. "I am Henry Wilson, Senator Henry Wilson, and I am ordering you off the road and out of my way." He struck Ol' Mex in the head a couple of times.

"Damn you, you bastard!" Ol' Mex said, "stop whipping me! I don't give a good goddamn who you are. I am not a horse for the beating!"

"No," Wilson said, "You and the rest of your kind are something far less. You are losers, quitters, you can't fight worth a damn! And now your cowardice is going to get us all killed."

"You pushy son of a bitch. This whole god awful mess wouldn't even have never happened if it wasn't for the likes of you and the rest of you government men who sent us out here before we was ready. Why, I've got half a notion to climb up there and..."

"Get out of my way, chicken-heart. I have no time for you." The Senator spotted an opening and snapped the reins, nearly trampling Ol' Mex beneath his horse's hooves.

Mex sizzled but he was just too tired to do anything about it. He let the tirading fat man auger his way into the mass of blue. Looking back, he did have the consolation of one sight. The ball of the sun had disappeared beyond the mountains. Perhaps he might make it yet. Perhaps darkness would fall before the marauding Confederates could cut off his escape. At least he allowed himself to hope that as he re-entered the stinking current of humankind.

CHAPTER FIFTY-EIGHT

Portici
7:30 p.m.

By the time Lucas had led President Davis' entourage to the estate house, the celebration there was even more raucous. Men with mouths blackened from biting off cartridges were shooting their weapons into the sky, yelling wildly and banging on tin cups and plates. "We won! We beat the Yankees!" came the shouts in all their varieties. The only one who was attempting to restore order was General Jackson and he was not having much success.

"Line up, men," Jackson was saying as loudly as his monotone would allow. "Form ranks and rally on me."

But the frolic whirled on around him, now exacerbated by the arrival of Davis.

"Where are the officers for these men?" Jackson said, refusing to slacken his discipline simply because the President was there. "I need officers to organize them. Officers. Where are the officers?"

When none appeared, it occurred to Lucas that he was an officer, albeit a junior one. That was an idea he had not entertained this day, usually feeling more like a private or a cadet than a lieutenant, especially when it came to dealing with Jackson. After pointing out General Johnston to President Davis and receiving the man's thanks, he strangely felt an urge to go to his old professor rather than join the scores of Confederate soldiers ecstatically swarming their commander-in-chief.

Nudging his horse alongside Jackson's, he shouted into the crowd, "Rally, men, rally!" He seemed to surprise himself. It was the first command he had issued to a body of soldiers since accepting his commission. Feeling a near out-of-body numbness, he glanced at the General and saw a man he had never seen before, strong-jawed, stout, face ruddy with the day's sun. "Rally around General Jackson!" he heard himself cry as if from a well. "Rally on Stonewall, the hero of Manassas!"

Jackson sat quietly on his horse, taking it all in with a quizzical look He noticed that the boy's exhortations were having some effect on the joy-crazed mass. Other officers soon appeared and carried the rallying calls farther down the forming lines.

"Rally on Stonewall!" Lucas called, peeling his mount back into the ruckus and herding the partying men into formation. "Rally! Rally! There is still time to catch the Yankees before nightfall! Rally! Rally! Rally on Stonewall Jackson!"

He circled his horse back to Jackson, perhaps expecting praise, perhaps condemnation. He never knew what to expect from this man. What he got was nothing: no thanks, no ridicule, no anything. As more men began to settle down and form up under the re-emerging discipline, Jackson dismounted and started toward General Johnston. Lucas dismounted and followed, still oddly drawn to this man he had so long despised.

The two of them found Jefferson Davis shaking hands, profusely congratulating General Johnston for the victory. Johnston gave the President a quick overview of what had happened, being careful to accentuate his role as the overall architect of the triumph. The glad-handing went on for several moments before anyone even realized that General Jackson was present and waiting to report.

"General Jackson," Johnston said, finally noticing the dusty man in blue. "You know President Davis, of course."

"I know of the President," Jackson droned sleepily, his eyes back to their usual dull blue.

"He is here to get a report on our victory," Johnston said. "Can you add anything, especially on the fighting on Henry Hill?"

"Only that our win there was God's will, sir."

President Davis nodded, "Well, yes, General, but certainly some of the credit must go to commanders such as yourself. I heard them calling you

Stonewall, for your stubborn defense of that hill, I presume."

Jackson shifted uncomfortably and said, "The name, sir, if it belongs to anyone, belongs to my brigade. The glory belongs to our Heavenly Father. But His work is not yet complete here."

"Are you referring to the pursuit of the Federals?" Davis said.

"I am."

"It is getting too dark for that," Johnston said. "I have already sent a courier to recall Generals Longstreet and Bonham in front of Centreville. I don't want anyone to engage the enemy in the dark. Besides, this victory of ours has left our army as disorganized and exhausted as the enemy's."

"Disorganized men can be organized, sir," Jackson said. "Exhausted men can be driven. Battles can be won night and day."

"Well, perhaps, but..."

"Give me 10,000 men, General Johnston, some from here and some from the uncommitted reserves, and I will be in Washington tomorrow, our independence achieved."

"Why that is quite a boast, General," Johnston said, "especially coming from such a humble man."

"I would take none of the credit, sir," Jackson replied. "It would be..."

"God's will," Johnston said. "Yes, I know."

President Davis spoke up. "I like this man. And I, too, believe we have an opportunity here to achieve our independence this evening, in one fell swoop if we act quickly."

"It is too late to pursue, Mr. President," Johnston said. "Disaster would befall us if we did, perhaps reversing the gains we have achieved here today."

Hearing but not listening, present yet absent, Lucas felt an emptiness expand in him like a sea sponge being stuffed inside his gut. It was part anxiety, regret, disgrace, and dishonor, an overriding sense that he had years of wrongs to right and so little time in which to right it. He blurted, "General Jackson can do it if he says he can. I saw him in action today. And I can attest to his bravery and resolve."

"Silence, Lieutenant," Jackson said, taken aback and embarrassed by the outburst.

"Indeed," General Johnston added with a throttling glance at the youth. "I am in command of the field, and I have already sent out orders to break off all attacks. Tomorrow is another day. We will have another opportunity then. General Jackson, see to these men you have so admirably organized. Set up camps for them as you see fit."

"Yes, sir," he said, ignoring the compliment and resigning himself to

Johnston's authority. He offered a tired salute and shuffled away. Lucas followed at a distance, apparently unbeknown to Jackson.

"President Davis," Lucas heard Johnston say, "would you please accompany me to General Beauregard's headquarters in Manassas? My officers will be sending in their initial reports there and you will, no doubt, be able to come by a broader understanding of today's events."

"It would be my honor, sir," he listened to Davis say, and he watched as the President and the commander of the army mounted their horses and waved to the cheering soldiers.

Watching them go, Lucas felt none of the happiness that they or the celebrating Rebels did. He felt a dull ache instead. And when he turned and saw that General Jackson had left, the ache turned jagged.

CHAPTER FIFTY-NINE

A Field Near Portici
7:45 p.m.

JACOB SEBASTIAN HOBBLED HIS HORSE AND LOOKED AROUND AT THE collected remnants of his cavalry company. "We're so damned spread out, I wouldn't begin to know where Colonel Stuart is camping tonight. There are less than half the troopers gathered here. And now to complicate matters, it looks like rain."

"I suppose it'll be every man for himself tonight," John Mosby said, "with whatever cover he can get over his head."

"I've got two oilcloths. I suppose we could put them together and form a lean-to of sorts for the both of us, maybe in that fence corner over there." Sprinkles began to fall out of the darkening clouds.

"It never seems to fail," Mosby said. "I've read dozens of times how it rains hard after big battles. Maybe it's God's way of washing the blood off the land."

Jacob explained that it was caused by the smoke rising up into the sky. Moisture in the atmosphere bonded with the ash particles and formed rain drops, he said, heavy rain drops that fell in torrents.

"Leave it to you, marm, to give me a scientific brief on the subject." He shook his head and spit hard on the ground.

The bookish young man pushed up his spectacles and said nothing.

"No matter," the lawyer said, "let's get the lean-to set up before I decide I don't want to spend another night with a coward." He laughed gruffly believing, correctly, that Jacob would not defend himself.

Once under cover, Mosby took out a piece of paper and a small pencil and began to scribble in the dimming light.

"Who are you writing to?" Jacob said.

"My wife."

"So, are you going to tell her what a hero you were today?" He dug him with a faint smile.

"No, you son of a bitch, I'm going to tell her what a hero I am going to be."

"Is that right?" Jacob said.

"Yes, that's right, marm. I might not have gotten in much of the fighting today, but I sure as hell discovered something about it. And about me."

"And what is that?"

Mosby glinted hungry eyes. "I discovered that I love it."

The schoolmaster was shaking his head doubtfully when someone threw open the lean-to and barked in, "Hey, Mosby. Is that you in there?"

"Hell yes, it's me. What of it?"

"Get up and get mounted. Colonel Stuart sent me down here from Sudley Ford to find you. It seems you made some kind of an impression on him today, and he wants you to do some scouting for him."

Mosby looked out and noticed that the man giving orders was a lieutenant. "Scouting, sir?"

"You heard me."

"But aren't most of his scouts officers, sir? Does this mean that there is a promotion in it for me?"

"You figure it out, Private. Now get up and get moving. If you don't talk to him before he gets his sing-along band going, he may forget that he sent for you."

Mosby broke out in a cocky grin and said, "Well, school marm, I guess this is where we part. I told you I was going places in this army. And, by God, I am. As for you, well, I think maybe you ought to just fold up and go home. I don't believe this warring business has any place in it for the likes of you." He laughed out loud.

Jacob did not argue. He was too beaten and exhausted for that. Even the last source of his strength, his resentment, had dissipated. Listening to the lawyer and the lieutenant ride off, he sunk into the darkness beneath his oilcloth and wondered if maybe Mosby was not right. He flashed on images of the blood and splintered bones he had seen this day and shuddered. His 90-day enlistment would be up soon, he thought, and teaching children, even disinterested, unappreciative, bad behaving children had never sounded so good to him. As the rain fell harder and battle's horrors chaffed his tender mind, a rivulet of water drained through a bullet hole in his oilcloth and chilled his shaken soul.

CHAPTER SIXTY

---◆•◆---

One Mile South of Centreville
8:00 p.m.

SITTING BOLDLY ATOP HIS HORSE, GENERAL JAMES LONGSTREET SAT WITH his fist cocked into his right hip and swore to a mounted aide, "Goddamn it! Why are we still here? It's damn near dark, it's starting to rain, and we haven't done a thing all day! Beauregard held us here in the middle well after it was clear that the Yankees weren't going to attack us, and then he marched us back and forth across the run how many goddamned times trying to decide if he was going launch his own attack. I've got good men here, tried and true men, and I want to use them!"

Longstreet's brigade was indeed made up of good men, the victors of the fight at Blackburn's Ford three days earlier. There were nearly two thousand of them, rested and eager, packed shoulder-to-shoulder on a bare slope facing Centreville, awaiting the order to advance up to the wooded crest and beyond. They had their own quiet comments about their soaked shoes, socks, and about how poorly General Beauregard had used their muskets this day, but they knew, as did Longstreet, that guarding Blackburn's Ford had been important and necessary duty during the morning, remaining in position to prevent a Unionist force from breaking through the Confederate middle while the majority of the Southern troops hurried to the endangered left. But when the Unionist assault did not come and word of the rout reached them, they were impatient to get into the chase. Time was waning, though, and they and their General were hoping to squeeze every hue out of the fading dusk in order to take a final, and hopefully climactic, part in the battle.

Longstreet was anticipating a courier from his superior officer on this part of the field, General Milledge Bonham, carrying orders for him to advance against Centreville with his brigade in conjunction with Bonham's, a total of four thousand fresh men. He knew the fleeing Yankees would have to pass through the tiny village on their way back to Washington and that many could still be cut off and captured, perhaps ending the war right then and there. Out of the darkening horizon he saw not one rider approaching, but two. They reined up in front of him and offered salutes.

"General Longstreet," the aging Bonham said, "you know Major Whiting, General Johnston's chief engineer."

"Yes, sir," Longstreet said, glinting a suspicious eye.

"He says that there are reports of a Federal advance on Union Mills, trying to turn our right."

"That is correct," the professorial major said. "And I understand that General Johnston has issued orders for you and General Bonham to return to your original positions across Bull Run in preparation to meet such an advance."

Longstreet, ever the brooding bear, scoffed and said, "First off, Whiting, I haven't gotten any orders like that from General Johnston and second, I've been hearing those rumors about Union Mills all day long, and there's not a one of them that's had a lick of truth to it."

"But we cannot jeopardize our gains here today," Whiting said, "with unnecessary heroics."

Longstreet leaned forward in the saddle and fumed, "We're not jeopardizing anything, Major. The Yankees are played out and in full retreat. I know a rout when I see one and maybe you would, too, if you'd have ever been in any real fighting instead of burying your nose in those damned engineering books of yours. Now, get out of the way so we can finish these Yankee bastards off. Let the batteries open fire!"

Major Whiting stiffened. "In the name of General Johnston, I order that the batteries shall not open fire!"

"Did General Johnston send you to communicate that order?"

"No," Whiting said, "but I take the responsibility to give it."

"Major," the General growled, "unless you are carrying direct orders from

General Johnston, General Bonham has the responsibility of this field and he agrees with me. Now, get out of the way. You are wasting precious time."

"Now, let's not be rash here, General," Bonham said. "I am becoming disposed to agree with Major Whiting on this. I sent one of my officers out to scout, and he saw a line of artillery supported by blue infantry. And we don't know how many there might be formed up behind them."

"But General Bonham," Longstreet said, "this is the best chance we may ever have to completely crush the enemy army. I strongly advise that you order the attack."

General Bonham was rubbing his white beard as if reconsidering when a rider galloped up and reared his mount to a stop. It was Archie Bagwell. Breathless, he sprung a salute and said, "General Bonham! General Longstreet! I come from General Johnston with his latest dispatch!"

Bonham read it and said, "Well, here it is, General Longstreet, direct orders from General Johnston for us to pull back across the creek."

Major Whiting slipped Longstreet a self-satisfied look that made the big general sizzle.

Longstreet slapped his own thigh and said, "Damn it! Damn it to hell! General Johnston is going to regret this later. I guarantee it."

"But, General Longstreet," Archie spoke up. "We have beaten the Yankees so badly today that they will never be able to mount an invasion of our sacred soil again. Our independence is already assured."

Longstreet snapped, "Oh shut up, you goddamned little fool. Wouldn't you know that the first time you'd do your damned job right all day would have to be now." And he rode off by himself to prepare his wet-legged troops for yet another splash back across Bull Run.

CHAPTER SIXTY-ONE

Colonel Nathan Evans' Camp
8:15 p.m.

THE BATTLE WAS OVER. THE SOUTH HAD WON AND SOUTHERN WHISKEY had finally conquered at least one of the day's heroes. "Goddamn it to hell," Shanks Evans slurred as he stumbled among his adoring men, slapping backs and shaking hands. "You boys are the best goddamned killers in this entire army and I'm proud of you. I'm so goddamned proud I could shit!" While the equally inebriated soldiers yelled and shot their weapons into the falling rain, the orderly with the barrelita shared the contents freely with those pushing to get a second or a third cupful.

"Take it easy, take it easy," Evans said. "There's more where that came from. Hell, you don't think I'd come all the way up here from South Carolina with less than a wagon load of the golden nectar, now do you?" He laughed coarsely

The drunken men shouted out their glee at having a colonel who would look out for them so; a brigade commander who would set aside an entire wagon, two drivers, and a team of six mules just to haul their spirits right along with their ammunition, food, and artillery pieces. Evans shouted back that they deserved every drop, every logistical hurdle, and every quartermaster he had bribed to get the medicine through to the front.

The sloppy colonel cried, "And the boys that ain't with us tonight deserve it most of all! If they hadn't of given up their lives to hold the line this morning, Johnston and Beauregard and all the rest of those perfumed generals could have never gotten there in time to do a dram of good! And speaking of a dram, let's toast one up to the fallen heroes! You'd best believe that that's the way they'd like it!" The crowd cheered as he gulped down the lead toast.

"That's right," Evans said, wiping his scraggly beard. "And I don't mind telling you boys that it's no use for any of those goddamned commanders to brag about what they did in this here battle. We started the fight and we fought it through and whipped those sons of bitchin' Yankees before any sizable number of reinforcements even showed up. And that's an ass-kickin' fact!"

The cheering and gunshots increased until the throng parted to allow an old, uniformed gentleman with long, silvery white hair through the crowd. The rowdies began chanting the name Ruffin, Edmund Ruffin.

"Now, let's not you take all the credit for winning this little scrape, Colonel," the old man said over the noise. "You may not be aware of it yet, but it was I who fired the first cannon shot on the retreating Yankees, the one that hit Cub Run Bridge and turned the retreat into a complete rout, just like I fired the first shot at Fort Sumter!"

The wet-headed soldiers cheered Ruffin as Evans staggered up and hugged him tightly. "I should've known you'd find your way to the front again, Ruffin. Damn your eyes, you are sprightly for an old man, hoppin' from Sumter up to here."

Ruffin struggled free and said, "If you want to see me sprightly, how about sharing a couple of mouthfuls from your man's back keg there. You'd be amazed at the number of officers in this army tonight who cannot offer a gentleman even a taste."

"Yeah, it's good this war's over, Ruffin. It scares me to think what a teetotaling officer corps would do to the morale of an army if it had to fight for very damned long." He put an arm around the old man's shoulder and began walking him toward his tent, turning only to order his orderly to tap another couple of barrelitas for the men.

"You are right about that, Colonel," Ruffin said. "And if there ever was a night fit for toasting, this glorious night, this achievement of Southern independence would have to be it."

"Here-here," Evans said and he lowered his voice. "Come on inside. I've got a bottle of the good stuff stored away just for my special guests."

Ruffin rubbed his hands together and said, "Fine, that sounds just fine."

They ducked out of the rain and into the tent.

"But let me ask you one thing," Evans said.

"Certainly, Colonel, anything."

"Did I hear you right? Are you still sayin' that you fired the first shot at Sumter even when you and I both know it was somebody else altogether?"

Ruffin gave his hair a nervous flip backward and tugged at his cravat. "Well, I..."

Evans grinned lasciviously. "Aw, no matter, no matter. Your dirty little secret is safe with me. But you'd best hurry up and write your memoirs before somebody else beats you to the punch, and his name instead of yours goes down in history as being the one who started the War for Southern Independence."

The gentleman assumed a proud posture and harrumphed, "Well, I hardly think that..."

But before he could finish, the tent filled with Evans' vulgar laughter and the sound of the old man's back being slapped.

CHAPTER SIXTY-TWO

Fairfax Court House
8:30 p.m.

OL' MEX SLOWED TO A SHAMBLE IN THIS ONCE-TIDY VILLAGE CONSISTING of a colonnaded courthouse, a steepled church, and a few short streets lined with pleasant homes (those that had not been burned and looted by his comrades on their way out to the battle). He felt like he was suffocating in the retreating mob so he stopped in the darkness for another rest. He joined dozens of other exhausted men sprawled out on the wide steps of the courthouse. There was no sound except for rain pattering on the leaves, the low rumble of dragging feet, and the voices of two mounted officers whose conversation he could hear, but cared little about.

"Quite a sight, is it not, General Tyler?"

"It is, Colonel Sherman," Tyler said. "The whole thing disgusts me and could have been prevented."

"By McDowell, sir?"

"That's right, Sherman, and he knows it, too. You should have seen him slouching by here a few minutes ago. Hell, the man is so crestfallen he would not even look me in the eye."

Preoccupied with the morose parade, Sherman said, "He is a beaten man and we are a beaten army, there is no doubt of that."

"Hell, yes, he is beaten and for good reason," Tyler said, beginning to count on his gauntleted fingers. "He was late launching the attack, the road he used for the flanking action was nothing more than a goat path, and he sent in his troops piecemeal. He did not even bring my men across the Stone Bridge until it was too late for them to do any good at all. We are beaten all right. Just look at these poor souls slipping and sliding in the mud trying to get to safety. They can't look me in the eye either, and it's not even their damned fault."

"Well," Colonel Sherman said, "I would also add that our army was green, green as grass."

"Bah, that argument will not wash, Sherman," Tyler said. "The Rebel army was just as green as we were."

"True enough, General, but they were defending, we were on the offensive. I do not have to tell you what a disadvantage that puts even veteran armies in."

"So, Colonel, are you saying that you would not have done it differently than McDowell did?"

"The biggest thing I would have done differently would have been to fight with an army of Regulars or, led by Regulars or, at least, trained by Regulars, and that was simply not possible for McDowell, although I imagine the President and General Scott will settle down to the job of finding a man to drill that kind of army into shape now."

"Well, Sherman, since McDowell will no doubt be removed as commander, maybe that man will be you." Tyler smiled wryly.

Sherman reached for his canteen and said, "Oh, not me, General Tyler. Right now I feel sufficiently disgraced that all I want is to sneak into some quiet corner and stay there." He raised the canteen to his lips and chugged down several gulps.

"My God, Sherman," Tyler said. "Why is your hand shaking that way?"

Sherman quickly returned the canteen and hid his hands. "Oh, that's nothing, nothing new anyway, though it might be a bit worse today than usual. It's just the way God made me, I guess. My nerves. It's nothing. I'm fine." A flutter of visible tics flinched across his face.

"If you insist, Colonel. But if I were you, I'd check into that when we get back. It looks like the beginnings of melancholia or the like."

"Don't worry about me, General," Sherman said. "I'll be all right. Now, if you will excuse me, sir." He saluted, hand still trembling, and spurred his horse out into the muddy river of gaunt, unkempt men.

Once Sherman was out if earshot, Tyler shook his head and said to himself, "That man has no future in this army...no future whatsoever."

For his part, Ol' Mex dragged himself back into the crowd of shockworn refugees and added his aching feet to the shuffle.

CHAPTER SIXTY-THREE

South of Henry Hill
8:45 p.m.

RED O'RILEY HAD BEEN WANDERING ACROSS THE FIELDS, VALLEYS, AND HILL-tops of the day's fighting in search of the confidence he had lost. He felt a hollowness, a confusion, a disappointment with himself for his qualms about killing. They had kept him from joining in his company's songs and celebrations; he had not wanted to be around any of the victorious, the happy, the living. In the last gray of daylight, he had tried to toughen himself by opening the shirts of the dead still strewn about in hopes of facing and overcoming his shameful repugnance at the ravaged bodies. He had even helped load some of the moaning wounded into wagons for their agonizing ride off the field. There were no hospitals that he had heard of, but he assumed the army must have provided some place for the treatment of the injured.

Now, stumbling and fuzzy in the rain, he focused on a low constellation of lamps shining around what appeared to be a barn up ahead. He set a direct course for them, impeded by fences, ditches, and rutted cart paths. Before long, he could smell the place and hear it, the sticky-sweet blood, the feces, and the cries. He was soon stepping over bodies, alive and dead, and was nearly to the barn when he heard a familiar voice call out.

"Hey...Red...is that you?"

He looked around at the scores of wounded men who might have spoken to him and heard the voice again, pained, weak, and groggy.

"Red...down here..."

"Is that you, Slim?" Red asked, moving toward the blanketed boy.

"Yeah...help me...you've gotta make 'em give me more for the pain...the pain..." Slim whimpered like a child, clutching the blanket with white knuckles.

Red crouched down tentatively, shocked to see how old and ghastly pale his drinking mate from Harper's Ferry had become. His voice hitched in his throat and he had to push the words out. "W-where are you hit, Slim? H-how bad is it?"

"My legs...my feet...hurt somethin' fierce...more for the pain...tell them...please..." His sobs and cries rose above those of the other stricken men.

Red started to reach out to give Slim's shoulder a comforting squeeze but he drew back, frightened, when his friend let out a doleful wail. He searched for something to say. "When was the last time they done give you anything, Slim? Maybe they can only give it every now an' again."

"No...now...I've got to have it now...please..." Slim suddenly grabbed Red's leg and clung to it.

"All right," Red said. "I'll try and get something for you. Goddamn, if a soul in this world needs it tonight it'd be you. I'll be right back." He pulled his leg free and went in search of a doctor, aghast at the carnage along the way.

Hurrying into the glowing barn, he backpedaled to a stop. An amputation was about to begin and the victim was completely awake. Four ruffians were holding down the wounded man's limbs while a bloody-aproned surgeon, taking a swig from a whiskey bottle, observed a grisly gash in the man's left knee.

"Hold him down," he heard the stubby doctor snarl. "Hold him the hell down so I can cut straight."

Mouth agape, Red watched the blood-blackened orderlies tighten their grips to allow the surgeon to begin. The little bald man took a long, slender knife to the victim's left thigh just above the knee and sliced up from underneath. The victim screamed hideously. Red cringed. The doctor slivered the blade in deep until it clicked against the bone. Working the knife out, he cut in on the opposite side of the leg from the top down. The screaming nearly burst the victim's throat. Red turned away and pressed his ears shut, hoping for the torture to end. It did not. The victim thrashed his head about and shrieked higher and longer.

"Hold the son of a bitch down!" the surgeon ordered. Red looked back in time to see the little doctor straining to pry both of his hands into the gaping crevice he had created and rip the connective flesh apart. Red could see the bone now and hear the wounded man howling louder. The doctor then took a hacksaw and began grinding it back and forth.

Red grimaced at the sound, the grating, granulating, rasping sound of metal against bone. Only the tormented wailing of the victim was louder. Red's face pinched and his gut churned, but he forced himself to look and listen.

At last, he heard the bone snap and saw the leg fall free. The man's cries subsided. The pain and loss of blood had apparently rendered him unconscious. The surgeon quickly tied a belt around the gushing stub to bring the bleeding under control, and one of the ruffians grabbed the naked, hairy leg and started outside with it. Red was following him when he heard the doctor shout behind him, "Next!"

Red caught up to the bloody-handed orderly as he was tossing the leg onto a fly-blackened pile of previous discards. "Mister, you've got to give my mate more laudanum or chloroform or something. He's in an awful way over yonder. Please, you've gotta take heart."

Angrily, the man said, "Damn you, boy, don't you think I'd give that shit to everybody if I had it to give. Hell, your mate's lucky if he got any at all 'cause there ain't no more laudanum or chloroform or nothing now. Them glory boys down Richmond way must of figured that nobody was gonna get shot in this here scrape today 'cause they didn't send us shit." Hellish groans arose from all around them as if to underscore his point.

"Well, what's he supposed to do then?"

The ruffian jabbed a blackened finger into Red's chest and snapped, "He's supposed to do the only damn thing he can do and that's to lie there and suffer like all the rest and pray to still be alive tomorrow. Now get out of my way, you son of a bitch. They need me inside."

Rattled and shaking, Red returned to his friend and crouched beside him, this time a little farther away to avoid his clutches. With a complete sense of helplessness, he told him what he had found out, that there was nothing for the pain, that he was one of the lucky ones to have gotten any earlier and that he would have to gut it out, to take the pain, to somehow endure the anguish on his own.

"No..." Slim sobbed. "It hurts too much...they gotta give me something...help me up...get me outta here...get me home...I want my Ma..." He tried to struggle up but fell back howling. He threw his blanket off, revealing nothing of his legs but two bloody-bandaged stumps cut off below the knees.

"My God!" Slim exclaimed. "My legs...they cut off my legs...my legs!"

Red lurched up. He stared hard down at the sloppy mess and stumbled backwards, tripping over other thrashing men. Regaining his balance, he said nothing: not goodbye, not farewell, nothing about returning later to nurse him or write a letter to his family, nothing. He started running as if from a burning house, running from the pain, running from the heartache, running from the fear that he, just as easily as Slim, could have been the poor, legless bastard lying there in his blood. He ran and ran, grappled, and groped until he had hurdled the last blanketed form.

He did not stop running until he had found his company celebrating boisterously around a bonfire; the men who still had all of their parts, their liquor, and their laughter. There was escape here among the living, the uninjured, and it drew him nearer the blaze. Here he would stay. These were his people, not Slim, not the dead, not the dying, not even the folks back home who could never believe, never imagine all that he had seen and experienced this day along Bull Run creek. He had killed and nearly been killed. He had seen death and knew what it looked like, even if it had not made him feel the way he thought that it would, and he would find a place before the flames with these other killers who knew the same, the only ones who could understand him and what being a killer really meant.

But he feared that he might never shake the memory of Slim's bloody stumps and his pleas and the stink inside that barn or the tearing feel of his bayonet going through that Yankee boy. His gaze weary and mind drifting into the fire, he thought of his family in Alabama, hundreds of miles and his youth away. His little brothers and sisters and his Mama, too, would be sitting out on the porch about now, he thought, watching the fireflies and listening to the frogs, all laughing at his father's stories as he enjoyed his evening nip. He yearned to be back there on the farm, laughing and nipping along, telling stories just as funny as his Pap's.

That is the way it had been before Fort Sumter, before he left, before this terrible day, and he wondered if it would ever be that way again. He knew it would not tonight. But with a little coaxing from these filthy, blooded men around him, these initiates who had become his brothers today, he managed to join in on a chorus of *The Bonnie Blue Flag* in an earnest, yet failed, attempt to chase his pain away.

CHAPTER SIXTY-FOUR

Jackson's Headquarters
9:00 p.m.

STONEWALL JACKSON SAT ERECT IN HIS TENT LABORING OVER A LETTER TO his wife. The walk-in had just been set up so it lacked any appointments other than a cot, a chair, and the small correspondence table at which he was seated, but at least it was keeping out the increasing rain. Even the lighting was dimmer than usual because he had not yet had a chance to ignite an oil lamp and was writing by the glow of a single candle.

Looking up from his paper, he closed his eyes and shook his head. "A lost opportunity. Heavenly Father, you could have smitten the enemy and forever kept them from invading our sacred homeland had you but removed the scales from General Johnston's eyes. And now the rain will reduce the roads to impassable mires by tomorrow."

He drew a deep breath and started to write again but he suddenly crumpled the stationery, dissatisfied with his words and himself. Kneeling by the chair and bowing his head, he began to pray. "Heavenly Father, forgive me for my impertinence, my impatience, my failure to accept what must certainly be your will for me and for our beloved Country. Forgive my ungratefulness for the many blessings you have bestowed upon us this day and for my wanting more than you have chosen to give us at this time. Help me, Heavenly Father, to offer up the praise, which you so richly deserve for our victory and reaffirm my faith that whatever you bequeath upon us is always, in the end, the most beneficent. In the beloved name of your Son, Christ Jesus, I pray. Amen."

Slowly reseating himself, General Jackson took up his pen and began the letter to his wife on a fresh sheet of paper. This time the pen flowed smoothly and when he had signed it, he read the last paragraph aloud to see if, perhaps, it was too boastful.

"Whilst great credit is due to other parts of our gallant army, God made my brigade more instrumental than any other in repulsing the main attack. But say nothing of this. Let others speak praise, not you or I. All the glory is due to God alone. Your loving husband, Thomas."

He was sealing the letter for transit when he glanced up and saw Lucas Ashcroft, hat in hand, standing in the entrance to the tent. "Why are you here, Lieutenant," he said. "Are you carrying a dispatch?"

"Uh, well no, sir," Lucas said. "Not exactly. I, uh, was hoping perhaps I could maybe have a word with you, sir. I mean if you can find a minute for me."

Abruptly, a staff officer outside grabbed Lucas' arm and started to pull him back, "I'm sorry about the intrusion, General. He must have gotten by me when I was unloading your wagon. I'll take care him."

"That will not be necessary, Captain," Jackson said. "I will see the boy."

Once inside, Lucas came to respectful attention and saluted. Jackson was rubbing the fatigue from his eyes and did not return the salute. Lucas kept his salute rigidly in place, waiting until the General returned a limp one of his own.

"So, what is it that you want, Lieutenant?" Jackson asked with an exhausted sigh.

The look of fatigue in Jackson's dull eyes gave Lucas pause. He thought it was more the way he had looked as the inept professor at VMI rather than the fighting general on Henry Hill, and the reversion confused him to the point of silence.

"Well, Lieutenant, why are you here?"

Why indeed, he quickly thought, his eyes darting about the Spartan interior. He felt his heart race and his palms getting sweaty. Did he really intend to apologize to this man, to offer some concession or explanation?

"Speak your piece, Lieutenant," Jackson said. "It is late."

"Well, sir," Lucas managed, not yet able to dredge up a complete admission of wrongdoing, "what I would like to know is...well...how were you able to transform yourself out there from a mere professor, and, forgive me, sir, but not a very good one, into a commander capable of inspiring men to such a great victory as was ours today." Lucas braced himself for a discourteous response but it did not come.

Jackson did not speak for a long moment. Then he looked up and said simply, "You may be whatever you resolve to be, Lieutenant."

Lucas waited for more but he did not get it. "That's it? You may be whatever you resolve to be?"

Jackson glanced away and said no more.

"But what about your personal courage?" Lucas said. "Nowhere today did I witness such absolute fearlessness under fire as you showed. How do you account for that?"

Jackson closed his eyes and mumbled a prayer. When it ended, he said flatly, "Lieutenant, Our Heavenly Father has a plan for me. He has a plan for us all. When He decides that He will end my life on this Earth, He will take me to the unspeakable glories of Heaven. I have every assurance of that. Why, then, would I fear death?" He looked Lucas in the eyes as if there were nothing more to say. The look gave no indication that he had softened his heart toward his old class clown. "Will that be all, Lieutenant?"

That was not all and Lucas knew it. The reasons he had come to this tent tonight were coalescing from thoughts into words, and those words were about to tumble out of his mouth with the uncertainty of dice. "Well, sir, there is one more thing. I...I am sorry for the way I acted at the Institute. I am sorry that I disrupted your classes. And treated you disrespectfully. I mean, you seemed like the farthest thing from a soldier and even a professor back then, I just...I just..."

"You just acted like a child, Lieutenant," Jackson said coldly, "a spoiled child without a thought for anyone but yourself. Your deportment was absolutely reprehensible. You were a vexation to me and an embarrassment to the Institute. You acted the fool for laughter and petty attention. You acted the fool because you are a fool, Lieutenant."

Stunned and reeling, Lucas could only say, "But...but how was I to know back then what a great soldier you would become when under fire, your fiery eyes, your bravery, your fearlessness. I just wish you would have shown that back at the Institute. Then maybe..."

"Then maybe what, Lieutenant, you would have treated me with the respect that our Heavenly Father expects us to treat all people? That is what offends me most about you, Lieutenant, your callous disregard for the feelings of those whom you think are somehow less than you, those who did not grow up with your advantages. That is what offends me most."

Lucas hung his head. "I'm sorry, sir. You're right. You always were right. I know that now. I learned an awful lot today, about you and about me. I was scared out there, scared to death. And you weren't. You were the hero and I was the scared boy. I was just hoping that you might be able to forgive me for all the disrespect I've shown you."

"It matters little whether I forgive you or not," Jackson said, unmoved, "but, rather, whether our Father in Heaven forgives you?"

Lucas nodded glumly, expecting a sermon that never came. Instead, the General took up his ink pen and addressed the letter to his wife. He set it aside and drifted off again in prayer or some thought his face did not reveal. After Lucas had squirmed beneath the weight of the long silence, Jackson finally spoke.

"Lieutenant Ashcroft, I have a job for you."

"A job, sir?" Lucas said, his tone brightening.

"Yes. Take this letter and see that it is properly posted."

"Why, yes, sir. I would be happy to do that, sir." He took the letter, saluted, and started out of the tent.

"And, Lieutenant."

"Sir?"

"Return to me at dawn. If your repentance proves sincere, and that remains to be seen, then I may have some use for you as a courier. I imagine I could arrange your transfer over to me from General Beauregard should such a move be ordained."

Lucas grinned big and saluted another time. "Yes, sir. I would be deeply honored to serve under you, sir. Thank you, sir." He nearly tripped, bounding out of the tent with visions of redemption in the eyes of the greatest hero of the Confederacy and of proving himself worthy of the title *soldier.*

For his part, Stonewall Jackson sat braced in his chair with the faintest of smiles on his thin lips. The smile passed quickly, though, when Jackson went to his knees again to pray. This time he offered the Lord's Prayer, adding particular emphasis to the line, "...and forgive us our debts as we forgive our debtors..."

CHAPTER SIXTY-FIVE

General Beauregard's Headquarters
The McLean House
9:30 p.m.

JEFFERSON DAVIS, JOSEPH JOHNSTON, AND GUSTAVE BEAUREGARD SAT IN the lamp-lit parlor and toasted their victory with fine brandy. Their exhaustion and an ample supply of the liquor had finally toned down their excitement a bit, as had the soothing rainfall on the house's tin roof, but there was still glory and ambition dancing in their eyes.

"I think, gentlemen," Davis said, "that we should waste no time in communicating the news of our great success to Richmond and all the South. General Lee will be awaiting the news at the War Department, I am sure."

"I agree, Mr. President," Johnston said. "Perhaps I, as the overall commander, should draft and sign such a document."

"That will not be necessary," General Beauregard said. "I can do that. I was in tactical command, you know. I actually led most of the fighting."

"No," Davis said emphatically. "I am the commander-in-chief. It is fitting that I draft the telegram."

Beauregard took a drink. He noticed Johnston take a bigger one.

President Davis seated himself at a small writing table and began scratching out his dispatch. When finished, he read it aloud.

Beauregard considered it drivel, flowery prose, filled with the inaccuracies and generalities of a man who had not been at the fighting but who wanted someone to think that he had. He received the distinct impression that considerable political self-promotion was prominent among the President's motives. When Davis finished reading and signed his name alone, Beauregard was certain of it. Mastering his impulse to speak, he said nothing, leaning over to pour himself another brandy instead.

Davis stood and started gesticulating as if on the Old Senate floor. His face was aglow with confidence and the warm rush of spirits. "Tell me again, gentlemen, why we cannot press the pursuit tonight. With the Unionists as disorganized as they are, we could catch them in the moonlight if need be. Do not forget, I was a soldier long before I was a statesman, and I have a firm grasp of the logistics required."

General Johnston said, "No one here denies your military sagacity, Mr. President, I least of all, having served with you, but last reports place at least two fresh Federal brigades strongly positioned at Centreville covering their retreat."

Colonel Thomas Jordan stepped into the room and said, "I could not help but overhear, General, but a report just did come in from an officer saying that he was in Centreville not long ago and found it deserted except for abandoned caissons and wagons and such. He said that there was not a trace of any resisting troops."

"You see," Davis said. "We could have Bonham and Longstreet up there in an hour and walk into the place. Then we would have a clear road to catch up with the Unionists before they can get back to Washington." He sat down and began writing the orders for the advance himself.

Beauregard did not feel at all happy about what was transpiring, but neither he nor General Johnston objected.

"Who was the officer that sent in that report, Colonel Jordan?" Davis asked, "I want to commend him."

"Major R.C. Hill, sir."

Davis suddenly looked up. "R.C. Hill? Crazy Hill?"

"Major Hill, sir. I know him by no other name."

Davis crumpled up the order he was writing and said, "I remember Crazy Hill from the Old Army. You could not trust a thing he said due to his excitability."

Beauregard sighed relief and sipped his brandy.

"But I will write orders," Davis said, "for General Bonham to pursue at first light and for every available unit to follow." He scratched out the commands on a new sheet of paper.

Satisfied that he had done all that could be done for the night, he filled his glass and began probing his generals. "How much discarded Unionist equipment have we been able to secure thus far?"

"The reports are still coming in," General Beauregard said, "but I know we captured close to thirty cannon and all the caissons and ammunition to put them into immediate use if necessary, plus hundreds of wagons, many with their horses still in trace, five or six hundred rifles and enough rounds to keep them firing far longer than this war will require. In addition, we gathered accoutrements of every description: jackets, coats, blankets, sabers, and pistols all in small mountains."

"Glorious," President Davis said, "simply glorious."

"There were even reports that the Unionists left behind a wagon filled with thousands of manacles and leg irons, presumably to march our men through the streets of Washington as prisoners."

"The audacity," Davis said. "The blind arrogance. But clearly representative of the barbarous Northern spirit."

"I think it is important to remember, sir," General Johnston said, "that we have not confirmed that rumor. We are still looking into it."

"No matter," Davis said. "Our newspapers should be made aware of the reports, the treachery. It could have morale value."

"Yes, sir," Johnston said, sounding doubtful.

"And do we have any estimates as to enemy losses?"

"It is too early to know for certain," General Beauregard said, "but we are guessing that their losses were high, far higher than ours. It would appear that we captured somewhere around 1,500 of them alone."

"And what of our losses," Davis said soberly.

"They were considerable," Beauregard said. "But for the gain, acceptable, I think. Probably 400 killed and another 1,500 wounded. We are hearing very few reports of captured or missing men."

"And casualties among our commanders?"

General Johnston spoke up. "We lost many good and promising regimental and brigade commanders, Mr. President. Bernard Bee and Francis Bartow were killed. Roberdeau Wheat, Wade Hampton, and Kirby Smith were severely wounded. There were others, I am sure. The list will grow as reports come in."

Davis reflected in silence.

"There was great confusion on the field, Mr. President," General Beauregard said. "Our flag, for example, the Stars and Bars, looked like the Federal Stars and Stripes from a distance. If this struggle continues, I should design a new, more easily recognizable banner for use on the field."

"That is an interesting idea," Johnston said. "Perhaps I could help you in your design."

Beauregard nodded politely but noncommittally. He was not about to let the glory of designing a battle flag go to anyone else.

The usual amount of gunplay and hooting outside intensified. General Johnston got up and peered out the front window. "Those boys are having a bit too much amusement, I fear. Perhaps we should do something to settle them down."

"Oh, let them have their fun, General," Davis said. "They deserve it."

There was a loud rapping at the door. A guard appeared in the hallway and opened up. Triple-buttoned Archie Bagwell came rushing in. "I must see Colonel Jordan. I have a message for him of great importance, great importance indeed."

"Lieutenant," General Beauregard snapped. "I don't care who you are here to see and I don't care who your daddy is, when you enter into my headquarters you will do so with the proper military bearing."

"Yes, sir. It's just that I come from a young lady who says that she brought us the first warning of the Unionist attack. She says a lady spy in Washington sent her and that Colonel Jordan knows her."

Colonel Jordan appeared from the back and said cooly, "I will see him, General Beauregard, if you are through with him."

Beauregard waved Archie off and said, "Very well, Colonel, if you are telling me that this boy may be of some use to you, you may have him. Please, take him."

Archie followed Jordan into a small room with a table and two chairs. He saluted and sat down, flinching when a rowdy soldier shot off his musket just outside the only window in the room.

Jordan returned the salute and said, "You have a message for me?"

"Well, not actually a written message, sir, but a spoken one."

"Well, what is it, boy? Speak up."

"This girl, this young lady, she is down at General Ewell's headquarters right now. She said she is a spy for us and that she is going to make her way back to Washington tonight. She wants to know if you have a message for her to take back to a Mrs. Greenhow. Sir."

Jordan took out a locket with a woman's picture in it and seemed to drift for a moment before saying, "Yes, yes I do." He wrote for a minute or two warning Mrs. Greenhow of the increased danger she would be in of being captured and imprisoned if she was not especially careful. She would certainly be watched more closely. By the Secret Service. Probably by Allen Pinkerton himself. He wrote of his concern that she might be apprehended before he could get a chance to spirit her to safety in Richmond to the glory and gratitude she deserved and ended by saying how much he loved her, how he had never loved a woman more, how he could not live without her. He then took several more minutes to transpose the note into code. When finished, he folded the paper several times and said, "This message is exceedingly important, Lieutenant. Can you assure me that you will see it properly delivered? Because if you should fail, I…"

"I know I can deliver it, sir. Just give me the chance." He was grinning irrepressibly at the thought. Now he would show his father and his older brothers and everyone at the Citadel and in the army, too, everyone who had ever held him down and told him he would never amount to anything more than a silly boy. Now he was not just an officer or even an officer on the staff of an important general. He was part of a spy ring, just like the ones he had read about in books, the most daring, romantic, adventuresome elite of any fighting force.

Warily, Jordan sized him up and said, "All right then, maybe I'll take a chance on you. But first, wipe that goddamned childish grin off your face. You are supposed to be a soldier not a circus clown."

Archie struggled with the order but managed to obey.

"Now, boy, take this message to that little lady and find her a horse. One without a CS brand, for god's sake. And see her through the lines. Down by Union Mills Ford would most likely be the safest route. Then return to me as soon as you know that she is on her way."

"Yes, sir. I'll do everything you said, sir. Thank you, sir." He sprang to his feet and saluted eagerly, nearly smiling but quickly suppressing it into a ridiculous scowl. He then hurried out of the room and the house.

Moments later, there was a commotion outside, a tumbling down, a tumult of curses and shouts.

General Beauregard rushed out into the rain with Davis and Johnston following. He looked down at the bloody heap sprawled across the bottom step. "Dear God in Heaven, what has that damned boy gone and done to himself now?" But he became concerned when several nearby soldiers could not rouse him.

One of them said, "Christ Almighty. This feller's shot clean through the top of his head. Damnation, would you look at them brains."

"Who shot him?" Beauregard ordered. "I want you to find the man who shot this boy."

"Why, hell, General, it weren't none of us," another soldier said. "We've been out here for quite a spell. We would've saw a plum murderer."

"Perhaps it was a bullet falling out of the sky from all of this celebrating," General Johnston said. "It was bound to happen. You would think these men would know that whatever goes up must come down."

"Damnation," Beauregard said, "now I must come up with something to tell his father, that he was a son of a bitching hero on the battlefield or some such blather."

"What a shame," President Davis said, leaning over Archie's draining body, "to die in such a needless manner. Who is the boy's father anyway, a man of any useful political influence?"

While Beauregard explained, Colonel Jordan went to Archie's side and snatched the note from his hand. Without a thought for the boy or his brains, he shouted, "I need a courier here!"

CHAPTER SIXTY-SIX

The Executive Mansion
Washington City, D.C.
July 22, 1861
Dawn

PRESIDENT ABRAHAM LINCOLN LAY RESTING ON THE CHAISE IN HIS OFFICE overlooking muddy Pennsylvania Avenue. His head was propped up on the arm of one end, his legs dangled over the other. He was awake enough to hear the patter of rain against the window and the ponderous footsteps of someone entering the room.

"Mr. President," General Winfield Scott said. "I am sorry to awaken you but I have received another telegram from General McDowell."

Lincoln sat up, rubbing at his bleary eyes. "Quite all right, General. What's this one say?"

"It is all bad, I am afraid, all bad indeed."

"Let me see it," Lincoln said, donning his spectacles. He read aloud. "The battle is lost. Save Washington and the remnants of the army. The routed troops will not reform." He sighed deeply and stepped over to the window.

"Where did we go wrong, General?" Lincoln said. "Was it me? Did I make the wrong decisions?"

"There is plenty of blame to go around, Mr. President, and as surely as I am speaking to you now, the press and the Congress will point it all out. I would bet that Horace Greeley and his 'On to Richmond' crowd will be the first to say we should not have tried to go on to Richmond as early as they insisted."

The President nodded tiredly and said, "Could I have chosen a more qualified commanding officer for the operation? Did McDowell let us down?"

"No, sir," Scott said. "I think General McDowell did as well as anyone could have under the circumstances."

"Who then? Who is responsible for a debacle of this magnitude, his subordinates, Hunter, Heintzelman, Tyler? I must know who to keep and who to replace."

Scott shifted his huge mass and said, "Well, sir, if I had to blame anyone in particular, and this is not easy for me to say, it would have to be my old comrade, Rob Patterson, up in the Shenandoah Valley. It is confirmed now that he allowed the Confederates under Joe Johnston, to give him the slip and reinforce General Beauregard along Bull Run while he himself was fooled into remaining up there."

Lincoln watched stragglers dragging themselves up rain-splattered Pennsylvania Avenue. Most had no equipment or weapons. Many had collapsed in yards, in gutters, and under porch stoops. A crowd of exhausted men was even sprawling on the mansion lawn below. "Do we know yet about our losses, how many dead, wounded, missing, and whatever else they tabulate to tell how badly an army is whipped?"

"We won't know that for weeks, sir, at least not with any certainty."

"Could you at least give me your best estimate?"

"Well, sir. I would guess that some 500 or more were killed, maybe another 1,500 wounded, and that many captured, but I am just estimating, sir."

"What about our divisional and brigade commanders? Would you have any idea how many of them were casualties?"

"Reports are incomplete, sir, but I understand that Hunter and Heintzelman were badly wounded, James Cameron, Secretary Cameron's brother, was killed. I am certain there were more whom we have not yet heard anything about."

The President kneaded his aching neck and said, "Too many. And to lose the fight on top of it."

"And, of course, there are the stores of weapons and supplies that the men apparently discarded in their rush to save themselves. But, Mr. President, I believe the greatest loss we suffered was to the morale and spirit of our men. I would guess that most of the ninety-day enlistments will go home now and properly training those who stay will require a Herculean effort. Have you given any thought to whom you might appoint for that task should you choose to replace General McDowell?"

"Yes. But I have made no decision. You and others have told me good things about this McClellan fellow. The one who cleared the secessionist out of northwest Virginia. Perhaps I should call him over and have a look at him."

"Very well, sir, I can see to it."

"And I want to make another call for volunteers, three-year volunteers, if, God forbid, we should need them for that long. The summer-war is over, General Scott, the time when war was glory. We have been baptized at Bull Run, and we must now christen this war a holy crusade. He glanced around sheepishly. "Sorry to wax eloquent on you, General. Sometimes I forget myself."

"No apology required, Mr. President. It is one of your finer qualities, I think."

Lincoln chuckled mirthlessly and said, "A two-edged quality, I fear, General. It's probably what got me into this god-awful office in the first place. Now, if you will excuse me, I want to go out and talk to a few of these men about what happened out there. Please keep me informed."

CHAPTER SIXTY-SEVEN

The Executive Mansion Lawn
6:15 a.m.

OL' MEX WAS ALREADY TOSSING IN A FITFUL SLEEP, CURLED UP UNDER A tree, when he heard a voice from somewhere high above him. He jerked alert and saw a tall, bearded man in a black frock coat and a top hat looking down on him.

"Sorry to awaken you, soldier," the tall man said. "I just wanted to have a brief word with you, if you would permit me."

The veteran jumped up, trying to wipe the mud off of his uniform. "Why you're...I'm sorry, Mr. Lincoln, I guess I was so tired I didn't know where I was. I'll be moving along now."

"No, private," Lincoln said. "Please stay. I would like to ask you your personal opinion, your expert opinion on what happened out there, at the battle."

"Oh, I can't tell you nothing, sir. I was just a foot soldier, a ninety-day man. I only seen what was right around me."

"What was it like there, Private, right around you."

"Oh, hell's fire, I mean...sorry, sir."

"That's all right, Private. Go on."

"Well, sir, I don't know what to say. Everything was just smoke and noise and screaming and blood. That's all I can recollect of it, and I wish I couldn't recollect that."

"From your uniform it looks like you fought in Mexico. Was it something akin to that?"

"No, sir. I was scared in Mexico, believe me, but nothing like I was out at Bull Run. Hell, I mean heck, I was only eighteen in Mexico. I'm thirty-one now and maybe I got more to lose than I did then. Or maybe I'm not as reckless as I was then. I don't know. But either way, the fight yesterday was just plain worse than anything I ever seen in Mexico. Yesterday was the first panic I was ever in and it was the panic, even more than the fightin', that was the worst of it."

Lincoln gazed around at the tattered remains of the army struggling up the street. "I can only imagine, Private."

Ol' Mex took off his forage cap and rubbed at the bloody bandage around his head.

Lincoln said, "How did you get that wound, Private?"

The veteran shook his head and said, "I don't know, sir. The whole fight is just a blur to me. I'm not trying to keep nothing from you. It's just that I can't sort nothing out of it. Maybe I'll be able to later, I don't know. All I know is that we were winning at first, but then they started winning, and then we started running. You'd best talk to some officer type if you want to get the details. Like I say, I don't know nothing. I'm just a foot soldier."

Lincoln clasped the veteran's shoulders firmly, his eyes moistening, and said, "Private, it is men like you, the foot soldiers, who are going to end up doing the most to preserve this Union. It is men like you, and I thank you from the depths of my heart for the sacrifices you made on that battlefield yesterday."

Ol' Mex did not know what to say or how to react and he was simply too fatigued to care much about it. All he could manage was, "Thank you, sir."

After a pause, Lincoln said, "Well, I'm certain you're tired and would like to find a dry place to rest. I'll let you be on your way or you can stay here, if you want. Again, thank you, Private. For everything."

Slouching, the veteran nodded and sloshed off toward the street.

"Oh, Private," Lincoln called after him.

Ol' Mex turned slowly. "Sir?"

"Do you think that you will be re-enlisting for a three-year term?"

The veteran thought for a time before saying, "I don't know, sir, I just don't know."

Lincoln sagged a little and said, "Well, you've been through a horror out there. I am certain of that. Perhaps you have done all that the country can ask of any one man."

Ol' Mex nodded and started to leave a second time but stopped and turned. "You know, Mr. Lincoln. I can tell you this much."

"What's that, Private?"

"I had a whole mess of time to think on the way back here, and there was one thought I just couldn't shake out of my head. A young friend of mine most likely got killed out there or worse. If floggin' the scoundrels that done that to him means me re-enlisting, then maybe that's what I'll have to do. But for now, I want nothing more than to find some place to crawl into and sleep there till I can't sleep no more."

At that, the President smiled wanly and tipped his hat, but Ol' Mex was too tired to respond. He just headed for the street, turning his collar to the rain.